Limited Classical Reprint Library

THE

ASCENSION

OF

CHRIST

By WILLIAM MILLIGAN, D.D.

LATE PROFESSOR OF DIVINITY AND BIBLICAL CRITICISM IN THE UNIVERSITY
OF ABERDEEN

Foreword by
Dr. Cyril J. Barber

Klock & Klock Christian Publishers, Inc.
2527 GIRARD AVE. N.
MINNEAPOLIS, MINNESOTA 55411

Originally published by
MacMillan and Co., Limited
London, 1891

ISBN: 0-86524-061-2

Printed by Klock & Klock in the U.S.A.
1980 Reprint

FOREWORD

Future historians, as they look back on the closing decades of this century, will probably describe our age as one of crisis, and particularly as an era characterized by a crisis in authority. The inroads of biblical criticism in America shortly before the turn of this century produced, in the 1920's and 30's, a parting of the ways. Our educational institutions continued in the "liberal" tradition and "conservatives" were content to concentrate on evangelizing the masses. In the course of time, however, except for a few institutions who ably combined scholarship with a loyalty to the integrity of the Word of God, the majority of denominations followed the lead of those who had been trained in the theological mores of the times. This included an abandoning of Scripture as the authoritative revelation of God to man. The result as we are able to see it today is a crisis in which people have lost their bearings and are looking for someone to lead them.

Happily, according to a recent nationally publicized Gallup Poll, a reversal of the previous trend is evident:

- Today's young people are spiritually "charged up" and ready for religious instruction.

- There is a definite return to the traditional biblical views of marriage, the family, and morals.

- Unchurched Americans are surprisingly traditional in their views on religion.

Apparently, after fifty years, people have begun to find out that a humanistic theology does not have the answer to their problems. The need of the hour, therefore, is for pastors and Bible teachers who are committed to the authority of the Scriptures and are able to teach and train those who are so desirous to learn. The problem facing many today, however, is that they do not know how to relate the truths of God's inspired revelation to the needs of their hearers. They lack a good model.

Those who wish to know how to relate truth to life will find that William Milligan (1821-1893) serves as a good example. Educated at the universities of St. Andrews and Edinburgh in Scotland, and Halle in Germany, Dr. Milligan pastored two churches for a total of sixteen years before being appointed to the chair of Divinity and Biblical Criticism, University of Aberdeen--a position he held for thirty-three years!

Professor Milligan developed such a reputation throughout the United Kingdom that, in time, he was invited to deliver the Croall Lectures at the University of Edinburgh (1879-1880) and later gave the Baird Lectures at the University of Glasgow. These lectures were subsequently published under the titles *The Resurrection of Our Lord* and *The Ascension and Heavenly Priesthood of Our Lord.* Dr. Milligan authored numerous books and Bible commentariees. Each of his works is marked by a careful analysis of the original text together with an awareness of the theological issues involved. As a result, his writing is characterized by an unction which is at once compelling and uplifting. It is no wonder that a reviewer said of his works:

> There is a fulness of treatment which is not systematic, and there is a systematic treatment which is not full. Dr. Milligan's method is as thorough in range as in affiliation. His thought moves on patient and undaunted, unresting, unhasting, careful to include and discuss all points and finer aspects of the subject as they legitimately arise, especially alert to all illumination derivable from luminous exegesis. The style, too, fits the method like a glove; it is at once clear and full and serious and stately, argumentative but not tiresome, with a certain big-bodiedness and affable dignity....

The spiritual truths which permeate William Milligan's handling of Christ's ascension and heavenly Priesthood cannot fail to inspire and uplift. He masterfully blends biblical truth and theological perception, with the result that he has produced a work of rare merit.

Cyril J. Barber
Author, *The Minister's Library*

PREFACE

THE following Lectures are intended to be a sequel to those on the Resurrection of our Lord published by the same writer a few years ago. He need not hesitate to say that he has felt his present subject to be as difficult as it is important; and he can only therefore hope that, though he has endeavoured to express himself as clearly as possible, there will be found in his language no trace of dogmatism. Such a spirit would be peculiarly unsuitable to the treatment of the Theme with which he deals,—the Ascension of the Redeemer and His heavenly Priesthood. In those parts of the volume, more especially, which have occasioned the author most anxiety, when he has to speak of the Offering of our Lord, of the Gift of the Spirit, and of the essentially super-earthly or heavenly nature of the whole Christian dispensation, his aim has rather been to stimulate inquiry, and to encourage students of theology to prosecute the subject. Good which he has himself been unable to effect may thus be done by others. Few will deny that fresh investigation into the fundamental truths of the Christian system, to be in all probability followed by a restatement of many of them, is needed in our day.

At the time when the volume on the Resurrection of our Lord appeared, the writer had no thought of again turning to a subject so much akin to it as that with which the following Lectures are occupied. He has accordingly found it difficult to avoid a repetition of some things that had been previously said. Should it be thought that he has been only partially successful in this, he can assure his readers that the failure has not resulted from want of effort to effect his end. It will be seen, too, as in the discussion regarding the Offering of our Lord in heaven, that, even when a view taken in his former work recurs, it is stated in a different relation and for a different purpose. In these circumstances he ventures to hope that there may be little ground for complaint upon this point. Of what he had written in occasional papers in Theological Journals he has felt entitled to make freer use. Such papers are for the most part unconnected with each other, and are often forgotten as soon as read. He regrets that the fear of unduly increasing the size of the volume has made it necessary to suppress, at least in the meantime, many Notes which he should have wished to add to the Lectures.

In conclusion, the author acknowledges the kindness

of the Rev. James Cooper, East Church, Aberdeen, in supplying him with several valuable hints for the Lectures. He desires also to take this opportunity of recording his gratitude to his old and venerated friend, now gone to his rest, the Rev. Dr. Alexander Anderson of the Gymnasium, Old Aberdeen, a conversation with whom first led him into one of the most important lines of inquiry connected with the Offering of Christ, and whose warm-hearted encouragement, while he pursued the subject, he will never be able to forget.

THE UNIVERSITY, ABERDEEN,
December 1891.

CONTENTS

LECTURE I

The Ascension of our Lord

LECTURE III

The Heavenly Priesthood of our Lord,—in Heaven

LECTURE V

The Heavenly Priesthood of our Lord,—on Earth

LECTURE VI

The Heavenly Priesthood of our Lord,—on Earth

LECTURE I

"And He led them out until they were over against Bethany; and He lifted up His hands, and blessed them. And it came to pass, while He blessed them, He was parted from them, and carried up into heaven."—LUKE xxiv. 50, 51.

THE Resurrection of our Lord was not the completion of His glory. His glorification indeed then began.* He then burst for ever those bonds of the finite and the temporal within which, in carrying out the work of the world's redemption, He had previously, for three-and-thirty years, confined Himself. He received that "spiritual body," and entered upon that state of existence in "spirit," in which alone it was possible for Him perfectly to reconcile and to unite the material and the spiritual—man and nature upon the one hand and God upon the other. He reached a stage in the development of God's great plan of salvation for His creatures, at which He could penetrate all things with the influences of the Spirit. From that moment He could rule His people, not by the exercise of outward authority alone, but by inwardly assimilating them to Himself. From that moment He was in a position

B

to present His "many brethren" along with Him, amidst the sanctities of a new creation and in eternal submission to the Father, to Him who, alike in the natural and in the spiritual world, must be "all in all."[1] When Jesus rose from the dead, the kingdom of God was no longer future, a thing of promise and of hope. It was no longer merely "at hand." Though not in all the extent of its dominion, it was present; it was come. But inasmuch as He in whom the kingdom was summed up was still in the midst of disciples who had not been transfigured into a perfect likeness with Himself, and who could not therefore behold Him in His unclouded majesty; as He had still to take His place amongst those who were unable to comprehend all the excellency of His power, it was necessary for Him to restrain, in some degree and for a time, the full manifestation of what He was. In order to satisfy them as to the identity of His person He needed to speak and walk and eat with them; while they again needed to hear Him, to see Him with their eyes, and to handle Him with their hands.[2] For their sakes, not for His own, He had to pause before entering on that culminating stage of His development to which the voice of prophecy pointed, and for which creation waited.

Forty days therefore passed during which the Risen Lord appeared again and again to His disciples, "speaking unto them the things concerning the kingdom of God";[3] instructing, strengthening, comforting them, pointing out to them both the duties and the trials that

---

[1] 1 Cor. xv. 28,   [2] 1 John i. 1.   [3] Acts i. 3,

were before them, and making them "polished shafts"
in His quiver. Then His personal presence could be
dispensed with. It was to be replaced by that of One
who should train them with a more powerful discipline;
and He might "ascend to His Father and their Father,
to His God and their God."

On what Jesus was during these forty days, the
same, yet not the same, as He had been before His
crucifixion, it is unnecessary to dwell.[1]   It may be
enough to remember that the statements of Scripture
leave no room for the conception of a body becoming
more and more spiritualised and glorified during forty
days. Besides which, that period is too short for the
accomplishment of such a process. The analogies of
nature teach us to understand either a gradual development extending over ages of unknown length, or a
change effected in a moment; but not one where the
shortness of the time is altogether incommensurable
with the greatness of the result. The language of St.
Paul, too, when that Apostle speaks of the change to be
made on believers alive at the last day, establishes the
same conclusion : "Behold, I show you a mystery : We
shall not all sleep, but we shall all be changed, in a
moment, in the twinkling of an eye, at the last trump:
for the trumpet shall sound, and the dead shall be raised
incorruptible, and we shall be changed." [2]

Whatever, therefore, our Lord was during the forty

---

[1] The author has treated of this   book on *The Resurrection of our
point at sufficient length in his   *Lord*, Lect. i.
[2] 1 Cor. xv. 51, 52.

days which separated His Resurrection from His Ascension, He was at least essentially the same; and if at any
instant of that time He appeared to be in no respect
different from what He had been while He tabernacled
in the flesh, it was because He willed it. As on the
Mount of Transfiguration, immediately before entering
on the last and most trying scenes of His Passion, He
showed Himself in the glory originally belonging to
Him, so during the forty days He occasionally laid
aside His glory, and assumed a humiliation which was
no longer the chief characteristic of His state. In
Himself He was as much prepared to "leave the world
and go to the Father" on the Resurrection morning as
He was on the day of His Ascension.

These considerations, it may be remarked in passing,
throw light upon the special object which our Lord
seems to have had in view in thus making Himself
manifest to His disciples during the forty days. It
was less to give them a general training for their future
work than to convey to them a full assurance that He
had risen from the dead, and that He was the very
same Redeemer from whom they had long been learning what they were to teach and do. Conviction upon
this point was what they especially required. Had
they beheld Him only in His glorified condition, they
might have separated the present from the past. They
might have thought of Him as an altogether new revelation of God; and they might have lost sight of the
very essence of the Christian system—the necessity of
suffering and self-sacrifice as the preparation for its

rewards.[1] On all points of the Christian faith indeed, even on the full meaning and force of the Ascension, the Spirit afterwards given by their Lord was to be their trainer.[2] But as the fact of the Resurrection lay at the bottom of the training, it was necessary to bring it home to them with all the power which sensible demonstration could afford. Not to undergo any gradual development Himself, but to bind together in His own Person, in indissoluble union, the thoughts of suffering and glory, of humiliation and exaltation, did Jesus tarry with His disciples for a time after His Resurrection.

The question has been often asked by theologians whether our Lord did not return to His Father immediately after His Resurrection from the grave, and whether each of His subsequent appearances upon earth was not a new descent from heaven. What we call the Ascension would then become not His first but His public, formal, and final departure from the world. The question thus raised cannot be properly answered without an examination of the Scriptural meaning of the word "heaven"; for the conception commonly entertained of heaven seems to be different from that of Scripture. Yet nothing further need be said upon the point just now. No result of the inquiry would affect the main question with which we have to do. The Ascension of our Lord would still remain substantially the same, in the fact of its occurrence, in the views of His work with which it is associated, and in the lessons which it conveys.

[1] Comp. Luke xxiv. 26, where read "the Christ," not "Christ."
[2] John xvi. 13, 14.

I. The first thing to be considered is the fact. The details of the Ascension are not given either by St. Matthew or St. John, while St. Mark makes only a brief allusion to it in those closing verses of his Gospel, the genuineness of which is a matter of dispute.[1] We owe our knowledge of the particulars wholly to St. Luke, who, alike in his Gospel and in the Acts of the Apostles, has related them with the same clearness and circumstantiality as distinguish the other portions of his narrative. That Evangelist closes his Gospel with the words, "And He led them out until they were over against Bethany; and He lifted up His hands, and blessed them. And it came to pass, while He blessed them, He was parted from them, and carried up into heaven. And they worshipped Him, and returned to Jerusalem with great joy, and were continually in the temple, blessing God."[2] To a similar effect, the same Evangelist speaks in the Acts of the Apostles, "And when He had said these things, as they were looking, He was taken up; and a cloud received Him out of their sight. And while they were looking stedfastly into heaven as He went, behold, two men stood by them in white apparel; which also said, Ye men of Galilee, why stand ye looking into heaven? This Jesus, which was received up from you into heaven, shall so come in like manner as ye beheld Him going into heaven."[3] The testimony of St. Luke, however, does not stand alone. We know the belief of the early

---

[1] Mark xvi. 19.   [2] Luke xxiv. 50-53.
[3] Acts i. 9-11 ; see Note A.

Christian Church from sources in all probability even
earlier than the Gospels. Thus it is that St. Paul says
in his Epistle to the Philippians, " Wherefore also God
highly exalted Him," an exaltation spoken of in direct
contrast to that emptying of Himself and taking upon
Him the form of a servant, and being made in the likeness of men described immediately before;[1] thus that
in the same epistle he speaks of " heaven, from whence
also we wait for a Saviour, the Lord Jesus Christ";[2]
and thus that, enumerating in his first Epistle to
Timothy six leading particulars of the " great mystery
of godliness," he mentions as the last, still applicable
to Him who had been manifested in flesh, " received up
in glory."[3] Other not less explicit passages from his
writings might easily be quoted.[4] St. Peter also adds
his testimony to the fact, when he refers to " Jesus
Christ, who is on the right hand of God, having gone
into heaven; angels and principalities and powers being
made subject unto Him";[5] while the writer of the
Epistle to the Hebrews with no less distinctness says,
" But we behold Him who hath been made a little lower
than the angels, even Jesus, for the suffering of death
crowned with glory and honour"; and again, " Who
for the joy that was set before Him endured the cross,
despising shame, and hath sat down at the right hand
of the throne of God."[6] Even the Gospels which omit
any narrative of the Ascension imply it, as when the

[1] Phil. ii. 6-9.
[2] Phil. iii. 20.
[3] 1 Tim. iii. 16.

[4] For example, Eph. iv. 8-10.
[5] 1 Pet. iii. 22; comp. Acts ii. 33.
[6] Heb. ii. 9; xii. 2.

first Gospel quotes the words of Jesus to the high-priest, "Henceforth (ἀπ’ ἄρτι) ye shall see the Son of man sitting at the right hand of power, and coming on the clouds of heaven";[1] or as when the fourth tells us how He said, "What then if ye should behold the Son of man ascending where He was before?"[2] and makes such frequent reference to the declaration of our Lord that He was "going to the Father."[3]   In several of his apocalyptic visions also, St. John beholds the exalted "Son of man" encompassed by the splendour of His heavenly abode.[4]

Passages such as these take for granted the Ascension of our Lord with the same quiet and deliberate conviction as the ordinary events of His earthly history; and it is impossible to explain them in any other than their literal and historical acceptation.   They cannot be understood to express only the spiritual and ideal nature of the Christian faith.   More than this was certainly intended by their writers.   Nowhere do we meet with more specific statements as to any fact of the Redeemer's life.   The evidence is thus abundantly sufficient to show both what the first authorised and authoritative proclaimers of Christianity believed, and that their belief was formed under circumstances in the highest degree calculated to illustrate its reasonable-ness and to lend it weight.   If we refuse to credit them we must base our refusal either on the incredibility of

[1] Matt. xxvi. 64.   [2] John vi. 62.
[3] John xiv. 28 ; xvi. 5, 10, 17, 28.
[4] Rev. i. 13 ; v. 11-13 ; vi. 9-17 ; xiv. 1-5.

the events themselves, or on the assertion that they who have witnessed to them were so much under the influence of prepossession and prejudice as to believe that they saw what they did not see, and heard what they did not hear.   Neither of these points can be discussed now.   The first of them really resolves itself into the incredibility of everything miraculous.   The second takes for granted, what nothing but profound ignorance can assume, that the ascensions of Elijah[1] and of our Lord stand essentially on the same footing, and that they bear a similar relation to the systems of faith to which they respectively belong.   At present it is enough to say that, so far as the direct evidence of the men of our Lord's generation on any point can satisfy us, the witnesses to His Ascension could have had no better opportunities than they enjoyed, could not have been more capable of profiting by them, could not have spoken more clearly than they have done, and could, by neither word nor deed, have given more conclusive evidence as to their own convictions.   So far as evidence handed down from a remote past can carry conviction with it, that evidence is here.

We are not, however, without evidence of a still more convincing kind; for the sacred writers do more than presuppose our Lord's Ascension as a fact.   In the passages quoted, and in many others, they regard it as one without which the Christian Church could not have come into existence ; and than which no fact

---

[1] See Strauss, *Leben Jesu*, and Schenkel, *Bibel-Lexikon*, under the word "Himmelfahrt."

of Christianity had a stronger hold upon the gratitude
and joy and hope and exaltation of the Christian mind.
No one, indeed, will deny that at the very time when
the Gospels were penned (and the remark is the more
undeniable the farther we bring down that date), the
Ascension of our Lord stood side by side with His
Incarnation, Crucifixion, and Resurrection as a constituent element of Christian belief. In the light of
the Higher Criticism such testimony is of peculiar
value. It is not, that of one or two witnesses who
might be credulous or mistaken. It is that of com-
munities, of widespread bodies of men, whose life
had been changed by what they had felt compelled
to receive as facts, and to whom the conviction that a
particular event had really happened proved no principle slumbering in their breasts, but one pervading
their whole being and making it what it was. As
nothing could persuade us, so nothing could have persuaded them, to enter upon a new, and in most respects
far more trying life than that previously led by them,
except a deliberate assurance that the events upon
which their faith rested could be thoroughly relied on.

Why, indeed, should we show more hesitation about
accepting the Ascension than any other great fact of the
life of our Lord, such as His Incarnation or Resurrection?
It is not in itself more wonderful than these. It implies
no greater exercise of Divine power, and no greater departure from the laws by which nature and humanity
are governed. It is even less difficult to conceive that
the already glorified body of the Redeemer should have

been taken up to heaven in the sight of the disciples than that the Second Person of the Godhead should have come into the world as a child; or that, after having died on Calvary, He should have burst the bonds of death, and risen on the third morning from the grave without having seen corruption. An Ascension, or something of a similar nature, is indeed necessary to the verisimilitude of the life of Jesus as a whole; although not in the sense that His early followers might naturally imagine it, as they strove to fashion for their Master a closing scene worthy of all that had preceded. Even had imagination thus played its part in their account of their Lord's Ascension, it would but tend to show how thoroughly they were convinced of His Resurrection; for no thought of an Ascension could have entered into their minds had they not been persuaded that He had risen from the dead.

There is still another and a deeper sense in which the Ascension has always been demanded by believers. Without it we should have introduced into Christian history a problem of a kind altogether insoluble, and the existence of which could not fail to prevent its other truths from producing their legitimate effect upon us. If the Lord of the Church, if He in whom her life and hope are gathered up, had, after His Resurrection, been again compelled to submit to the sentence of mortality, that strength of Christian faith which springs from its being rooted in a heavenly world would disappear. How then could men either have believed in the past, or believe now, that Jesus was indeed the

Only Begotten of the Father, the Giver and the Prince of Life—life Divine, spiritual, unchangeable, and everlasting? Could He have bestowed that life and yet Himself have died? Could He have taken victory from the grave, and yet have lain in it for centuries— earth returned to earth, dust to dust, and ashes to ashes? Could He have said, "He that believeth on Me, though he die, yet shall he live; and whosoever liveth and believeth on Me shall never die,"[1] and yet be at this moment held fast under the dominion of death? The conception is impossible. Besides which, if the Lord Jesus did again die, where and under what circumstances did His death take place? Was it in the city or the country, amid the crowded haunts of men or in some distant solitude? Was He alone or surrounded by His friends? What was the last message sent by Him to His disciples? or what the last prayer he offered to His Father in heaven? To none of these questions can a reply be given; and an event so much more incomprehensible than (if we admit the Resurrection) the Resurrection itself—the death, in some ordinary way, of One who had been so preternaturally recalled from the grave, has no word spoken regarding it, and no ray of light thrown upon the darkness in which it is involved.

Here indeed lies the main weight of the evidence for the Ascension of our Lord. It follows from His Resurrection. It is inseparably connected with it. It is a corollary dependent upon it. We cannot indeed deduce

---

[1] John xi. 25, 26.

from the earlier event the precise circumstances attending the later. But that in the Resurrection the Ascension is implicitly involved will be granted by every one who, whether in a spirit of faith or unbelief, reflects upon the subject. If there be sufficient proof that Jesus rose from the grave the unbeliever has no interest in denying the Ascension; and, on the other hand, the believer has no need to ask more in order to satisfy himself that the Ascension really happened. From the very nature of the case he must conclude that, if our Lord rose from the dead, and that in a glorified condition, He could neither have continued to live as an inhabitant of this earth nor have again died. In one way or another He must have passed into the spiritual and eternal world, and must have returned to His God and Father.[1] Any difficulties connected with the evidence may be ascribed to our imperfect knowledge of the circumstances; and the reality of the fact itself may be accepted without hesitation.

What has now been said is, to a large extent at least, recognised by the most recent modern inquiry. Keim admits that "the Ascension of Jesus follows from all the facts of His career"; and, although he regards it as "not in a strict sense demonstrable," and distinguishes between "a general belief in the exaltation of Jesus and the materialistic description given of it in the New Testament," he can only sum up his discussion in the words, "The modern Christian consciousness is

---

[1] Comp. Martensen, *Dogmatik*, § 173 ; and especially Neander, *Das Leben Jesu*, 4th edition, p. 785, etc.

mature enough to dispense with these pictures, and
without seeing to believe with the earliest accounts
themselves that the sphere of the departing Jesus was
from the very hour of death the higher world of God." [1]
Weiss, who deals in the freest manner with the details
of the Ascension given by the Evangelists, is not less
explicit: "As certainly," he says, "as Jesus rose in the
body, *i.e.* in a glorified body, so certainly was He raised
to heaven in that body which was destined for the
heavenly life, and the Apostles thought of Him as
continuing to inhabit that glorified body in heaven
(Colossians ii. 9; Philippians iii. 21). In this sense
the corporeal Ascension of Jesus is of course produced
by His Resurrection, and with this it stands and falls.
To him who believes in a resurrection, as Scripture
understands it, and who, taking the Resurrection of
Jesus as a pledge thereof, believes in a real and therefore corporeal state of existence beyond the grave, to
him there is nothing in the Ascension of Jesus to
heaven which could be shown to be contrary to the
divinely-appointed laws for the government of this
world." [2]

With admissions of this kind we may be satisfied.
Once grant that the grave is not the termination of our
being, but that there is a "higher world of God" in
which the departed live, and both the Resurrection and
Ascension of Jesus, when looked at in their true light,
become matter for an intelligent rather than an un-

---

[1] *Jesus of Nazareth*, vi. pp. 365, 366, 382.
[2] *The Life of Christ*, translated by M. G. Hope, iii. 409.

reasoning faith. The materialistic details may be aban-
doned by those who think that the proof is not sufficient,
and the mere fact may be enough, that He who came
forth a living person from the tomb in the garden
ascended in due season to His Father in heaven, and
that He is now with Him. Let this much, moreover,
be allowed, and the details will soon cease to be a
difficulty. Returning in thought to the time when the
event took place, we shall see in the Risen Saviour the
marks of One who is preparing for His departure. The
strangely intermittent character of His visits and the
nature of the instructions He delivers will awaken the
suspicion that ere long we shall be left without Him.
At His call we shall accompany Him towards Bethany
with a vague presentiment of what is to happen. He
has vanished suddenly before now : to a final parting
a slow and gradual disappearance will be more suitable.
He has laid His hands before now on the heads of
children and blessed them : there will be nothing unnatural in His lifting up His hands and blessing us.
The upward movement will then begin : we shall direct
our gaze to heaven with astonishment and awe as He
ascends : a cloud will receive Him out of our sight : we
shall worship Him, and return to Jerusalem with great
joy. No one, in short, who accepts the fact will long
hesitate as to the details.

Two difficulties are still urged to which it is desirable to advert. They are stated with his usual clearness and emphasis by Strauss.

1. It is said that a tangible or palpable body is not

adapted to a superterrestrial abode.[1]   But the word
"tangible" may be used in two different senses, and we
may deny its applicability in one sense to our Lord's
risen body, while we admit it in another.   It may
mean either subject to be touched apart altogether from
the will of him whose body is spoken of, or capable of
being touched according to his will, and in such
manner as he may choose.   In the first of these senses
it has no application to the body of the Risen Lord.
There is no reason to think that at the moment when
Jesus ascended to heaven His body possessed those
properties of matter to which the word "tangible"
belongs.   The contrary would rather seem to have
been the case.   Our Lord's body was obviously not
tangible in the ordinary sense when, on the day of His
Resurrection, He twice appeared suddenly in the midst
of His disciples in the upper room at Jerusalem, though
the doors were shut.   Or, if it be said that it must
have been tangible, when St. Thomas was on one of
these occasions instructed to put his fingers and his
hand into the wounds inflicted on the cross, it is sufficient to reply that, just as the body taken as a whole
could be recognised though changed, so the marks of
its sufferings might remain, though changed in the same
direction and to the same extent as the whole body.
We are apt to forget that the wounds were a part of
the body, and that if the body was recognisable, though
not tangible in the sense of the objector, the same thing

[1] Strauss, *Life of Jesus*, Eng-   Schenkel, *B. Lexikon*, "Himmel
lish Translation, iii. 384. Comp.   fahrt."

may be said of the wounds. Besides this, there is much in the narrative of this particular appearance of the Risen Lord leading to the belief that the conviction ultimately forced upon the doubting Apostle was dependent, not merely upon the sight presented to him, but upon his own preparation for it. The week previous to that appearance had not been lost upon him: he had been passing through a process of education during that time. When, too, our Lord speaks of his faith, He does not say, "Because thou hast seen My wounds," but "because thou hast seen *Me*, thou hast believed"; and under the words addressed to him, "Be not faithless but *believing*," and "Thou hast *believed*," we are certainly not to think of a faith now first formed but, as so often in St. John, of a faith purified, strengthened, and deepened.[1] All this leads to the conclusion that, in the same way as Jesus had said to Mary Magdalene a week before, "Touch Me not, for I am not yet ascended to My Father," and had thus implied that, when known in the power of His Ascension, He might be touched, so the sensible proof offered to Thomas would be different from that given of the presence of any ordinary material object, and would be largely dependent for its efficacy on the Apostle's own state of mind. In itself the glorified condition of the body of our Lord, as that of One who had been made "a quickening Spirit," may have even been invisible to

---

[1] For a fuller exposition of these points and of this whole passage, reference may be made to the *Commentary on St. John* by Milligan and Moulton, published by Messrs. T. and T. Clark, Edinburgh.

the merely human eye, as it was, without doubt, intangible to the merely human hand. But it does not follow that it would be equally invisible or intangible to the eye or the hand of one who had been prepared by a spiritualising process for its perception. It would rather appear that our Lord designed expressly to distinguish between the tangibility of His own body and that of ordinary matter; and any objection, therefore, resting on the supposition that by tangibility the same thing is meant in both cases, rests upon preconceptions of the objector and not upon the facts presented to him.

This conclusion is confirmed by the consideration that with His body as the perfected instrument of His will, our Lord was wont to " show," or rather " manifest " Himself to His disciples only when He was pleased to do so; for the word "manifest," so often employed in connexion with His appearances after His Resurrection, expresses more than the word " show." It means at one time to bring out of the invisible into the visible, at another to reveal to man in a particular condition of his being what in a previous condition he would have been unable to take note of.[1] An entirely new state of things is thus presupposed, not only in the bodily condition of Jesus, but in the mental attitude of believers, when we speak of the body of the Risen Lord as " manifested "; and in that state the common qualities of material objects cannot be thought of as either exhibited or perceived. Something of a similar kind

---

[1] Comp. Col. iii. 4 (where it is opposed to κέκρυπται); John ii. 11, xxi. 1; 1 John iii. 2.

holds good with regard to the bodies of Christians in
the future world.   When the Apostle Paul gives particulars of their resurrection, he tells us that, on their
rising again at the last day, each of them shall possess
"a spiritual body";[1] and by this he means neither
that their bodies shall wholly evaporate into spirit, nor
that they shall lose the marks by which upon earth
they were distinguished from one another.   He means
rather that, when raised from their graves or changed,
their bodies shall be what they are not now, a full and
appropriate expression and organ of their spiritual life,
still indeed retaining their individuality, but independent of the limitations by which in our terrestrial state
matter is confined.   Unless, therefore, the words of the
Apostle, "a spiritual body," have no meaning, and some
distinct and intelligible meaning they must have had
to him who used them, they settle the question.   Such
a body, being the framework in and by which the Spirit
works, must be conformed to the Spirit which rules in all
its members.   It must interpose no obstacle to the accomplishment of the Spirit's aim.   It must rather obey its
every impulse, and must accompany it in its every flight.

A body of this kind, however, must be widely different from our present bodies, and language applicable
to them may be unsuitable to it.   If our Lord in His
superterrestrial estate has a body,—and one of the fundamental conceptions of humanity as well as the spirit
and aim of the Christian system are overthrown if He
has not,—this body must be in one way or another

---

[1] 1 Cor. xv. 44.

adapted to the sphere in which He is now living.   The
question, in the form in which it has been raised, is
thus not as to any inconsistency between the qualities
of body as we know it, and a heavenly sphere of existence.   It really raises a further question, whether the
conditions of our terrestrial being are so unchangeable as
absolutely to preclude all thought of a future different
from the present, or whether it is possible to accept any
such revelation of a bodily not less than a spiritual
immortality as must form a part of every just conception of our Christian hope.   Who shall venture to say
that we may not thus look forward to the future ?
And this the more when we consider that, in doing so,
the probabilities of the case are on the side of change.
If the future life is either to be in harmony with the
"increasing purpose" of God, or an object of our desire,
we must think of the body of man as there entirely different from what it is here; and any denial of the possibility of its being so, while personal identity is preserved,
would be tantamount to an assertion that at death
we return to the dust for ever.   Thus then it was with
the body of our Lord.   Either He does not still live, or if
He does live, His body is not subject to the same tests
as those applicable to it when He was on earth ; and,
with the same body which He possesses in heaven, He
might and naturally would ascend from Olivet.

2. A second difficulty is urged—that to speak of our
Lord's Ascension into heaven is to imply that heaven
is a locality circumscribed by definite boundaries, and
that of such a heavenly locality we can form no con-

ception.[1] When Jesus goes to Heaven, it is said, He goes to God, and God is everywhere.[2] He, therefore, who is to be ever with God can be confined to no particular spot, and there is no such place as heaven to which He may ascend. The difficulty springs from too materialistic a view of those expressions which the poverty of human thought and language compels us to employ. It is unnecessary, in thinking of heaven, to confine ourselves to the thought of any particular locality. We have no need to imagine to ourselves a region either higher than the blue sky or situated in the centre of those millions of starry orbs which move around us in silent majesty. Nor have we to pass onward into that interminable space which, as we must suppose, stretches beyond the limits of all created things, in order that there at last we may enter into the abodes of everlasting bliss. If such conceptions appear to be demanded by some expressions of the Word of God, they are at variance with others as well as with its general drift and meaning. In the New Testament, in particular, heaven is contrasted with earth, less as one *place* than as one *state* is contrasted with another. When we say "Our Father which art in heaven" we cannot mean that the Father to whom we pray dwells only in some distant region of the universe. He must be also by our side, in this world as well as beyond it; and the thought of His nearness to us is one of the conditions of effectual prayer. By these words, "in heaven," therefore, we simply mean that the

---

[1] Strauss, u.s. iii. 385.   [2] Comp. Psalm cxxxix. 7-10.

Father to whom we pray is in a region purer, loftier, and brighter than ours. We are upon earth, bowed down under its weaknesses, beset by its temptations, stained by its sins, afflicted by its sorrows, hampered by its limitations. He is " in heaven," free from weaknesses, temptations, sins, sorrows, and limitations of every kind, full of infinite pity and unchanging love. The conception is the same as that embodied in the words, " Heavenly Father," so often used by Jesus in circumstances with which the thought of place has no connexion, and which take us into an entirely different circle of ideas: " Your Heavenly Father feedeth them "; " Your Heavenly Father knoweth that ye have need of all these things "; " Every plant which my Heavenly Father planted not, shall be rooted up." [1] The same use of the words " heaven " and " heavenly " is peculiarly marked in the writings of St. John and in the Epistle to the Hebrews. " And no man," Jesus says to Nicodemus, " hath ascended into heaven, but He that descended out of heaven, even the Son of man, which is in heaven." [2] In speaking thus our Lord cannot mean to say that he was both in earth and in heaven, as two different *localities,* at one time. He was before the eyes of Nicodemus when He spoke. He was there not only in His Divinity but in the limitations of the humanity which He had assumed; and it was in the nature of things impossible that he could be elsewhere at the same instant. In using the words " in heaven,"

---

[1] Matt. vi. 26-32 ; xv. 13.
[2] John iii. 13.   Westcott and Hort omit the last clause.

therefore, our Lord could only mean that the true
essence of His being belonged not to a material but a
spiritual world, a world it may be of unclouded majesty,
but especially, as shown by the context in which the
words occur, of that love which is the very ground and
fundamental element of the Divine existence.   The
words "which is in heaven" point to no locality, but to
the state or condition of being to which our Lord belonged.   Other words of Jesus in the same discourse
lead to a similar conclusion: "If I told you earthly
things, and ye believe not, how shall ye believe if I tell
you heavenly things?"[1]   The "earthly" things here
spoken of cannot mean things relating to the material
earth, or to the course of human history, for no such
things had been taught by Him who came down out of
heaven.   The "heavenly" things, in like manner, cannot
mean things relating to a local heaven, for no part
either of the remaining discourse with Nicodemus or
of our Lord's other discourses contained in the fourth
Gospel is occupied with that thought.   The "earthly
things" are the truths, the home of which, so to speak, is
earth, and which were known before God gave His final
and complete revelation of Himself.   The "heavenly
things" are those upon which Jesus immediately proceeds to dwell, including His revelation of Himself
and, in Himself, of the Father, now for the first time
given in fulness to the world.   It is in perfect harmony
with this that, throughout the Gospel and Epistles of
St. John, the life of union with Christ or the Divine

[1] John iii. 12.

life in the soul is always regarded as life in its most absolute sense, life not merely future but present, unchangeable, and everlasting.[1] So also in the Apocalypse the New Jerusalem, the ideal picture of the true Church in a present world, comes down " out of heaven from God." [2]

The same mode of thought marks the Epistle to the Hebrews. When we read that our great High-priest has been " made higher than the heavens," [3] the meaning obviously is, not that He has passed through or been made higher than the sky, but that He has been exalted far above all the material creation; and that, freed from every restraint, He has gone into the immediate presence of that God and Father who is everywhere and in all things.[4] When, too, we read of a " heavenly calling," [5] the context shows that we are to understand neither a calling from heaven nor to heaven, but one essentially spiritual in its nature, and in contrast with the calling of Israel by Moses, the representative of an outward and carnal economy. A similar remark applies to the " heavenly things," mentioned in the same Epistle,[6] which are in contrast not with earth as a locality but with the tabernacle as a material building. They are the spiritual, the Divine, ideas which an embodiment in form may symbolise but cannot adequately express. Finally, when we are told that the heroes of

---

[1] John xi. 25, 26, xvii. 3 ; 1 John ii. 17, 24, iii. 14.

[2] Rev. xxi. 10.

[3] Heb. vii. 26.

[4] Compare Riehm, *Lehrbegriff des Heb. Briefes*, i. 349; compare also Keil, *Heb. Brief.*, pp. 210, 266.

[5] Heb. iii. 1.

[6] Heb. viii. 5 ; ix. 23

the ancient faith desired "a better country, that is an
heavenly," [1] it seems as if the writer had in view not so
much a region beyond the grave as the spiritual blessings of the better covenant. [2]

In the light of passages such as these there is reason
to conclude that, according to the conception of the
sacred writers, "heaven" is a state rather than a place. [3]
The thought of locality may, no doubt, be involved in
it, but it is not the main thought.   "Heaven lies about
us" even now, and that not only "in our infancy," but
in our manhood and age.   Ideally we are in it when
we experience, with an immediateness unknown to us
in our common lives, the presence of God as a Father,
and when we open our hearts to the full manifestations
of His grace.   It is one of the "many abiding places"
of that "Father's house" [4] which is not to be regarded
as a home in a distant land alone, but is to be found in
the universe around us when that universe is beheld
in the light of the Father's love.   In the meantime
"earth" and "heaven" are in Scripture contrasted with
one another; but the contrast will be removed, and
then the one will become, not less than the other, a
place for the perfect manifestation of God; in other
words, earth will be a heaven.   Even now there is a
true sense in which "God, being rich in mercy, for His

[1] Heb. xi. 16; comp. Westcott *in loc.*

[2] Comp. verses 39, 40.

[3] It has yet to be shown in
this lecture that the same remark
applies to the expression "Sitting
at the right hand of God." Of
the difference between what is
here said and the Lutheran doctrine of the ubiquity of Christ's
glorified body it ought not to be
necessary to speak.

[4] John xiv. 2.

great love wherewith He loved us . . . hath made us to sit in the heavenly places in Christ Jesus." [1] Even now " our citizenship is in heaven," and what we wait for is not removal from one limited locality to another, but " the fashioning anew of our body of humiliation, that it may be conformed to the body of Christ's glory, according to the working whereby He is able to subject all things unto Himself." [2]

When, therefore, we speak of our Lord's Ascension into heaven we have to think less of a transition from one locality than of a transition from one condition to another. A change of locality is indeed implied, but it need not be to a circumscribed habitation like that of earth ; it may be only to a boundless spiritual region above us and encompassing us on every side. The real meaning of the Ascension is that, in that closing act of His history upon earth, our Lord withdrew from a world of limitations and darkness and sorrows to that higher existence where " in the presence of God there is fulness of joy, and where at His right hand there are pleasures for evermore." [3]

If these things be so it will be seen that the ques- tion alluded to in a previous part of this lecture, as to the precise point of time when Jesus returned to His Father, loses its importance. No sooner did He shake off the bonds of earth, and take His place in the higher spiritual world to which He was ever afterwards to belong, than He may be said to have ascended into heaven. When for a special purpose He again appeared to His

---

[1] Eph. ii. 4-6.   [2] Phil. iii. 20, 21.   [3] Ps. xvi. 11.

disciples as they had known Him during His earthly
ministry, He may be said to have descended out of
heaven. Wherever He was in that glorified condition
which began at His Resurrection, there heaven in its
Scripture sense also was ; and His very presence with
the Father was the rendering of His account. No
words needed to be uttered either by the Father or by
Him. From the first moment of His entrance into
heaven, its inhabitants beheld in Him the Captain of
salvation, who had accomplished His appointed work,
and in whom the Father was well pleased.

II. We have spoken of the Ascension of our Lord as a
fact of actual occurrence, assuring us that, when He
passed out of the sight of His Apostles on the Mount
of Olives, it was to enter a new sphere of spiritual
existence, where He was to live and where He still lives
for ever. To consider the most important purpose of
that life, and the manner in which it is accomplished,
both in heaven and upon earth, is the main object of
these lectures. But, before entering upon this, one or
two aspects of the Ascension itself demand attention.

1. It was the completion of all that was involved
in the Incarnation. There is no need to dwell upon
the fact that, when our Lord ascended into heaven, He
did so in His human as well as in His Divine nature ;
or that, in laying aside the garment of " flesh " in which
He had been clothed, He did not lay aside the humanity
which He had assumed. That Incarnation constitutes
the basis of the Christian faith, the foundation of the
whole Christian system, in its bearing both upon time

and upon eternity.   The assumption of that human
nature which was involved in it was not to come to an
end when Jesus died on Calvary, or when He rose from
the dead.   Whenever He spoke to His disciples of His
going away it was the same "I" then before them who
was to go; the same "I" who would afterwards remember them and dwell with them, and at last come for
them again.   The thought could not by possibility
enter into their minds that after His departure He was
to be a different being, to be no longer the human Master
and Friend and Brother whom they had honoured and
loved and clung to during the days of His flesh.   His
words could convey but one impression to their minds,
that even after His exaltation and glorification He
would be still what He was then.   This indeed was
the impression which they did convey.   When St.
Paul breaks forth into his triumphant strain of joy for
the blessings of redemption, he speaks of Christ Jesus
who died and rose again as at the right hand of God,
and also making intercession for us;[1] and the writer of
the Epistle to the Hebrews declares that the High-
priest in heaven who is touched with the feeling of
our infirmities is the same Jesus who had been "in
all points tempted like as we are."[2]   So clear and
explicit indeed is the language of Scripture upon this
point that no one who accepts the fact of the Ascension
will deny that, if our Lord is now in the heavenly
world at all, He is there not as God only, but as man.

   Without further delay, therefore, we may proceed

[1] Romans viii. 34.   [2] Heb. iv. 14, 15

to ask, What is the relation between the two stupendous events, the one at the beginning and the other at
the close of the earthly life of Jesus—His Incarnation
and His Ascension? The answer is, that the latter
completes what was aimed at by the former, and was
even to a certain extent involved in it. For the object
of the Incarnation was not simply to make it possible
for the Eternal Son to labour and suffer and die. Had
no more than this been necessary for the accomplishment of His work, it would be difficult to understand
why His human nature should not have been a merely
temporary possession, and after having been united to
His Divine nature during the days of His humiliation,
been laid aside at His exaltation. His mission, upon
this view, was executed when He bowed His head and
gave up the ghost. The great sacrifice had been offered.
The way to the Father had been opened up. Why
should the Conqueror retain what in this case could
only have been the memorial of His low estate? Why
should He not divest Himself of the garments in which
He had borne the burden and heat of the day? and,
Why should He not return to every particular of that
condition in which before He became poor He had been
rich?

But we are not led to think that the sole or even
the great object of the Incarnation was to prepare our
Lord as a victim for the sacrifice. Scripture everywhere implies that, necessary as was His suffering of
death to procure the pardon of sin, and precious as are
its fruits, it was only a step towards the attainment of

a still higher end—an end contemplated from the
beginning, corresponding more closely to the nature of
God Himself, and alone able to satisfy our need.
That end was to bring us into a state of perfect union
with the Father of our spirits, and so to introduce
into our weak human nature the strength of the
Divine nature, that not in name only, or outwardly, or
by a figure, but in truth, inwardly, and in reality, we
might receive the right to become children of God.[1]
The Incarnation by itself could not have effected this,
because it could only bring the Eternal Son into "the
flesh," and flesh is a barrier to that free communication
of the Spirit by which alone we can be united to Him
who is Spirit.[2] The Incarnation could only identify
the Redeemer with the essential elements of humanity.
It could not spiritualise that bodily organisation which
is no less a part of the true being of man than his
intellectual and moral gifts. It could not provide for
the unity of his nature as a whole without failing
to be a genuine Incarnation. The Resurrection and
Ascension needed to follow, that the "quickening
Spirit" of Jesus, thus set free, might enter into our
spirits, and make us sharers of its victory. Up to that
point in His history, the Son "had been learning
obedience by the things which He suffered."[3] He
had been effecting an actual identification of Himself
with every weakness and temptation and sorrow of our

---

[1] John i. 12. The word τέκνα
here used deserves attention, not
"sons," which we may become
by adoption, but "children," implying actual (though spiritual)
paternity.

[2] John iii. 6 ; iv. 24.

[3] Heb. v. 8.

present lot. He had even borne our sins in His own body on the tree, and had accepted that death which is the wages of sin. Then, still as man, He rose victorious over sin and death; and, still as man, ascended to the Father that, with our nature spiritualised and glorified, He might pass into the sphere where nothing but the Father's will is done, and where the Father's immediate presence is the fountain of perpetual joy.

Even in the creation of man, therefore, the Ascension of our Lord, and not merely His Incarnation, must have been part of the Divine Counsel. Our first parents, though in an estate of innocence, could not perfectly fulfil the idea of human nature. It may be true, as the Church seems always to have held, that " besides the seeds of natural virtue and religion sown in their minds, they were endowed with certain gifts and powers supernatural infused by the Spirit of God; and that in these their perfection consisted." [1] Yet, although they possessed these " gifts and powers supernatural," it could only be as gifts. They had not been made a part of their nature in the intimate sense in which, as we have yet to see, they have been made ours in the glorified Redeemer. The ultimate idea of human nature had not yet been fulfilled, and the consequence was, that when assailed by temptation our first parents fell. They had not received that " indissoluble life " which no power of the enemy can touch. Satan had not been trodden down. The Spirit of a victorious

---

[1] Bull's *Works*, Oxford, 1837, vol. ii. p. 82. Archer Butler takes an opposite view, *Sermons*, 1st series, p. 325.

Redeemer had not taken full possession of their spirits. For these results a " new birth,"[1] a " new creation,"[2] was needed—a birth and a creation to be reached only when the Spirit of One at once Divine and human was made their spirit, the human giving the connecting point, the Divine the ruling power.   In other words, they could be reached only when our Lord was glorified.

It is important to dwell upon this point because, in the revived interest which has been taken in modern times in the great doctrine of the Incarnation, it may be doubted whether full justice has been done to that of the Ascension.   In Christian truth, as taught and applied by the Apostles, the latter is always connected with the former by the closest bonds; and, even when not stated in express terms, it always underlies their thoughts.   It is not enough to say that the Incarnation is the keystone of the Christian system.   In a certain sense, indeed, it is so, for it is the foundation of Christian history.   But, *taken by itself*, it is not the centre of Christian doctrine or the mainspring of Christian life. When St. Paul speaks of the Redeemer, it is seldom in any other light than as One who has not only assumed humanity, but in whom humanity has been glorified.[3]   When he describes " the exceeding greatness of God's power to us-ward who believe," he has in his mind a power not exhibited only in the earthly life of the Redeemer, but " the strength of that might which God wrought in Christ, when He raised Him from the dead and made Him to sit at His right hand in the

---

[1] John iii. 3.   [2] Eph. ii. 10.   [3] Phil. ii. 7-9.

heavenly places."[1] And, when he sums up the doctrine which he had preached to the Corinthians in its two main branches, one of which is that "Christ died for our sins according to the Scriptures," he is careful, in mentioning the other, to change the tense in which he sets it forth, so that we may rest on the thought not only of the past but of the present, who "hath been raised (not 'was raised') on the third day according to the Scriptures."[2] Nor is it otherwise with St. John. His ideas of "life" and "light" as applied to Jesus are those of eternal life and unfading light;[3] and his main conception of the Lord who guides the fortunes of the Church is expressed by him in the words which he bids us hear from the Son of man Himself: "I am the first and the last, and the living One; and I was dead, and behold, I am alive for evermore."[4] A similar line of thought runs throughout the whole New Testament. Christ is not merely the Incarnate Son; He is in His human nature exalted and glorified. When we would regard Him either as the foundation or as the life of the Church, we cannot separate the Ascension and the Incarnation. As the Ascension necessarily presupposes the Incarnation, so without the Ascension the Incarnation is incomplete. In the teaching of Scripture the two events are complementary to one another. Our conception of the Christ, therefore, ought to be the same. Unless it be so, there is no small danger that,

---

[1] Eph. i. 20.
[2] 1 Cor. xv. 4.
[3] Compare the contrasted description of the Baptist in John v. 35.
[4] Rev. i. 18.

notwithstanding the immense advance lately made by
theology, from the manner in which, after having long
devoted itself too exclusively to man and his salvation,
it has turned to Christ,[1] a most important part of the
gain may be lost sight of. Occupying itself with the
Incarnation alone, theology and along with it religion
will be deprived of its most essential characteristic. It
will fail to dwell amidst those superearthly realities
which it is the object of the New Testament to make
our daily food; and, though man and the world may
still be elevated, they will not be pervaded by the light
and the spirit of heaven.[2] The Ascension must thus
be combined with the Incarnation if we would understand the process by which the Almighty designs to
realise His final purpose with regard to humanity.[3] In
the Incarnate and Ascended Lord, we have all that the
human heart expects with unquenchable instinct and
undying hope. Seated on the throne of that heavenly
world which is above us and around us on every side is
One in whom the human nature has been closely and
indissolubly united with the Divine; and from that
time onward humanity is filled with its loftiest potencies
and most glorious prospects. At the Ascension the
goal of humanity is reached.

How elevating and stimulating is the thought!
Even in fallen man we often see much that reminds us
of his high original,—intellectual powers which seem

---

[1] Comp. Rev. J. R. Illingworth, in *Lux Mundi*, 3rd ed. p. 133.
[2] Comp. Hare, *Mission of the Comforter*, Serm. I.
[3] Comp. Godet *On Luke* xxv. 50-53.

to penetrate into the deepest secrets of the universe, wisdom before which the future unfolds itself as before the prophet's eye, the heart that throbs with generous and self-denying love, the saintliness of character that commands our admiration or our awe. Yet when we endeavour to extend these blessings how much cause have we often to despond! Every effort made by us seems to be in vain. We fail; others fail. We see that even Jesus failed; and we listen with melancholy sympathy to the pathetic words of the beloved disciple when he brings to an end his account of his Master's struggle: "But though He had done so many signs before them, yet they believed not on Him." [1] In the Ascended Lord all weakness passes away; all that limits the universal diffusion of His Spirit is removed; and human nature glorified with the glory of the Divine may become the portion of every child of Adam. In that nature the Lord Jesus Christ has ascended to His Father. We who are partakers of it are His "brethren." [2] And as He ascends before our eyes, we behold the pledge of perfect and everlasting communion established between God and man.

2. The Ascension of our Lord was His entrance into the reward prepared for Him after the accomplishment of His work. We are not, indeed, to imagine that even amidst the pains and sorrows of earth our Lord had no reward. Never at one single point of the *via dolorosa* trodden by Him from the manger to the cross did the joyful confidence desert Him that, in the obedience of perfect sonship, He was doing the Father's will; and

[1] John xii. 37.   [2] John xx. 17.

never did He lose sight of the glorious results He was
to secure.　Thoughts like these were always present to
His mind, and even in themselves they were a reward
for the sufferings He endured.　He saw in them of the
travail of His soul, and He was satisfied.　More than
once, when hours of thickest darkness gathered round
Him, He spoke of " My peace " [1] and " My joy." [2]　And
when He reflected on the wisdom of the Divine Counsels,
so inscrutable by man, we are told that He " rejoiced
in the Holy Spirit." [3]　The mystery of His sorrow is
familiar to us; we think too little of the mystery of
His joy.

But this joy was not His sole encouragement.　He
looked forward to another and a higher joy.　" For the
joy that was set before Him He endured the cross, despising the shame." [4]　He spoke of the " Son of man
coming in His kingdom," [5] of " the new fruit of the
vine " [6] that He would then drink with His disciples,
of the " regeneration " [7] that was to mark the close of
the present state of things; and, when He referred to
the future in parables, it was under such joyful figures
as those of a banquet or a marriage feast. [8]　More particularly this reward seems to be presented to us in the
New Testament under three points of view, all of which
are immediately connected with the condition of the
Ascended Lord.　It was reward,—in relation to Himself, to the members of His body, and to His enemies.

---

[1] John xiv. 27.　　　　　　　[2] John xvii. 13.
[3] Luke x. 21.　　[4] Heb. xii. 2.　　[5] Matt. xvi. 28.　　[6] Mark xiv. 25
[7] Matt. xix. 28,　　　　　　　[8] Luke xiii. 29 ; Matt. xxii. 2.

(1.) In relation to Himself, our Lord was to be glorified," that is, He was not only to be crowned with glory, but with glory seen and acknowledged by the world. Under this point of view His reward is especially spoken of in the fourth Gospel; and the passages relating to it, when looked at in the light of their context, are so remarkable that they ought to be examined. They are mainly these. When Andrew and Peter told Jesus of the Greeks who would see Him, He answered them, "The hour is come, that the Son of Man should be glorified," and He ended with the prayer, "Father, glorify Thy name." When at the Last Supper Judas had gone out, our Lord immediately exclaimed, "Now is the Son of man glorified, and God is glorified in Him; and God shall glorify Him in Himself, and straightway shall He glorify Him." Finally, our Lord thus pours forth the longings of His heart in His High-priestly prayer, "Father, the hour is come; glorify Thy Son, that the Son also may glorify Thee"; "I glorified Thee on the earth, having accomplished the work which Thou hast given Me to do. And now, O Father, glorify Thou Me with Thine Own Self, with the glory which I had with Thee before the world was": "The glory which Thou hast given unto Me I have given unto them, that they may be one, even as we are one": "Father, that which Thou hast given Me, I will that where I am, they also may be with Me; that they may behold My glory which Thou hast given Me; for Thou lovedst Me before the foundation of the world." [1]

---

[1] John xii. 23, 28 ; xiii. 31, 32 ; xvii. 1, 4, 5, 22, 24.

Let us put these passages together, and look at them in their connexion with the position of Jesus when He uttered them, and we shall learn the true nature of the "glorifying" and the "glory" of which they speak. No mere material glory is alluded to, no mere outward blessedness, no mere homage of angels or of men; it is in another direction altogether that we must seek their meaning.

Before our Lord came into the world His glory had been that of Divine Sonship. He had been " the effulgence of the Father's glory";[1] and, as the essence of the Divine character is love, He had been the expression, the impersonation of that love. From eternity He had been the Father's delight, rejoicing always before Him; and with no disturbing element to cloud their blessed fellowship, the ages of the ages had passed away, love ever flowing forth from the Father to the Son, and returning from the Son to the Father, nothing within, above, around, except the glorious and, as soon as there were eyes to see them, the visible harmonies of love. That time came to an end. Man was created and fell; and, in order to redeem him, the Eternal Word became flesh and tabernacled among us. Where was the glory of the Divine Son then? It was there—more, it may be said, than ever there; for the work of the Son upon earth was the highest conceivable manifestation of the love of God. But the glory, though there, was hidden in the lowliness and humiliations of a suffering life. Men could not believe that the Son of Mary, " the Man of

[1] Heb. i. 3.

sorrows and acquainted with grief," was the beloved
Son of the Father in whom He was well pleased.
They rejected Him, and thinking that they were doing
service to God they nailed Him to the cross.[1] A third
and last stage in the history of Jesus followed. He
who had been crucified in weakness, was raised by the
power of God, ascended to the right hand of the
Majesty on high, and sent down the gift of His Holy
Spirit to complete the redemption of the world. That
was the rolling back of the clouds which had interrupted
the vision of Christ's glory upon earth. He was not
something different then from what He had previously
been. As human, not less than Divine, He was essentially the same—the revelation of the love of God. But
now He was seen by human eyes to be so, as " before
the world was " He had been seen by the Father.
The thought of His Incarnation, of His humiliation, of
His tears and agonies and cries, of His death and burial,
no longer dimmed His glory ; and this lesson was proclaimed as one of the eternal verities, that not earthly
power or greatness, but love and self-sacrifice, are the
highest expression of what God is, and true glory.

When, therefore, our Lord prays, " Father, glorify
Thy Son, that the Son also may glorify Thee," we are
not to think chiefly of outward glory. There may be,
doubtless there will be, such. Outward glory surrounded
Jesus and the two Old Testament saints on the Mount
of Transfiguration. The Shechinah, which was the manifestation of the Divine glory in the Tabernacle, shed

[1] Comp. John xvi. 2.

a brilliant light over the Most Holy place. And it is not possible for us to think of " the glory to be revealed " except as accompanied by light and splendour. Yet, whatever outward glory may surround our Lord, what He speaks of as His reward is mainly inward. It is the glory of Divine Sonship. It is the glory of the most intimate union and communion with that God who is the sum and the substance of all being in its holiest and happiest estate. It is the fellowship with God of One who is not only the coequal and coeternal Word, but who is also Man. And, finally, it is this glory manifested to the eyes of all, the veil being with-drawn which had hitherto obscured or concealed the Son's unity of relation to the Father, in order that that glory of the Father Himself, which is the end of all existence, and which can be seen only in the Son, may shine forth in the sight of His creatures. Thus the exalted Redeemer vindicates the ways of God to man ; and, as no loftier task can be imagined, so there can be no greater reward than to be owned, alike of God and man, as successful in accomplishing it. This is our Lord's reward when it is viewed as " glory." The Son glorified the Father, and the Father glorifies His Son.

(2.) In relation to the members of His body, our Lord was to be the fulness, the *pleroma*, of all Divine blessing to His people. This aspect of His reward is often spoken of in the New Testament, and especially in St. Paul's Epistles to the Ephesians and Colossians. In the first of these Epistles we read, as part of a de-scription of the glory of the Lord Jesus Christ, that we are "blessed with every spiritual blessing in the heavenly places in Him"; that it was the good pleasure of the Father, "in the dispensation of the fulness of the times, to sum up all things in Christ, the things in the heavens and the things upon the earth"; and that "He put all things in subjection under His feet, and gave Him to be Head over all things to the Church, which is His body, the fulness of Him that filleth all in all." [1] In like manner, although still more directly, in the Epistle to the Colossians, which, as distinguished from the Ephesian Epistle, is occupied with the glory of the Head rather than of the members of the Body, we are told that Christ is "the Head of the body, the Church: who is the beginning, the firstborn from the dead; that in all things He might have the pre-eminence. For it was the good pleasure of the Father that in Him should all the fulness dwell; and through Him to reconcile all things unto Himself, whether things upon the earth or things in the heavens"; and again, that "in Him dwelleth all the fulness of the Godhead bodily"; and that "in Him we are made full, who is the Head of all principality and power." [2] In passages such as these, the context distinctly shows that it is not the pre-incarnate, but the Risen and Ascended Lord of whom the Apostle speaks. No doubt, in immediate connexion with some of them, the glorious attributes of the preincarnate Son are described, and we are taken back to a time before the foundation of the world, that we may behold in Him "the image of the invisible God, the

---

[1] Eph. i. 3, 10, 22, 23.   [2] Col. i. 18-20; ii. 9, 10.

firstborn of all creation, in whom all things were created, in the heavens and upon the earth, things visible and things invisible, whether thrones or dominions or principalities or powers; all things have been created through Him and unto Him; and He is before all things, and in Him all things consist." [1] But in the words to which special reference has been made, St. Paul passes beyond the thought of the pre-incarnate Christ to the thought of Him as He is now in heaven. He speaks of Him as one who has both died and risen again, not only as the firstborn " of all creation " but as the firstborn " from the dead," and of His seat in the " heavenly places "; while in another part of his Epistle to the Ephesians he expressly mentions His Ascension, " Now, this that He ascended, what is it but that He also descended into the lower parts of the earth ? He that descended is the same also that ascended far above all the heavens, that He might fill all things," after which the Apostle proceeds to enlarge upon the gifts bestowed by the Ascended Lord, and the end to be attained by them. [2]

These passages present us with a very striking picture of the reward now enjoyed by Him who on earth had been humbled even unto death. He has received far more than outward glory or material recompense for His previous pain. From eternity the grand Original in whom the Almighty had beheld and planned the universe of created things, and " without whom," to use the similar language of St. John, " was not anything made

[1] Col. i. 15-17.   [2] Eph. iv. 9-16.

that hath been made: that which hath been made was life in Him,"[1] He, in His human as well as His Divine nature, has been, is now, and will ever be, the centre not only of the natural but of the redeemed creation. In Him, as in one great fountain-head, are stored up those waters of Divine grace that, throughout the ages, are to flow forth in every direction, and to fertilise every department of the life both of men and nature, so that they may produce, instead of bitter fruits, the sweet fruits of righteousness and peace and joy. From Him and through Him alone are to come all holy thoughts, all heavenly aspirations, and all just works, everything that makes life desirable, lends brightness to existence, and fills us with the hope of immortality. Nor is He presented to us in these passages as if He were only some abstract idea of the Godhead, some hardly comprehensible conception of a purely spiritual Being filling all space and time, to which in our hours of need we are to flee, but as a living personality whose possession of irresistible power is associated with human affections and human sympathies, as the Divine Man who can be touched with a feeling of our infirmities, and can enter into all our varying emotions whether of sorrow or gladness. In Him as such dwells the fulness of all perfection, of the very perfection after which, by the law of their existence, man and nature strive. The full store of heavenly gifts has been placed at His disposal; and when the glory of " God the Father " is consummated in the happiness of everything created by Him, it will be

[1] John i. 3, R. V. margin.

in the name of Jesus that every knee shall bow; and
Him will every tongue confess.[1]   Our Lord, in short, was
exalted, not to be separated for ever from a world which
crucified Him, from a world with the weaknesses and
sorrows and sins of which He was once in contact, but
that He may apply to it His ample and free forgiveness,
together with the inexhaustible resources of His power.

As this too was the purpose of the Almighty, so also
has it been fulfilled in the whole history of the Christian Church.   On its larger scale that history has been
summed up in the Revelation of St. John under the
light of the manifestation of the Ascended Lord.   In
her aims and teaching and labours and prayers the
Church of Christ has acknowledged but one source of
illumination and quickening and guidance—even Christ.
She may not always have been true to the source of her
strength, but in no land or century has she owned any
other principle or declared that she was dependent on
any other helper.   In the darkest as well as the
brightest, in the most ignorant as well as the most
enlightened periods of the past, her one symbol has
been the Cross.   Everything around her may have
changed; in this she has not changed.   In her most
mistaken or faithless moods she has rested upon this
rock, and has desired to do honour to her One Head.
When we turn to private Christian life, it has not been
otherwise.   The faith that has removed mountains, the
hope that has lightened suffering, the love that has run

---

[1] Phil. ii. 10, 11.   For force of the verb "confess" see Lightfoot
in loc.

like a golden thread through the otherwise dark web of human wrongs, have all been confessed by those who have exhibited them to be the gift of Christ. In Christ each believer has lived. Out of His fulness each would say that he had received his patience in affliction, his meekness under provocation, his spirit of toil amidst discouragement, his readiness to sacrifice himself amidst misinterpretation and thanklessness, his heavenly-mindedness under the pressure of the outward world. In Christ each has died. One voice alone reaches us from the depths of every Christian heart, "To me to live is Christ"; "God forbid that I should glory save in the cross of Christ."[1] The same feelings animate the Christian's heart when he looks forward to the future. His Ascended Lord is to him the model of all excellence, the ideal of all perfection: His highest aim is so to live by Him that he may be like Him. Is not all this a great reward, and one in the very spirit of the Redeemer's mission?

Again, let us dwell for a moment on the thought that this reward in its fullest extent belongs to One not less human than Divine—our Brother! We know what Jesus was when upon earth. But whatever men beheld in Him then they may still behold in Him, though in indefinitely increased measure, and with means of easier application to their wants. If, as the Lamb that had been slain, He bears upon His Person the marks of Calvary, He bears also in His heart the memories of Cana of Galilee, of Simon's house, of the spot outside

[1] Comp an eloquent passage in Dale *On Ephesians*, p. 96.

the little town of Bethany where Mary wept beside her
brother's grave and He wept with her. He is "Jesus
Christ, the same yesterday, to-day, and for ever"—the
same, that is, while other teachers are removed by
death; but not the same, in so far as He can now do
for us what He could not do on earth, and can secure
for us a triumph which could not be ours had He not
first realised it in Himself.

(3.) In relation to His enemies our Lord was to be
their Conqueror and Judge. As He looked forward to
the future He often spoke of the "kingdom" upon
which He was ere long to enter. When He shadowed
forth in parables the nature of His work and His future
glory He was wont to employ the figure of a king;[1]
and He accepted the homage of the penitent thief in
his prayer to be remembered when He should "come
in His kingdom."[2] He held out to His followers the
hope of eating and drinking "at His table in His kingdom";[3] and at the sounding of the seventh angel in
the Apocalypse there "followed great voices in heaven,
and they said, The kingdom of the world is become the
kingdom of our Lord, and of His Christ: and He shall
reign for ever and ever."[4] We lose the full force of
such passages by substituting our own ideas of a king
and of a kingdom for those of the Jews in our Lord's day.
We think of exaltation in earthly dignity, of a brilliant
court, of crowds of attendants, of wealth, luxury, and
splendour. These conceptions were not indeed strange

---

[1] Matt. xviii. 23, xxii. 11 ; Luke xiv. 31.

[2] Luke xxiii. 42.   [3] Luke xxii. 30.   [4] Rev. xi. 15.

to the mind of a Jew when Jesus was upon earth, but they were not the prominent ones which he connected with the term king. To him a king was more especially the representative of two ideas, victory over enemies and judgment.

When wearied with the rule of the judges it was partly in the first of these lights that Israel cried out for a king, that " he might go before them and fight their battles." [1] Thus also the Hope of Israel is often celebrated in the Psalms, " Yet I have set my King upon my holy hill of Sion. Ask of me, and I will give Thee the nations for Thine inheritance, and the uttermost parts of the earth for Thy possession. Thou shalt break them with a rod of iron ; Thou shalt dash them in pieces like a potter's vessel ; " [2] " I speak the things which I have made touching the King. Gird Thy sword upon Thy thigh, O Mighty One, Thy glory and Thy majesty. Thine arrows are sharp ; the peoples fall under Thee ; they are in the hearts of the King's enemies ; " [3] " He shall have dominion from sea to sea, and from the river unto the ends of the earth. They that dwell in the wilderness shall bow before Him, and His enemies shall lick the dust." [4] To such passages we may also add the favourite designation of the Almighty by the Jews—the Lord of Sabaoth, the Lord of hosts.

But in the eyes of Israel a great king was not only a victorious conqueror, he was also a judge of men. Again, it was partly in this aspect that Israel desired a king.

[1] 1 Sam, viii. 20.   [2] Ps. ii. 6, 8, 9.   [3] Ps. xlv. 1, 3, 5.
[4] Ps. lxxii. 8, 9.

"Now make us a king to judge us like all the nations." [1]
In the Psalms also this kingly prerogative of judgment
is associated in the closest manner with that of victory
over foes.   Immediately following one of the descriptions of the "king" already quoted we read, "Thy throne,
O God, is for ever and ever : a sceptre of equity is the
sceptre of Thy kingdom.   Thou hast loved righteousness,
and hated wickedness : therefore God, Thy God, hath
anointed Thee with the oil of gladness above Thy
fellows." [2]   So also elsewhere.   The combination of in-
flicting disaster upon enemies and executing judgment
for the poor and needy often meets us in the same
Psalm, and strikingly illustrates the ideas of Israel
upon this point : "The King's strength also loveth
judgment." [3]

When, in the light of these passages, we turn to our
Lord's reward in the aspect in which we are now considering it, we are met, in the first place, by the assurance that it is victory.   Victory, indeed, presupposes
war ; but war is the characteristic of the present Christian dispensation.   That dispensation is not one of rest.
It is one of struggle, a struggle with evil, carried on no
doubt by the instrumentality of the Church, but in
which the Head of the Church shares, and for which
He supplies the needful strength—"Rule Thou in the
midst of Thine enemies." [4]   In this aspect it is particularly set before us in the Apocalypse, where the
Captain of Salvation rides forth at the head of His
armies, arrayed in a garment sprinkled with blood and

---

[1] 1 Sam viii. 5.   [2] Ps. xlv. 6, 7.   [3] Ps. xcix. 4.   [4] Ps. cx. 2.

with a sharp sword proceeding out of His mouth.[1] In
the same aspect also we read of His kingdom, in the
first epistle to the Corinthians, that a time is coming
when He shall deliver up the kingdom to God, even the
Father; when He shall have abolished all rule and all
authority and power.[2] The kingdom here alluded to by
the Apostle is no kingdom of mere honour and glory.
It is rather one in which our Lord contends with His
foes until He makes them His footstool, and which,
therefore, He naturally lays down when there are no
more foes to overcome. Such has been the history of
the whole Christian age. "The light has shined in the
darkness, and the darkness overcame it not."[3] The
struggle of our Lord with "the Jews" during the days
of His flesh, described in the fourth Gospel, has never
ceased to be a struggle upon the wider area of the
world.

Our Lord's kingdom, however, is one of victory as
well as war. Many indeed, when they look back upon
the past, may be of opinion that it has been marked by
defeat rather than victory. Why, they may ask, unless
it were so, should not all opposition have been long
since overcome? Yet in the same sense the issue of
our Lord's own struggle upon earth may seem to have
been defeat. He was rejected and despised and per-
secuted, sentenced by the tribunals of His own land to
death, and nailed to the cross where He bowed His
head and died. Was not that defeat? It was really
victory. St. John brings it before us under the aspect

[1] Rev. xix. 13, 15.   [2] 1 Cor. xv. 24.   [3] John i. 5.

of "glory," of a "lifting up on high out of the earth,"
of a life willingly surrendered which no man could
have taken from Him, of a corn of wheat sown in the
ground, not to perish, but to spring up in fresh and
more abundant forms of loveliness.[1]   All that was
victory.[2]   It has not been otherwise since then.
Amidst all its struggles Christian truth has never lost
its spirit of confidence and hope.   It has never failed
to meet its opponents in controversy, or to maintain
its testimony, though called to face discouragements
of every kind.   It has subdued one form of evil after
another; it has redressed many of the most terrible
grievances under which men have suffered; and it has
secured the homage of the most civilised and advancing
nations of the globe, entering into their laws, elevating
the tone of their society, enriching them in every
department of their public and private life.

The objection may indeed be urged that this has not
been accomplished by Christian truth spoken in simple
purity; but that in successive ages that truth has been
accommodated by worldly prudence to the temper of
the day, and that therefore it has not been the same
Christ, the same truth, that has prevailed.   But this is
the very glory of the Christian system, that, while remaining essentially the same, it has in every age been
able to present itself in a form the power of which the
age was compelled to acknowledge, and that as each
age closed it entered with weapons at least in some
degree new upon a new career.   Its hidden force lay

---

[1] John x. 18 ; xii. 24, 28, 32   [2] Comp. 1 John v. 4.

in the fact that it had been made manifest in a personality, a life—the personality, the life of the Lord of
glory. Life changes while remaining the same, and
the better it adapts itself to its environment while
retaining its fundamental principles, the more powerful
does it prove itself to be. All that we have to ask of
any particular period is whether the aspect of Christian
truth then presented to the world was a legitimate
deduction from the life of Christ, and suited to the
wants of the men then living ? If it was so, then, however different in different ages its accidents or its mould,
the truth itself may have preserved its unity. It may
have changed only as the Life from which it came
would, had it continued to be on earth, have changed
and have been seen to change in the same successive
epochs. It may have changed only to such an extent,
and in such a way, as life, if really life and not death,
changes. It may have changed no further than to
show that it embodied throughout the ages a power of
growth adapted to the growth of man, while yet in its
inner nature it was one—one in origin, in aim, and in
effect. This has actually been the case with Christian
truth ; and it has been so because, however often supposed to be a dogma, it never was in reality a dogma.
It was always a life, the life of the Living Lord.
Therein lay its secret, and to that its success was due.
We are, therefore, entitled to maintain that whatever its
changing forms, or the changing thoughts with which
it has been associated, Christian truth has been always
essentially one, and that its conquests in every separate

age go to swell the record of the victories of its one victorious Head.[1]

The "kingdom," however, which our Lord has received as His reward does not lie only in war and victory.   When we recall the ideas already spoken of as connected in the Jewish mind with a king and a kingdom we see, in the second place, that the reward lies also in judgment.   Nor is that judgment which Jesus exercises confined to one great day at the end of the present dispensation.   He judges now.   When He stood before the tribunal of the High Priest He said, " Henceforth (that is, from this moment onwards)[2] ye shall see the Son of Man sitting at the right hand of power, and coming on the clouds of heaven."[3]   When He is described in the first Apocalyptic vision as the glorified " Son of man," the marks of His appearance, with almost no exception, indicate judgment.[4]   And when He sets before His disciples that heavenly work which, after His departure, was to be carried on through the instrumentality of His Church, a main part of that work is judgment: " The Advocate shall convict the world of judgment, because the Prince of this world hath been judged."[5]   This judgment is not necessarily eternal condemnation.   Properly speaking, it is that protest for wisdom against folly, and for righteousness against unrighteousness, which may either find an approving answer from " the world," or rouse it to a more determined rebellion against God.   It is a vin-

[1] Comp. Canon Holland in *Lux Mundi*, p. 34.

[2] Not ''hereafter'' as in A.V.

[3] Matt. xxvi. 64.

[4] Rev. i. 13-17.

[5] John xvi. 11.

dication of the Divine Justice. Herein lies its glory.
Justice! judgment! There is nothing nobler in the
universe of being or of thought. They may not always,
at first sight, attract us like the mercy of which we say
that it is " twice blessed." But, except on a foundation
laid in them, there can be no mercy.

> Hatred of sin, and zeal, and fear
>   Lead up the holy hill ;
> Track them till Charity appear
>   A self-denial still.

They are the upholders of that law the majesty of
which is not less to be seen in the spiritual than
in the natural world. As principles of action they
penetrate beneath outward appearances, and deal with
the realities not the shows of things. To them
the poor and weak are as precious as the rich and
powerful, and with solemn joy they raise the worthy
poor man out of the dust, and lift up the needy from
the dunghill, that they may set him with princes, even
with the princes of God's people.[1] Justice and judgment! let us bow before them with reverence, let us
pay to them the loftiest tribute of admiration which
the tongue can speak. They are the foundation of all
moral order and, therefore, of all happiness. Upon them
rests the highest conception which the human mind is
capable of forming, that of the government of God.

These attributes of a righteous rule also our Lord
did not exercise only when He was on earth, He has
continued to exercise them through the instrumentality

---

[1] Ps. cxiii. 7, 8.

of His Church. She, too, has judged the world. In the darkest ages we turn to her as the deliverer of the oppressed; and, if she sometimes went beyond her commission, put her foot upon the neck of kings, and made licentious and cruel barons beg as suppliants at her gates, it is only fair to bear in mind that in the eyes of eternal righteousness these men for the most part deserved their fate. It would be well for the Church of our own day if she would return to more of that sternness, and be less tolerant of the worldliness and gross sins of society, especially high society, than she is. In a sinful world sternness is a necessary element of Christian truth; and in the history of the past there have been no struggles for human progress so worthy of admiration, and no sacrifices for the suffering so great, as those of the unflinching champions of righteousness. Our Lord's reward is to be the Judge of men; and the members of His body deny Him His reward when they, in His stead, are afraid to judge righteous judgment.

Finally, we ought not upon this point to forget how intimate is the connexion between our Lord's humanity in His state of glory and the judgment part of His reward. "God hath given Him authority to execute judgment also, because He is a (not 'the') Son of man." [1] Because He has been in the same position, has fought the same battles, and endured the same trials as those standing at His bar; because He entirely knows them, and they by the instinct of a common

[1] John v. 27.

nature know that He knows them, His judgment finds
an echo in their hearts as no simply divine judgment
would. Is it a sentence of condemnation ? They are
speechless,[1] and judgment, by awakening the conscience, becomes judgment, instead of a mere verdict
of irresistible power against which we can rebel. Or is
it a sentence of pardon ? Then that that pardon should
be pronounced by One who, in human love and pity,
has followed every false winding of their hearts and
yet forgives, fills them, even in their forgiven state,
with remorse and shame and humility and tender
longing to draw still nearer Him.

> When thou seest thy Judge
> The sight of Him will kindle in thy heart
> All tender, gracious, reverential thoughts.
> Thou wilt be sick with love, and yearn for Him,
> And feel as though thou couldst but pity Him.
> There is a pleading in His gracious eyes
> Will pierce thee to the quick and trouble thee,
> And thou wilt hate and loathe thyself ; for though
> Now sinless, thou wilt feel that thou hast sinned
> As never thou didst feel ; and wilt desire
> To slink away, and hide thee from His sight.
> And yet thou wilt have a longing aye to dwell
> Within the beauty of His countenance.

Such then is the reward of the Risen and glorified
Lord. His own glory is acknowledged; He is the
fulness of Divine blessing to His people; He is the
Conqueror and Judge of every hostile power.

One thing still remained to be done. It concerned

[1] Matt. xxii. 12.

the proprieties of the case that into this reward, into the possession of this kingdom, our Lord should be solemnly inaugurated.   The sovereign of a great nation may exercise every royal prerogative from the date of his succession to the kingdom.   But his people cannot be satisfied until he is crowned with every demonstration by which they may either give utterance to their feelings or have their feelings deepened.   In a relation similar to this the Ascension of Jesus stands to His Resurrection.   Between His absolute authority and right to rule there was probably, on the two occasions, little or no difference.   What He was at the Ascension He was also on the Resurrection morning, and we have already rejected the idea that, during the forty days, there was development either of His body or His Spirit. Yet the Ascension was not without a supreme import- ance of its own.   It was the enthronement of the great King, when the words of the Psalmist were ful- filled, "I have set My King upon My holy hill of Zion"; "Lift up your heads, O ye gates; yea, lift them up, ye everlasting doors: and the King of glory shall come in."[1]

This, however, is not all that may be said.   Not only did it concern the proprieties of the case that there should be an enthronement or coronation of our Lord; it was also suitable that it should take place in the particular form of Ascension from the earth.   A coronation *upon* the earth might have confined men's thoughts of Him *to* the earth.   They might have honoured Him as a

---

[1] Ps. ii. 6 ; xxiv. 9.

human being like themselves, though higher, holier, and more powerful. It was of the utmost consequence to teach them that His earthly condition was to come to an end, and that a new era in His history was to be the beginning of a new experience in theirs. Not His enthronement alone, therefore, but that enthronement in the particular form in which it was effected, was essential to the teaching of this lesson. His upward movement from earth to heaven in the sight of His disciples showed where the real sphere of His existence was thenceforth to be.

3. A third aspect of the Ascension of our Lord has still to be noticed.

It was His entrance upon a new sphere of exertion for the good of man. Into the particulars of this we shall inquire hereafter. In the meantime it is enough to say that we are not to think of the glorified life to which our Lord ascended as a life of rest. Neither at the Resurrection nor the Ascension was His work completed. It is going on now, and it will continue to go on until, so far at least as the present dispensation is concerned, it closes with His manifestation in the glory of the Father, and the kingdom of the earth becomes, not by right only, but in reality, His kingdom.

No doubt Christ's life in the heavenly world is described, both in the Old and in the New Testaments, as a "sitting" at the right hand of God.[1] But we must be careful how we interpret such expressions.

---

[1] Ps. cx. 1; Heb. i. 3, viii. 1, x. 12, xii. 2; Rev. iii. 21.

" All local association must be excluded from them." [1]
They refer to honour and dignity, not locality. Were
we compelled to think that sitting, as an attitude, was
chiefly in view it would be difficult to resist the conclusion that that attitude must be perpetual; for the
writer of the Epistle to the Hebrews tells us, not that
Jesus " sat down," but that He " hath sat down at the
right hand of the throne of God"; and the tense thus
used indicates permanence. To entertain such an idea is
impossible. Not only so. It is worthy of notice that
the ordinary Scriptural representation of the position of
the glorified Redeemer is either standing or some other
attitude which invites to the thought of His being
engaged in work.

Thus the dying Stephen " being full of the Holy
Ghost, looked up stedfastly into heaven, and saw the
glory of God, and Jesus standing on the right hand of
God, and said, ' Behold, I see the heavens opened, and
the Son of man standing on the right hand of God.'" [2]
Thus when, in the first vision of the Apocalypse, the
beloved disciple beheld the Head and King of His
Church, it was as one " girt about at the breasts with a
golden girdle." [3]   And the girdle was worn in this
manner by priests when they were engaged in active
service. In the Epistle to the Church at Ephesus, too,
our Lord describes Himself, not as He that sitteth, but
as " He that walketh in the midst of the seven golden
candlesticks." [4]   In like manner St. Paul, describing

---

[1] Westcott on Hebrews, i. 3.   [2] Acts vii. 55, 56.
[3] Rev. i, 13.   [4] Rev. ii. 1.

the assistance given him when placed before the hostile
tribunals of the world, exclaimed, " At my first defence
no man took my part. . . . But the Lord stood by me
and strengthened me ";[1] while in his visions, recorded
in the Acts of the Apostles, commissions or encourage-
ments are so given him that it is hardly possible to
think of the Person giving them as sitting. Sitting at
the right hand of God, therefore, is not an attitude of
the glorified Lord, nor does it imply rest in His exalted
state. It is consistent with the idea of constant uninterrupted activity, and in such active exertions the
whole revelation of the New Testament tells us that
our Lord is now engaged.

We have considered the fact of the Ascension
together with one or two aspects of the great event.
It may be well to remember, before bringing this Lecture
to a close, that in the Ascension the Church of Christ has
always rejoiced with a joy unspeakable and glorified.
Though too little before her thoughts in later times, her
services bear constant and striking witness to the influence which she felt that it ought to exercise upon the
faith, the life, and the hope of her members. No festival
of her sacred year has had its details arranged with a
more profound sense of its importance or with more
loving care. She has beheld in it a ladder uniting
heaven and earth. Even when she has paused in
adoring wonder at the lowly life of Jesus of Nazareth,
she has raised her loudest songs of praise to Jesus
glorified; and she has listened to Him as if He were

[1] 2 Tim. iv. 16, 17.

still addressing her in the words in which He addressed Nathanael, " Thou shalt see greater things than these. Verily, verily, I say unto thee, Thou shalt see the heaven opened, and the angels of God ascending and descending upon the Son of man." [1]

[1] John i. 50, 51. For a very striking description of the feelings of the Church as they appear in the festival of the Ascension, see Liddon, *Univ. Sermons*, 1st series, p. 283.

LECTURE II

'It is witnessed of Him, Thou art a Priest for ever after the order of Melchizedek."—HEB. vii. 17.

THE Ascended and Glorified Lord is in Heaven. In what light are we mainly to regard Him, and what is the most essential characteristic of the work in which He is there engaged? Theologians have generally answered the first of these questions with the reply that, as on earth, so in heaven our Lord is Prophet, Priest, and King. But they have not uniformly observed this order,[1] nor does it commend itself either to the reason of the case or to the language of Scripture.

The reason of the case suggests a different arrangement; for that office ought certainly to have the pre-eminence assigned to it by which, more than by either of the other two, our Lord accomplishes the main object of His Coming; and there is no difference of opinion as to what that object was. It was to reunite God with man and man with God; to open up the way by which sinful creatures may return with confidence to the Holy One from whom they have alienated themselves,

---

[1] Thus Calvin brings the priestly office of Christ last.—*Institutio C. R.*, lib. ii. cap. 15.

and so to remove every obstacle standing in the way of
love and fellowship between them, that God may be
acknowledged as a Father, and men be children in a
Father's house.   To effect these ends is peculiarly the
office of the priest.   The prophetical and kingly offices
of Christ are indeed also necessary to the production of
the result.   From the first we must be taught in whom
we are to believe, and to teach is the prophet's work.
From the first we must obey the command " Believe,"
and to command is the prerogative of the king.   Even
when we believe, however, the object of our faith is the
Lord Jesus Christ in all that He is and does.   Even
when we obey, obedience can only be reasonable when
the grounds upon which it is enforced are understood.
At the very beginning of our Christian life, therefore,
we must learn to know the Lord in that priestly character which embraces the most essential particulars of
His work ; and, if it be so, such knowledge is still more
necessary in the later stages of our Christian progress.
Whatever be the relation of the glorified Lord to men
in their natural condition, His primary relation is to
the members of His Body.   In them His eternal purpose is fulfilled, and the actings of His heavenly life
have special reference to them.   Upon them, and upon
them alone, the fulness of His prophetic gifts is poured.
In them, and in them alone, the affections are awakened
which form a meet answer to His kingly rule.   But
Christians are what they are by being in Christ as their
Priest, by whom they draw near to God, and in whom
the chief end of their being is accomplished.   Know-

ledge of Him in that office thus precedes their full
experience of Him in the other offices discharged by
Him on their behalf. In the order of thought our Lord
is Priest in heaven before He is Prophet or King. His
prophetical and kingly offices are but the further issues
of what He accomplishes as Priest.

The teaching of Scripture confirms this conclusion.
In two at least of the most important books of the New
Testament, the Epistle to the Hebrews and the Revelation of St. John, the glorified Redeemer is set before
us as peculiarly the Priest or High-priest of our confession. In the first of these books the matter is so
plain that nothing need be said regarding it. In the
second the opening vision, in chap. i., of the glorious
Person spoken of as "like unto a son of man" is admitted by almost all, if not even all, commentators to
be the representation of a priest. Some traits of
royal dignity mingle with the description, and fittingly
belong to Him who is King as well as Priest. But
the particulars ascribed to Him, giving the key-note
of all that is to follow, and one or other of which is taken
up again in each of the seven Epistles representing together the universal Church, are sufficient to show that
He who sends these messages to the churches desires to be
especially known and listened to in His priestly character.

The supereminent importance of the priestly office,
as compared with every other position of authority, had
indeed been long impressed with the utmost clearness
upon the history of God's ancient people. More than
any other it had penetrated to the heart of their

national and religious existence. The conceptions attached to it, though at a lower spiritual stage than that reached under the Christian dispensation, were the fundamental and regulating principles of the whole economy of Israel. The first proclamation of the Almighty by Moses to the tribes assembled at Sinai was "Ye shall be unto Me a kingdom of priests and a holy nation." [1] This was their calling and the inspiration of the religious system under which they lived. Only when this end had been attained could they occupy the position, enjoy the privileges, and discharge the duties that had been assigned to them. Failing in this, they would have failed in everything.[2] Thus, without being first a priestly, Israel could not have been a kingly people; for in the fact that Jehovah was its King much more was implied than that it was ruled and protected by the Divine power. The righteous reign of the Heavenly King was to be reflected in it.[3] In no other way than as living in God its King could Israel be kingly; and before, therefore, it could be so it needed to be in the true sense of the word priestly. As with Israel's kingly, so also with its prophetical function. The people were to be a prophecy to the heathen by what they themselves were, if not by actual missionary preaching. Their national existence, the holiness and happiness of their obedience, the success which crowned their arms, the plenty which smiled

[1] Exod. xix. 6.

[2] "In the priests the ideal of the nation culminated ; they were in every sense its representa-tives."—Perowne, Introduction to *Commentary on Psalm cx.*

[3] Comp. Deut. xvi. 18, 19.

from their vineyards and oliveyards and fields,—these
and all the other outward features of their lot were to
be their message to the surrounding nations.[1] And
this prophecy they could not utter with effect until the
end of their priestly relation to God had been attained.
The priestly function, in short, lay deeper in Israel's constitution and history than either the prophetical or the
kingly.   Only as priest could Israel be prophet or king.

In strict conformity with this is the remarkable
statement of the Epistle to the Hebrews, that "the
priesthood being changed, there is made of necessity a
change also of the law."[2]   Under the word "law" the
whole Old Testament economy is embraced;[3] and the
statement is that, so essentially, so fundamentally, had
the idea of the Aaronic priesthood entered into Israel's
life that, when that priesthood was "changed," the life
of the people was necessarily changed along with it.[4]
There can be no doubt, therefore, that the idea of the
priesthood was the leading, forming, and controlling
idea of the Old Testament dispensation.

If it was so then, we may naturally expect it to be
so under that New Testament dispensation which proceeds upon the same lines, bringing with it only the
full accomplishment of what had been formerly presented in type and shadow.   But the Epistle to the

[1] Comp. Deut. iv. 6-8.
[2] Heb. vii. 12.
[3] Comp. ver. 11 ; chap. viii. 6.
[4] The word "changed" in
Heb. vii. 12 deserves to be
marked. The sacred writer does
not say "brought to an end."
Priesthood remains though it is
changed. 'Επ' αὐτῆς (later reading) ought also to be noted—not
"under it" but "upon it" as a
basis (ver. 11).

F

Hebrews is again decisive upon this point. The priesthood of Christ, together with the privileges and duties of the priestly office, as transferred to those who are united to Christ in faith, is the leading theme of the Epistle,—the spring out of which both its doctrinal and its practical teachings flow. Nor is this the case simply because the Epistle was addressed to a people familiar with priests and sacrifices. The object of the writer is not to pass from these to ideas of a different kind, for which it may be said that ancient arrangements had prepared the way. It is to confirm the ideas by which these arrangements are pervaded and explained, while it is at the same time to show that in Christ they had been transferred from an outward, material, and temporal, to an inward, spiritual, and eternal sphere. Blot out such ideas from the Epistle, or regard them as an accommodation to ignorant or childish conceptions, and the teaching of the writer would either become unintelligible or would leave us no alternative but to reject his canonical authority.

Thus then we reach the distinguishing characteristic of our Lord's life in heaven. Whatever work He may then engage in, whatever glory may surround Him in performing it, one work, one glory, chiefly meets our eye when we penetrate within the veil. We may often think of the exalted Redeemer as Prophet and King. We have mainly to think of Him as Priest. To Christ, therefore, as Priest in heaven, and to the functions discharged by Him in that office, these lectures will be devoted. The subject is one that ought to lead us into the very heart of the Christian dispensation, and to its most important bearing upon our privileges, our responsibilities, and our work as Christians. One or two preliminary remarks are necessary.

1. Whatever is said in Scripture of our Lord as High-priest may be used in illustration of what is said of Him as Priest. The duties and responsibilities of these two offices cannot be separated from each other. It matters not that, in the Epistle to the Hebrews, the work of Christ is mainly typified by that of the Jewish high-priest, and that the ritual of the Great Day of Atonement, more than that of any other holy day of Israel, lies at the bottom of the sacred writer's description of His service. In their essence the two offices of priest and high-priest were one. The holders of the two were indeed of unequal rank, but there was no fundamental difference between them. The office of the priest simply culminated in that of the high-priest, and all that was demanded of the latter was a sharper and more definite expression of what was demanded of the former. If the limitation of his office to the tribe of Levi and the descendants of Aaron showed that the priest was the possession of God in a deeper sense than the ordinary Israelite, this principle of Divine possession only received a still clearer illustration in the case of the high-priest by the restriction of his office to the first-born of Aaron's house through successive generations. If the ordinary priest was to be free from all uncleanness, but was permitted, notwithstanding this, though under the penalty of being unclean until

the evening, to touch the dead body of a relative, such touching of the body of even his father or mother was strictly forbidden to the high-priest,[1] while the general prescriptions for ceremonial purity were in his case more numerous and strict. If the ordinary priest was to be holy, and to have that feature of his office symbolically set forth by his garments, holiness was still more strikingly symbolised by the special vesture of the high-priest, and by the golden plate worn on his forehead, with the words HOLINESS TO THE LORD inscribed upon it. Finally, the consecration of the high-priest was effected in the same way as that of the priest, although it was more elaborate and minute. In all these respects the high-priesthood was simply a more marked expression of what was involved in the ordinary priesthood. Commentators, accordingly, have found it impossible to distinguish between the two terms as used in the Epistle to the Hebrews. Even when the high-priest performed duties beyond the province of the priest, it was as a priest that he performed them. He was only the first of the priesthood, just as the services of the Day of Atonement did not essentially differ from those of the other sacred services of the year, but were rather their culminating point. In everything pertaining to calling, privilege, and work, the commonest priest who ministered at the altar occupied the same ground as Israel's greatest, most unique, and most honoured functionary. In Christ as High-priest, therefore, not less than in Christ as Priest, the nature of His Priesthood is to be sought.

[1] Lev. xxi. 2, 11.

2. The Priesthood of our Lord was never a priest-hood after the order of Aaron.   That it is not so in His exalted and glorified condition is at once admitted by all inquirers.   But the writer of the Epistle to the Hebrews has made it equally clear that it was not so during His earthly life.   Referring to the exalted Lord, he says of Him on one occasion: "Now if He were on earth, He would not be a priest at all, seeing there are those who offer the gifts according to the law."[1]   It is not necessary to suppose that, in these words, the temple is thought of as still standing, or the Aaronic line of priests as still ministering within its precincts. The writer has in view the Levitical institutions in themselves, and his object is to show that such was the nature of Christ's Priesthood, and such its essential characteristics, that it was impossible to associate with Him, in any circumstances, the thought of a priesthood of the Aaronic line.   That priesthood was one "accord-ing to the law," and the law was no more than a type or shadow of "the heavenly things" with which the High-priest whose glory he would illustrate had to do. The idea, therefore, of our Lord's having been at any time possessed of an earthly or legal, or, in other words, of an Aaronic priesthood, was altogether incompatible with His true nature and work.   Again, on another occasion, referring to the words of the Psalm so often quoted by him, the same writer says: "For He of whom these things are said belongeth to another tribe, from which no man hath given attendance at the altar.   For

[1] Heb. viii. 4.

it is evident that our Lord hath sprung out of Judah; as to which tribe Moses spake nothing concerning priests."[1] These words are fatal to the supposition that our Lord could ever have been an Aaronic priest. The same person could not, in the nature of the case, even at different periods of his life, have belonged to different orders. His connexion with either depended upon conditions inherent in his personality, which could not be transferred without that personality being completely changed. By the strictest and most solemn sanctions, too, the priesthood in Israel was confined to the members of the tribe of Levi. Had our Lord claimed to be a priest of that house, the claim would have involved a positive breach of the Mosaic law, and would have been a violation instead of a fulfilling of "all righteousness."

That our Lord never was an Aaronic priest is further demonstrated by this, that if, in that capacity, He had made His great sacrifice upon the cross, then in the same capacity He must have presented it to His Father within the veil. It will not be contended that He could have died as a priest of one order and yet brought His death before God as a priest of a different order. Any such supposition would be at variance with the meaning of the different priestly actions and their relation to each other. These were too closely bound together to be separated. If, therefore, our Lord was an Aaronic priest on earth, He must have been the same when He entered heaven, and all will at once reject such

[1] Heb. vii. 13, 14.

an idea. Even more may be said. Distinguish the different priestly acts from one another, and it will not be disputed that the presentation of the offering is the more important of the two. In every ordinary sin-offering (that on the Day of Atonement forming no exception to the principle), not the slaying of the victim but the presentation of the blood was the essentially priestly act; and if, therefore, our Lord ever performed what was the priestly function in its deepest meaning, it must have been when He presented Himself with His offering in the heavenly sanctuary. That was the moment when His Aaronic priesthood, if He ever possessed it, must have appeared in its clearest light and highest potency. But this is precisely what the writer of the Epistle to the Hebrews is most concerned to deny. One of the leading points of his argument is, that with heaven, with the true tabernacle, the Aaronic priest had nothing to do. It was the distinguishing characteristic of the class of priests to which he belonged that they "serve that which is a copy and shadow of the heavenly things." [1] " The Aaronic priest ministers in the sanctuary of this world, the figure of the true, ix. 1, 23; if he could penetrate into 'heaven,' the true tabernacle, he would cease to be an Aaronic or figurative priest, he would be in the presence of God, into which he could enter only in virtue of having made a true atonement, which nu Aaronic priest could accomplish." [2] The conclusion is

[1] Heb. viii. 5.
[2] Davidson on Hebrews, p. 149. The whole Extended Note from which these words are taken deserves careful study.

irresistible.   Our Lord never was a priest after the
order of Aaron.   His priesthood is only after a higher
and more glorious order.   The unity of His Person and
Work cannot be preserved unless every priestly function
discharged by Him is brought under the notion of
another order than that of Aaron.   The point now
considered is thus not one of mere curiosity or minor
importance.   We shall see more clearly, as we proceed,
that a distinct recognition of the non-Aaronic character
of our Lord's Priesthood is essential to a clear perception of the nature of the Christian dispensation in its
most inward and peculiar characteristics.

3. A third question immediately suggests itself, to
which an answer must be given before we turn directly
to the qualifications of the heavenly High-priest and
to His priestly work.   When did the Priesthood of our
Lord begin ?   Was our Lord at any period of His earthly
life a Priest, or did He only enter upon His Priesthood
when He entered heaven ?   The question is one which
since the days of Grotius has engaged the attention of
not a few of the most eminent theologians and commentators.   It has justly done so; for, as may afterwards appear, the answer to be given it has a vital
bearing on our construction of a dogmatic theology, and
particularly on our conception of the great doctrine of
the Atonement.   In the meantime we have to do with
it only in its critical and historical aspect.

The difficulty of the question arises from the fact
that, in the Epistle to the Hebrews, there are two classes
of texts which it is not easy, at first sight, to bring

into perfect harmony. On the one hand, there are those which seem to declare with a clearness not to be misunderstood that our Lord was a priest only after the order of Melchizedek, and that His Melchizedek priesthood is connected with heaven alone. Such are the words in which our High-priest is said to have been solemnly "addressed" or "saluted"[1] as "a high-priest after that order," at a moment subsequent to the time when He had been "made perfect," at a moment when He had accomplished His earthly mission, and had been exalted to the glory of His reward.[2] The same designation is again applied to Him when He is thought of as One who had "entered within the veil," and had "become" what He then was.[3] Again, in contrast with the word of the law which makes men who have infirmity high-priests, the word of the oath which was after the law is declared to make the Son who is perfected for evermore High-priest;[4] and this "word of the oath" has no place in relation to "the law." It belongs only to a season of which the Gospel either in promise or fulfilment is the leading thought.[5] And, to quote only one passage more, Christ's having come as "a High-priest of good things to come" is closely associated with conditions expressly referring to His

---

[1] Heb. v. 10. Not as in Authorised Version "called," or in Revised Version "named."

[2] Comp. ver. 7-9.

[3] Heb. vi. 20. "From this passage it is clear that the eternal High-priesthood of the Lord 'after the order of Melchizedek,'

King and Priest, followed on His exaltation to the throne of God in His glorified humanity."— Westcott *in loc.*

[4] Heb. vii. 28.

[5] *Ibid.* It might here be well to translate "which *is*" rather than "which *was*" after the law.

exalted state, those of "the greater and more perfect tabernacle not made with hands, that is to say, not of this creation," and "His own blood," with which He "entered once for all into the Holy Place, having obtained an eternal redemption." [1]   The teaching of these and other similar passages of the Epistle to the Hebrews is so distinct as to admit of only one conclusion,—that the order of Melchizedek is the only order of priesthood to which our Lord belonged, and that that order has no connexion with earth.

On the other hand, there is not a little in the same Epistle which sets before us the sufferings and especially the death of Christ as priestly acts, thus leading to the inference that Christ was a Priest when He endured them.   "Wherefore in all things," we read, "it behoved Him to be made like unto His brethren, that He might be a merciful and faithful High-priest in things pertaining to God, to make propitiation for the sins of the people"; [2] where the words "through death," coming almost immediately before, seem to render it impossible to separate from the death of Christ the "propitiation" spoken of.   Again, even in one of the passages already quoted for the first view, it is the death of Christ upon the cross which it is natural to think of as the proper contrast to the death of "goats and bulls." [3]   And, once more, the same thought may appear to be prominent in the statements, "But now once at the end of the ages hath He been manifested to put away sin by the sacri-

---

[1] Heb. ix. 11, 12.   [2] Heb. ii. 17 ; comp. ver. 14.
[3] Heb. ix. 15

fice of Himself"; "By which will we have been sanctified through the offering of the body of Jesus Christ
once for all"; "Wherefore Jesus also, that He might
sanctify the people with His own blood, suffered
without the gate."[1] To all this may be added, as not
without force in a controversy of the kind, the conviction of the Christian Church in every land and age,
that the death of her Lord upon the cross was an
offering in which He was not merely a Victim but a
Priest, and, as a Priest, was engaged in carrying out
that mediatorship between God and man which always
has been, and must be, the leading function of any
priesthood either in its lowest or its highest form.
Must we then abandon this idea as has been done by
some?[2] Or is no reconciliation of the two views now
stated possible? Various solutions have been proposed.

It has been suggested that, during His earthly sufferings and at His death, our Lord is to be regarded as a
"destinated" rather than as a "consecrated" Priest;[3]
but for such an idea Scripture obviously supplies no
warrant. To a somewhat similar effect is the notion
that our Lord was indeed in Himself a High-priest on
earth while learning obedience by the things which He
suffered, but that He did not become *fully* High-priest
until, through that obedience, He had been perfected.[4]
It is enough to reply to this, that the conception

[1] Heb. ix. 26; x. 10; xiii. 12.
[2] See *e.g.* the words of Kurtz
in his able Excursus on the point.
Hebräer Brief., p. 152; comp.
Davidson on Hebrews, p. 151.

[3] Jackson, *Priesthood of Christ*,
ch. xi. 5.

[4] Hofmann, *Schriftbeweis*, ii. 1,
402.

attempted to be established of our Lord's gradually filling up His Priesthood to what it actually and really was, or, as it might perhaps be expressed, "verifying by actual fulfilling of its offices His true Priesthood," [1] is exposed to various objections. It is difficult to understand what is meant by a priesthood ideally possessed but actually involved in a process of "becoming"; nothing is gained by it, for an ideal priesthood is a real priesthood; and it is inconsistent with such language as that in which we are told that our Lord "having been perfected *became* the author of eternal salvation," where the word "became" must be expressive of one definite act.[2] Nor does the proposal to meet the difficulty by the supposition that our Lord may have been a priest on earth, though a priest after the order of Melchizedek only after He passed into the upper sanctuary, meet the case. We cannot understand the priesthood the thought of which it would thus be necessary to introduce. Not belonging while on earth to the order of Aaron, nor to that of Melchizedek till He had no more connexion with earth, to what order did our Lord belong upon the cross? We are no nearer a solution of the difficulty. Once more, the idea of "fulfilling" different orders of the priesthood has been substituted for that of belonging to them. At each of two different stages of His history, before and after His Glorification, our Lord "fulfils" a priestly order, and is thus at each a priest, though in a different aspect. "As High-priest

---

[1] Davidson, u.s., p. 152.

[2] Heb. v. 9. Ἐγένετο following τελειωθείς seems to leave no doubt that it must be so.

Christ fulfilled two types; and we must therefore distinguish two aspects of His High-priestly work: (1) as the fulfilment of the Levitical High-priesthood, and (2) as the fulfilment of the royal High-priesthood of Melchizedek—the first before His Session (as High-priest), and the second after His Session (as High-priest-King)." [1]   Two lines of priesthood are by this view placed in the same relation to our Lord, and He " fulfils" them both, though on each occasion in a different aspect,—that after the order of Aaron as Priest, that after the order of Melchizedek as Priest-King. Not even thus do we surmount the difficulty now dealt with; for (1) such a view lays too great an emphasis upon the kingship of Melchizedek, and assigns too subordinate a position to the priesthood of him who, though King of Salem, was " Priest of God Most High "; [2] and (2) it places our Lord in the same relation to the two orders spoken of. But, according to the teaching of the Epistle to the Hebrews, that relation is not the same. Our Lord no doubt "fulfils" the order of Aaron, just as He fulfilled the whole Old Testament economy, yet not in the same sense as that in which He may be loosely said to " fulfil" the earlier order. Strictly speaking He does not "fulfil" both orders. He *fulfils* the lower because He *is* of the higher.

Is there then no other means of meeting the difficulty? no common thought which may take up and

[1] Westcott on Hebrews, p. 227.

[2] " The kingly trait combined in the Melchizedek priesthood is little insisted on." Davidson on Hebrews, p. 78.

harmonise the two views by which it is occasioned?
no way by which to accept the teaching of the Epistle
to the Hebrews, that our Lord's only Priesthood is unconnected with this earth, and yet to hold, as demanded
by the ineradicable instinct of the Christian heart, that
in His death upon the cross our Lord was a Priest
offering Himself, as victim, a sacrifice for sin? Let the
answer now to be given to this question not be too
summarily dismissed. Fair consideration alone is
asked for it. If correct, it hangs together with other
important views of Christian truth.

The question then must be answered in the affirmative; and it is our Lord Himself who, in words of His
recorded by the fourth Evangelist, supplies the answer.
In a text already referred to, and which must be translated otherwise than either in the Authorised or the
Revised Version, the beloved disciple gives the words
of His Divine Master as follows: " And I, if I be lifted
up on high out of the earth, will draw all men unto
Myself." [1] The translation " lifted up," is too weak for
the original,[2] which ought to be rendered " lifted up on
high "; and the preposition employed [3] is not to be
translated " from," but (with the margin of the Revised
Version) " out of." So given, the words of Jesus can
have but one meaning, that His Glorification begins
not with the Resurrection but with the Crucifixion.
This is indeed one of the lessons of the fourth Gospel
to be learned both from individual texts and from its
general structure. The " glory " so often spoken of

---

[1] John xii. 32.   [2] ὑψωθῶ.   [3] ἐκ.

there includes not only that of the Resurrection but of the supreme act of love manifested on the cross; while the structure of the book [1] demands that the facts of the Crucifixion and Resurrection be considered as one whole. The dying Redeemer is glorified through death: the glorified Redeemer died that He might, in the path of death, find glory. The same point is illustrated by the striking words in which the Evangelist records the death of Jesus, " And He bowed His head, and delivered up His spirit." [2]   "No one taketh away His life from Him, but He lays it down of Himself. He has power to lay it down, and He has power to take it again." [3] Instead of the extremity of shame, a moment such as that brings with it a weight of glory. According to our Lord's own teaching the Crucifixion is thus the beginning of His Glorification, and the sacrifice upon the cross falls within the sphere of a superearthly or heavenly priesthood.

In the considerations now adduced we seem to find that common thought in which the two different aspects of the beginning of our Lord's priestly work, marking the Epistle to the Hebrews, are harmonised and unified. His priesthood begins with His Glorification, but of that Glorification the death upon the cross was part. The sacrifice which He then offered, the spirit of self-surrender in which He offered it, the loving submission to the Father which it illustrated, and the issue which it was to promote, were really " glory."

---

[1] John xviii.-xx. form a complete section.   [2] John xix. 30.
[3] John x. 18.

God's thoughts are not as our thoughts, nor His ways as our ways; and we have been looking at the death which Jesus died from the Divine rather than the human point of view.

It may perhaps be objected that the explanation now offered rests too much upon one passage of Scripture; that, if true, we might have expected allusion to be made to it in the Epistle to the Hebrews; and that it is inconsistent with that language of St. Paul, in which the cross of Christ is regarded as humiliation rather than exaltation, and as shame rather than glory. The first of these objections has no weight. The words upon which dependence has been placed are the words of our Lord Himself, and the only question regarding them is, Have they been properly interpreted? That there is a certain force in the second objection may be allowed. Yet it may be replied that by the writer of this Epistle the death of Christ is always regarded, even when he does not expressly say so, as a glory; that he dwells less upon it as a penal offering than as a consummation of the past, bringing us into a perfect communion with God; and that he is so much occupied with the great offering itself, by which the redeemed are for ever perfected, that the question as to the moment of Christ's entering upon His Priesthood probably never occurred to him in the form in which it presents itself to us.[1] Add to which that our right to take this view is confirmed by the singular affinity between this Epistle and the writings of St. John. Lastly, it may be urged in

---

[1] Davidson on Hebrews, p. 151; Farrar on Hebrews vii. 27.

reply to the third objection that, although St. Paul generally looks at our Lord's death from its side of humiliation and shame, he too sees the background of glory upon which it rested. He could not have gloried in a cross in which he saw no glory. He could not have declared to the Corinthians that he had determined to know nothing among them save Jesus Christ, and Him crucified, had he not felt that that subject was the power of God and the wisdom of God to all who would receive the message.[1]

To return directly to the question before us, When did the Priesthood of our Lord begin? We have already seen, at least in some degree, how much inquirers have differed upon the point, but the cause of the difference is plain. Such writers as Tholuck, Riehm, Hofmann, Delitzsch, Davidson, and Westcott admit with more or less distinctness that the High-priesthood of our Lord began with His Glorification; but they cannot allow that the death upon the cross was not " an essential part of His High-priest's work, performed in the outer court, that is, in this world," and they are thus driven to the expedient of saying that, High-priestly as that act was, the Priesthood of Christ only attained its completeness after His Resurrection. This distinction, however, between incompleteness and completeness cannot be maintained; and the true solution appears to be suggested by our Lord's own words. It began upon the cross, and the cross was the beginning of His glory.

[1] Comp. Dr. Matheson's deeply interesting work, *Spiritual Develop ment of St. Paul*, p. 162.

One point must still be noticed. In what light, it
may be asked, does the view now taken place the whole
of our Lord's life between the Incarnation and the Cross?
The answer is, It was the preparation for His priestly
work. On the one hand, He was Victim as well as
Priest. He was the true Paschal Lamb, and that Lamb
had to be separated from the flock days before the
Paschal Feast that it might be made ready for its fate.
On the other hand, He was to be a merciful and faithful
High-priest for ever, sympathising with all the trials
and sorrows of His people, and "able to succour them
that are tempted."[1] Through His whole earthly life,
therefore, He had to learn by personal experience the
nature of human weakness, and to bear the burden of
human woe, so that, even after He had returned to His
Father's house on high, the members of His Body still
on earth might know that they had in Him a Brother,
not only possessed of Almighty power, but touched with
a feeling of their infirmities. For both these parts of
His priestly work then our Lord was prepared by His
earthly life. Onward from the Incarnation, through the
humiliations and pains of His condition in this world, to
the instant when in spirit He bade farewell to earth
and took His place upon the cross, He was "learning
obedience through the things which He suffered." He
was realising in the increasing fulness of its meaning
what it was to be the "Sent" of God, and what to
sympathise, not by Divine insight alone but by human
fellowship, with all our varied wants, in order that

---

[1] Heb. ii. 18.

having been thus gradually perfected, He might enter upon a priesthood which embodies everything most full of love both to God and man.[1]

From these preliminary considerations we may now turn directly to the Priesthood or High-priesthood of our Lord in heaven. It is one after the order of Melchizedek, not of Aaron; and so frequently, and with such a marked solemnity and awe of manner,[2] does the writer of the Epistle to the Hebrews refer to it under this aspect, that it will be well to look briefly at his teaching on the point. What is said of the priesthood of Melchizedek may throw light upon that of Him to whom he was "made like."[3]

A single sentence may recall the only circumstances known to us of this mysterious personage. In the Book of Genesis we are told that, when Abram was returning in triumph from the overthrow of the five kings by whom Lot his nephew had been attacked and spoiled, "Melchizedek king of Salem brought forth bread and wine: and he was priest of God Most High. And he blessed him, and said, Blessed be Abram of God Most High, possessor of heaven and earth: and blessed be God Most High, which hath delivered thine enemies

[1] Those who wish to prosecute the inquiry as to the time when our Lord's Priesthood began may be referred to Riehm's chapter upon it in his *Lehrbegriff des Hebräer Briefes*, to a valuable Excursus by Kurtz in his *Commentary upon Hebrews*, p. 148, and to Davidson's Extended Note already spoken of.

[2] Heb. v. 6, 10; vi. 20; vii. 17, 21.

[3] ἀφωμοιωμένος, not merely made like, but made like as a copy to an original; comp. chap. viii. 5; also Keil, Kurtz, etc., on Heb. vii. 3.

into thy hand.   And he gave him a tenth of all." [1]   Who this Melchizedek was it is as needless to inquire as it is impossible to determine.   One of the most important facts, indeed, connected with him is that we know nothing of his history either before or after that moment when, like a sudden flash of light, he comes out of the unseen, fills the eye for an instant, and passes into the unseen again. Had any further revelation regarding him existed, the writer of the Epistle could not have reasoned as he does.

There is, no doubt, another passage of the Old Testament upon which his reasoning rests, the only other in which the name of Melchizedek occurs, but one regarded by the Jewish thought of our Lord's time as so central that "it is more frequently cited by the New Testament writers than any other single portion of the ancient Scriptures." [2]   In Psalm cx. the Psalmist is filled with the contemplation of Him in whom the highest hopes of His people were to be accomplished, and he celebrates His coming in the words, "Jehovah hath sworn and will not repent, Thou art a priest for ever after the order of Melchizedek." [3]   The Psalm begins with the thought of royal dominion and the triumphant over-throw of enemies.   It ends with the thought of the nations and their princes crushed beneath the power of one who, even in the thirsty East, will always find "a brook in the way" at which he may drink and recruit his strength.   In its very centre the words occur, "Thou art a priest for ever after the order of Melchizedek." Messiah shall come, the great Priest-King, surrounded

---

[1] Gen. xiv. 18-20.   [2] Perowne on Psalm cx.   [3] Ver. 4.

by His youthful warriors, plentiful and beautiful as drops of morning dew, clothed in " holy vestments," the white robes of the priesthood. But how strange a priesthood! Not that familiar to the Jews, and which they had been accustomed to regard with so much reverence, but another a higher and more glorious. How often must they have wondered what was meant; till now at last, in the light of our Lord's Ascension,[1] the meaning was made clear, and the most remarkable prophecy of the Psalms was seen to be fulfilled in Him who had gone victorious into the heavens, after a life of suffering and death on earth.

Upon these two passages of Scripture the reasoning of the writer of the Epistle to the Hebrews rests. At one moment he argues from considerations the force of which had been deeply impressed upon the Jewish people by the providential arrangements of the Almighty with their fathers; at another from the positive statements of Scripture as to the person of whom he speaks, and at yet another from its silence. But, whatever be the point from which he starts, he has one aim before him—not merely to establish the superiority of the priesthood of Melchizedek over that of Aaron, but to bring out its different and independent character, that character which belonged first and essentially to the High-priest of the Christian dispensation, although it had been shadowed forth, as in a preparatory copy, in His Melchizedekean forerunner. In order, therefore, to understand the Priesthood of our Lord, we have to pass

---

[1] Comp. Acts ii. 34-36

beyond the Old Testament arrangements for the Levitical priesthood, and to think of a still more ancient and famous "order." For this purpose the following points ought to be kept in view.

1. The object of the priesthood of Melchizedek. This was indicated by the mystery of his name. Every one knows how deeply such mysteries were impressed upon the history of God's dealings with His people, from the first book of the Old Testament to the last book of the New Testament Canon. We may not always be able to acknowledge the full weight of the argument connected with them; but it would be wrong to say that it has no weight. We may see in it one of the ways by which men were taught in ages different from our own.

Following then the analogy of so many names appointed by God for use under the old covenant, of the name of Jesus Christ Himself, and of names given by our Lord to some at least of His Apostles, the writer of the Epistle to the Hebrews beholds in the name " Melchizedek " a Divine revelation regarding the man, a revelation pregnant with the most important inferences as to both the person of whom he speaks and the ends to be attained by him. He was not merely a priest, but a priest-king. Nothing of the kind had been known before. There had been kings, but few of them had exhibited the priestly character. There had been priests, but they had wanted kingly power. The one had, for the most part, shown little desire to do good; the others, however eager to do good, had possessed no means of carrying out their wishes. Here was a new combination,—king and priest in one, the kingship sanctified, and the priesthood made effective. Not only so. By his very name this Melchizedek, who had shadowed forth the Messiah to come, was "king of righteousness," and also "king of Salem, which is king of peace." The two designations expressed alike what he was, and that part which in the providence of God he had been raised up to play. He was the embodiment, so far as it was possible for man to be it, of the two greatest blessings which were to flow to the human race through Him of whom, in that very aspect, the Psalmist and the Prophets had spoken in the most glowing terms.[1] The outward ceremonial observed by him as a priest, and the outward glory surrounding him as a king, sank into insignificance when compared with the moral and religious benefits he secured for men. Righteousness and peace met in him, and were dispensed by him to all who would accept his services or acknowledge his rule. The righteousness too preceded the peace. The foundations of the happiness of his priestly reign were laid in the holy dispositions and devout affections of his subjects. Because Melchizedek reigned in "righteousness," he "also" reigned in "peace."

2. The priesthood of Melchizedek belonged to an age anterior to the Judaic period, when the distinction between Jew and Gentile had not yet been introduced. Attention has before now been called to the Gentile character of his priesthood ;[2] and there can be no doubt

---

[1] Psalm lxxxv. 10 ; Isa. ix. 4-7, xi. 4-9.

[2] Pfleiderer, *Paulinism*, chap. ix. i. ; Perowne on Psalm cx. 4.

not only that it was Gentile, but that, fully cognisant of the fact, the writer of the Epistle to the Hebrews was deeply impressed by it. The main point, however, to be attended to is not that Melchizedek was a Gentile. That is simply introductory to a far more important thought—that, having exercised his office before Judaism existed, he was above the temporary provisions and aims of the Jewish dispensation, and that he belonged to a more spiritual and universal economy than that in which, for purposes subsidiary to the welfare of mankind, Israel had been placed. The principle lying at the bottom of this reasoning is strikingly illustrated both by our Lord and by St. Paul. By our Lord, in His language to the Pharisees, when they urged, with relation to divorce, that Moses had commanded to give the wife a bill of divorcement, and to put her away. Then Jesus said to them, "Moses for your hardness of heart suffered you to put away your wives: but from the beginning it hath not been so."[1] By St. Paul, when, in his Epistle to the Galatians, he argues that the law which came four hundred and thirty years after the promise, could not disannul the covenant confirmed beforehand by God, so as to make the promise of none effect.[2] In both cases there was a Divine order, older, larger, wider, and more enduring than that of Moses, one therefore in which the ultimate purpose of God had been more directly manifested. The economy brought in through Moses was a limitation of that plan, rendered

---

[1] Matt. xix. 8.
[2] Gal. iii. 17 ; comp. Bruce, *Expositor*, 3rd series, vol. x. p. 91.

necessary by circumstances and temporary in duration. For the real plan of God we must look to His dealings with men before the days of Moses, when the limitations were introduced.

The same principle is applicable to the point before us. Melchizedek was a priest in that earlier and better age, when no regular line of priesthood had been constituted, when the qualifications fitting any one for the office were individual and personal rather than ceremonial, when the father of the family, when the head of the tribe, when perhaps even any single individual might act as priest, and might become the religious guide and counsellor of all who desired his aid. Such a time there really was in the history of the world. It seems to be a mistake to imagine that, either amongst the ancestors of the Jews, or in heathen nations, no one could be a priest without belonging to a particular line. This idea was later, and in the judgment of the writer whose argument we are now considering, a judgment confirmed by the analogy of Scripture, it marked a lower not a higher stage of development than the earlier view. Melchizedek was thus the priest of humanity, not of Judaism alone. He belonged to a date when he could discharge the duties of a priesthood wide as the world, and when no member of the human family was excluded from the benefits of his priestly rule.

3. Melchizedek was free from those relations of family and tribal descent, of beginning and ending, of sense and time, which were inseparably connected with individuals belonging to this world. The reasoning

upon this point is indeed drawn from the silence, not the positive assertions of Scripture. But in the circumstances that silence was enough. That one claiming the position of an ordinary priest might have his claim recognised, more was necessary than that he should be supposed to possess the qualifications of our common humanity and of priestly lineage. Men needed to *know* that he did so, and to be able to lay their hand upon the proof. When, accordingly, the Most High God says of such or such an one, He is My Priest, giving us at the same time no information upon these points, our ignorance of them is, so far as we are concerned, equivalent to their non-existence. It may thus be said without hesitation of Melchizedek, in whose case all of them were absolutely unknown, that he was "without father, without mother, without genealogy, having neither beginning of days, nor end of life." Nothing but entire indifference to the spirit and meaning of the passage as a whole can demand a strictly literal interpretation of the particular statement. The words "without genealogy" are of themselves sufficient to indicate the direction in which the writer's thoughts are running, and to show that the different appellations used by him are designed simply to lead us out of that region of the carnal and the temporal in which the Jewish religion moved. Any other characteristics by which the same end might have been effected would have been of equal value. Their influence is, no doubt, at first negative and privative. They transcend sense and time; but by that very circumstance they gain a positive weight. No sooner do we leave sense and time behind us than we are in that sphere of the real which underlies the phenomenal, of the ideal which the visible only imperfectly expresses. We have entered the region of spiritual and eternal things. Our ignorance of the circumstances alluded to is not thought of as due to our distance from the period when they occurred. The darkness resting upon them is part of the Divine plan. It was never intended that we should know them because, if known, they would confine us to a lower range of thought than that which is beyond the darkness, and to which we can ascend only through the darkness.   Thus, the priesthood of Melchizedek, dissociated from the thought of an earthly parentage, and from the beginning and ending of earthly life, belongs to the real and the true which lie behind all we see. It springs out of eternity ; to eternity it returns ; when it rises before us we have no thought of the boundaries of either space or time.

4. The three particulars now mentioned illustrate a still more important characteristic of the priesthood of Melchizedek—its spirituality. The Levitical priests were made after " the law of a carnal commandment " ; Melchizedek was made after " the power of an endless (or rather of an indissoluble) life." [1]   The Levitical priesthood was constituted through observance of the manifold prescriptions of an external and burdensome ceremonial ; Melchizedek's priesthood through a living power inherent in his personality, and flowing not from

---

[1] Heb. vii. 16.

the letter but the spirit.[1]   As with the ancient priest
himself, so also with his work.   No rite or ordinance is
mentioned in connexion with him such as had always
been thought essential to the idea of priesthood; and
this is the more worthy of notice when we remember
that in the Book of Genesis Melchizedek is represented
as having brought forth bread and wine to Abram
and his band of followers.[2]   The writer of the Epistle
cannot have regarded that act as sacrificial in the ordinary acceptation of the term, or as equivalent to the
slaughter of a victim.   Had he done so he would have
used language leading more directly to the thought of
sacrifice.   In nothing, however, said of Melchizedek is
there the slightest allusion to death; and the reason
can only be, partly, that Melchizedek could not, like his
Antitype, give himself to death; partly, as has been
suggested, that " he purposely presents Melchizedek
as priest, not in sacrificing but in blessing, that is, in
communicating the fruits of an efficacious sacrifice
already made." [3]   Because, in short, he is the prefigura-
tion of a priesthood in heaven into which death does
not enter, no sacrifice of death is spoken of in connexion with him.   We know him only as a priest " of
whom it is witnessed that he liveth." [4]   The priesthood
of Melchizedek is thus simply a priesthood of life, of
spiritual and Divine life with God.   It has no connexion with what the writer to the Hebrews elsewhere

[1] Comp. Bruce in the *Expositor*, 3rd series, vol. x. p. 195.
[2] Gen. xiv. 18.
[3] Westcott on Hebrews, p. 201.

[4] Heb. vii. 8.   It will be seen
in the next lecture that this is
not inconsistent with the idea of
an offering of life in heaven.

calls "carnal ordinances."[1] It is a priesthood of "blessing" and of quickening to persons fainting and ready to die.

5. The priesthood of Melchizedek was further distinguished by every general characteristic which could enhance its glory. In particular, it was one, unchangeable, continuous, and royal. It was one. The Levitical priests were "many in number." Melchizedek was one. We read, it is true, of his "order," but of that order he is the single representative until Jesus came. Our Lord even was not, strictly speaking, his successor. His Priesthood was rather the perfect embodiment of all that His prototype had shadowed forth, the original pattern upon which His forerunner had been moulded. Melchizedek had neither predecessor nor successor in office, or, if he had, we do not know them, and the strain of the passage forbids our thinking of them. He gathered up into his single person, so far as was possible to a merely human personality, the whole idea of priesthood. In itself as well as numerically, his priesthood was one.

Thus one, it was also unchangeable. Absolute unity is in the nature of things unchangeable. A succession of individuals will vary with the varying traits of character and work produced in the course of generations by the ever-changing circumstances of the world. No flight of time brings with it any difference in our conception of that which can only possess its internal oneness by being the expression of some essential reality,

[1] Heb. ix. 10.

always abiding amidst accidental and temporary change. The more therefore these ideas can be embodied either in persons or institutions, the greater the glory that belongs to them, and the greater their value to creatures ever prone to fear that there is nothing either within or around them on which they can depend.

One and unchangeable, the priesthood of Melchizedek was further marked by uninterrupted continuity. It could be disturbed by no outward incident, not even by that law of death which everything of earth obeys. Having neither beginning of days nor end of life, Melchizedek "abideth a priest continually,"[1]— "continually," not exactly "for ever." The first of these two phrases is relative, the second absolute. The meaning is not necessarily that the priesthood spoken of is everlasting; but that, as long as there was any function to be discharged by it, nothing could interrupt its task.

Yet again, the priesthood of Melchizedek was royal. The Jewish view of royalty spoken of in the previous lecture ought to be here before our minds. According to it royalty was not simply elevation in rank, dignity, and splendour. It was power,—power to protect friends and to overthrow enemies. No power of this kind belonged to the Levitical priests. Notwithstanding their religious privileges, they were only citizens of the state. They could persuade or remonstrate, sacrifice or pray. They could instruct the people in times of peace, or in war they could accompany the armies of Israel to the field. But their province was

---

[1] Heb. vii. 3.

to serve and not to rule, to submit to authority, and, except in matters specially provided for by Divine appointment, not to control their brethren. The priesthood of Melchizedek was royal, and whatever he desired as a priest he could accomplish as a king.

6. Once more, both the Levitical priesthood and the whole Jewish economy acknowledged its inferiority to Melchizedek and bowed before him. The striking scene from the Book of Genesis appears to be especially quoted in order to illustrate this. Two figures are there introduced to us, and both are representative— the one, "priest of God Most High," representing the priestly idea in the purest form in which men were at the time capable of receiving it; the other, Abraham, "the patriarch," [1] "he that hath the promises," the illustrious father of the faithful, in whose loins was even then the priestly tribe which was afterwards to occupy so commanding a place in Jewish history. These two persons meet. Nay, more. The particular moment at which they meet is to be noted in order that the full meaning of the scene may be understood. It was when "Abraham was returning from the slaughter of the kings," [2] when he had proved himself to be the vindicator of the oppressed, and was flushed with victory. Yet even at that moment, with

[1] It is unfortunate that the Revised Version should have failed to give the emphasis of the original to the position of the word "patriarch" in Heb. vii. 4, the true translation, as we should say, being "unto whom Abraham gave a tenth out of the chief spoils—and he the patriarch." "A whole argument about the dignity of Abraham is condensed into the position of one emphatic word" (Farrar, *in loc.*).

[2] Heb. vii. 1.

no compulsion, with no commandment binding him, such as afterwards bound the people to pay tithes to the sons of Levi, he voluntarily gave to Melchizedek "a tenth out of the chief spoils." What a token of submission on the part of the one! What a proof of greatness in the other! Then Melchizedek "blessed" Abraham, that is, not merely uttered for him his friendly wishes or his prayers, but pronounced upon him his priestly blessing, and, along with him, upon Levi, Aaron, and the whole line of the Aaronic priesthood. Could there be the slightest hesitation in the mind of any one as to the superiority of the earlier to the later priesthood? The law is universal that "the less is blessed of the better." [1]

Two characteristics of the priesthood are not indeed distinctly mentioned in the account given us of Melchizedek—his appointment by God to his office and his human sympathy. Yet the first of these is indicated with sufficient clearness in the statement that he was "priest of God Most High"; for every Jew knew well that he could not have been so had he not been commissioned by Divine authority. The second again appears in what is said of the blessing bestowed on Abraham, for, whatever else that blessing may include, it seems designed to illustrate the human-hearted compassion of the priest when he supplied the wants of the patriarch and his exhausted warriors.

Such then is that priesthood of Melchizedek in which the writer of the Epistle to the Hebrews beholds reflected

[1] Heb. vii. 7.

the Priesthood of our Lord in heaven.   And now, combining the characteristics spoken of with the positive
statements of Scripture, and with the fact that the
Priesthood of our Lord, like every other part of the
Christian system, fulfils the imperfect ideas of the
ancient economy of Israel, we learn what the heavenly
Priesthood of our great High-priest is.   In the first
place, we have to mark the more general characteristics
of that Priesthood.   The Work in which its duties are
discharged must be reserved for another Lecture.

The more general characteristics of our Lord's
heavenly Priesthood.

1. The foundation of our Lord's Priesthood is
the constitution of His person, and not regularity of
descent from others.   No doubt it is " after the order of
Melchizedek," but the peculiar language of the sacred
writer is sufficient to prove that its fundamental ideas
pass from our Lord to Melchizedek, and not from
Melchizedek to our Lord.[1]   Melchizedek illustrates
rather than lays down the principles of the line to which
he belongs.   These in their originality are to be found in
the exalted and glorified Lord; and the first of them is
that the heavenly High-priest is what He is person-
ally, not by succession.   He is the Son, and this connexion between His Sonship and His heavenly Priesthood is brought out with remarkable force in the Epistle
to the Hebrews.   The very opening of the Epistle witnesses to the fact.   Few will doubt that the whole Old
Testament dispensation, and not merely words spoken

---

[1] Compare p. 83.

H

"in the prophets" in the narrower sense of that term, are there contrasted with the higher dispensation brought in "at the end of these days." If so, it must be the priestly arrangements of both dispensations that the writer has particularly in his eye; for, immediately afterwards, in drawing out the contrast between the past and the present, he fixes upon the priestly work of Christ as the leading and most essential characteristic of the Christian age, "who being the effulgence of His glory and the very image of His substance, and upholding all things by the word of His power, *when He had made purification of sins*, sat down on the right hand of the Majesty on high." The "purification of sins" was the work which Jesus, in passing on to His exaltation, accomplished; and He accomplished it as the "Son" whose eternal pre-existence and glorious position both in creation and providence are described in the preceding participial clauses.[1] Thus, in the Sonship of our Lord the foundation of His High-priestly work is laid. The same truth is not less clearly brought out in a later passage in which, calling us to consider Christ, "the Apostle and *High-priest* of our confession," and contrasting Him with Moses, in whom the whole ancient economy was summed up, the writer closes his comparison with the words that Christ was faithful "as a Son" over His house.[2] And, to refer only to one other passage, it is thus that when comparing the high-priests appointed by "the law" with the High-priest of the Christian Israel he describes the latter as a "Son."[3] In

[1] For connexion comp. Keil *in loc.*   [2] Heb. iii. 1-6.   [3] Heb. vii. 28

all these passages, too, it is to be particularly observed that Christ is spoken of not simply as the Incarnate, but as the exalted and glorified Son. In the first He has "sat down on the right hand of the Majesty on high": in the second He "hath been counted worthy of more glory than Moses," where the tense of the verb leads directly to the thought of His continually existing glory: in the third He is the Son "perfected for evermore." It is unnecessary to enlarge upon the point. No truth appears more clearly upon the face of the whole Epistle than that neither the pre-existent nor the incarnate Sonship of our Lord (although both are proceeded on and implied), but His Sonship in His now glorified condition constitutes Him to be our High-priest. The two conceptions of Son and Priest cannot, in His case, be separated from each other. Because He was to be the High-priest of humanity He assumed our human nature, and was afterwards elevated in that nature to the throne of the heavenly Majesty. Because He had assumed our human nature, and had been so elevated, He was fitted for His priestly function.

Nor is it difficult to conceive how it should be so. Our Lord was to be the one Mediator between God and man, thus fulfilling the office of a priest. But to effect a real mediation He must Himself be both Divine and human; and no inspiration, however high, can make a creature Divine. Impartation of nature alone can do so. No prophet of the Old Testament, therefore, no angel of God even, could have been a mediator in the highest sense of the term. He alone could be so who was the

Son "in the bosom of the Father,"[1] who also "became flesh and dwelt among us," and who in His two natures was lifted into that all-embracing spiritual world from which He can penetrate to the spirit of man as man, through the limitations and conditions of earthly circumstance. Whatever our Lord effects for His people in His heavenly Priesthood He effects by reason of the very constitution of His nature as the ascended and glorified Lord. His Priesthood is not merely an office conveyed to Him by the gift of God. Nor does He merely draw upon the resources of His Eternal Godhead in order that He may form the Divine life within us. "He bears the name of Mediator because He *is* what it expresses."[2] There is nothing arbitrary or artificial in the arrangement of the economy of grace. Its gifts are no other than the natural and necessary result of what He who is its substance *is* in relation to the Father upon the one hand, and to man upon the other. In Himself He fulfils the mediation at which priesthood aims. He is *the*[3] Mediator, the bond in which the mediation is actually accomplished and realised. Out of that truth every other truth connected with "so great salvation" flows. Hence, accordingly, the importance of maintaining, and of urging with persistent earnestness, as essential to any just thought of salvation, the twin truths of the Divinity and the glorified humanity of our Lord. Religion, if it have any meaning, means a union between God and man, penetrating to the very

---

[1] John i. 18.   [2] Wilberforce on the Incarnation, chap. vii.
[3] Wilberforce, u.s.

foundation of man's being.   Redemption is a state into which we are introduced with the full concurrence and co-operation of our nature, and where we become what we are through the processes of actual life.   Those, there-fore, who abandon either the doctrine of the Divinity or of the glorified Humanity of our Lord, do not simply abandon doctrines in the statement of which they believe that they see the imperfect working of the human intellect.   They abandon facts essential to the concep-tion of a perfect religion.   They hand us over to a religion of nature and humanity, to a religion which may be good (that is for them to prove), but from which all thought alike of Revelation and of God must needs be gradually excluded.   This aspect of the case ought to be fairly faced, and not evaded, as, at one time from prejudice, at another from self-interest, it so often is.

2. In its sphere of action, our Lord's Priesthood belongs to the heavenly region which the whole New Testament regards as that of the ultimate develop-ment of man.   "That is not first which is spiritual, but that which is natural; then that which is spiritual. The first man is of the earth, earthy; the second man is of heaven." [1]   The heavenly, the ideal, is that to which our nature points, and to which it continually aspires. In the Priesthood of our Lord these longings of the soul are met.   He Himself is heavenly; He ministers in a heavenly sanctuary; He offers Himself "through eternal spirit" to the Father who must be worshipped in spirit and in truth; He calls His people with a "heavenly

[1] Cor. xv. 46, 47.

calling"; He bestows upon them a "heavenly gift"; He enables them to offer up spiritual sacrifices acceptable to God through Him. The most essential characteristic of His work is not that He treads this earth of ours, engages in its labours, bears its burdens, encounters its temptations, and drinks its cup of sorrows. He does all this, it is true, and it was necessary for Him to do it in order that He might be prepared for His work in heaven. But, these things done, His real work is heavenly. It starts from a heavenly as distinguished from an earthly world. It belongs to a heavenly world, is wrought out in a heavenly world, leads to a heavenly world. While the Redeemer comes to us, made in all things like unto His brethren, He comes chiefly as the embodiment of a higher sphere, as One who, uniting us to Himself in a real, not a fictitious union, makes us members of a heavenly family gathered together in that House which is His own, and citizens of a heavenly City of which He is at once the Foundation and the Light. In His work as High-priest, and from the beginning to the end of that work, our Lord is not first of earth and afterwards of heaven. In this capacity He is first of heaven; and then He carries out His work on earth, in the meantime by His Spirit, afterwards by His personal presence, that He may change earth into the heaven of which He is Himself the only full and adequate expression. Herein, accordingly, lies the noblest trait of practical Christianity—its idealism. It is a system which no earthly reed can measure, an ocean which no earthly line can fathom. The ages press on in their effort to

realise the blessings of a perfect civilisation and brotherhood of man. They have as yet unfolded no thought
not contained in the heavenly Priesthood of our Lord,
and they have discovered no aim which does not proceed
directly from His heavenly life. They never will. In
the very nature of the case what is thus ideal or heavenly
must always be in advance of human effort. From it
we must ever draw our loftiest inspirations, and procure
for our activities their wisest guides.

> It needs the ideal to brush an hairbreadth's off
> The dust of the actual.

The loftiest aspirations of humanity have been realised
in the Son of man. Because they have been so we
believe and hope that they will be realised in humanity
as a whole.

3. Our Lord's Priesthood fulfils the idea of all priesthood, and more particularly of the priesthood instituted
under the earlier economy of the Law.

(1.) It is marked by Divine appointment and human
sympathy. "For every high-priest, being taken from
among men, is appointed for men in things pertaining to
God ... who can bear gently with the ignorant and erring,
for that he himself also is compassed with infirmity,"[1]
and thus was it with our Lord. "He also glorified not
Himself to be made a High-priest"; nor did He so
receive His office from men, or so do their will, that it
should be possible to say of Him that He was simply
the reflection of the longings and yearnings of the

[1] Heb. v. 1, 2.

human heart. He was appointed by Him "that spake unto Him, Thou art My Son, this day have I begotten Thee: as He saith also in another place, Thou art a Priest for ever after the order of Melchizedek."[1] The Father "sent" Him. No word fell from His lips which He did not hear from the Father. No work was done by His hands which was not the Father's work. In all His labours and sufferings there is a sense in which we may say that we behold the labours and sufferings of the Father. Not merely Christ but God, in whose love it is so difficult to believe, hath loved us; and, if we rejoice in the thought that Christ is love, His mission in every one of its particulars proclaims that God is love. While thus sent of God, our High-priest is also full of sympathy. He is "touched with a feeling of our infirmities." No suffering child of man can have a more bitter cup to drink than that which drew from Him His "strong crying and tears"; and when, therefore, His people cry or weep, He enters into their sorrows as His own. What is done to them, He testifies of Himself, is done to "Me."[2] Divine appointment, human sympathy! In these are to be found two of the most important characteristics of a perfect priest.

(2.) Our Lord's Priesthood elevates into the spiritual sphere the ideas that were only outwardly and carnally expressed in Israel. Was the priest of the Jewish economy the property of God in a deeper sense than the ordinary Israelite? It was thus in the highest possible degree with Him of whom it was declared by

---

[1] Heb. v. 5, 6.　　　[2] Matt. xxv. 40; Acts ix. 4.

the voice from heaven, " This is My beloved Son, in whom I am well pleased," [1] and who said of Himself, " I and My Father are one." [2]   Was it necessary that the Jewish priest should be free from every personal defect and uncleanness ?   Christ was " holy, guileless, undefiled, separated from sinners," One who was able to offer Himself " without blemish unto God." [3]   Did the priest of old require to be not only free from ceremonial defilement but to be positively cleansed ?   Christ could say of Himself, " Which of you convicteth Me of sin ? " " I do always the things that are pleasing to Him that sent Me." [4]   Or, finally, were Israel's priests not only divinely appointed but consecrated to their office ? Even upon earth Christ was not only the " Sent " of God, but was consecrated by the fullest and most perfect unction of that Spirit who descended upon Him at His Baptism, abode with Him then, and abides with Him for ever. [5]

(3.) As with the person of our great High-priest, so also with His priestly service.   In every essential particular it rises far above the priestly service of Israel, and is the fulfilment of the service which Israel enjoyed.   As contrasted with the Levitical system it is inward instead of outward, thus meeting those deeper wants of man to which the earlier system had failed to penetrate.   The gifts and sacrifices laid by the Israelite upon God's altar could not, " as touching the conscience," make the worshipper perfect, being only (with meats

---

[1] Matt. iii. 17.   [2] John x. 30.   [3] Heb. vii. 26 ; ix. 14
            [4] John viii. 46, 29.   [5] John i. 32.

and drinks and divers washings) cardinal ordinances imposed until a time of reformation." [1]   They had indeed served an important though a temporary purpose. While Israel was as yet unable to comprehend the true nature of God and of His worship, they had inspired powerful convictions as to the evil consequences of forsaking, and the blessedness of serving Him.   But it was necessary that the true nature of God should become better known, and that existing ideas of sin and holiness should be deepened.   Thus the whole Jewish system was doomed to break down.   " It is impossible that the blood of bulls and goats should take away sins," [2] or the observance of an outward ceremonial become a substitute for inward righteousness.   In the case of spiritual and free beings nothing can take away the sin or impart the righteousness but identification with One who is absolutely acceptable to God, and whose labours, sufferings, and self-surrender to the will of God may, through union with Him, be made also theirs.   Dumb animals incapable of thought and without intelligence or freedom could never meet that necessity; and a spiritual answer was wanted for a spiritual need.   That answer is given us in Christ, whose action at every step He took was spiritual, voluntary, free,—so that in His perfect will we may offer our wills to the Father, and in Him be accepted and complete.

As contrasted with the Levitical priestly service that of our Lord is also unchangeable.   One great weakness of the Levitical priesthood lay in this that,

[1] Heb. ix. 9, 10.   [2] Heb. x. 4.

held by mortal men, the office had to be continually surrendered at the call of death. There was thus in it that element of change and defeat by which the stamp of vanity is imprinted upon merely human things. At the moment when "old experience" best fitted him for the discharge of his varied and difficult duties the priest of Aaron's line was borne to the grave. At the moment when he had most completely succeeded in inspiring with confidence those who received the benefit of his ministrations his eyes closed upon their necessities and his ears to their cry. It is otherwise with the heavenly High-priest. In Him the thought of "many" is fulfilled in that of one, the thought of the changing in that of the unchanging, the thought of a past to be cherished by the memory into that of the same living and abiding presence. Nay more. The human spirit longs after the possession of life which shall rest upon something deeper than any outward promise, upon something which shall have the witness in itself, conveying with it an inward token that it shall never change. How could it obtain this through men whose own death showed that they had not themselves obtained that life, and that they therefore could not be the means of transmitting it to others? Such a gift He alone can bestow who can still say to us, with the same present power as that with which He first spoke the words in Bethany, "*I am* the Resurrection and the Life: whosoever liveth and believeth in Me shall never die." [1]

---

[1] John xi. 25, 26.

As contrasted with the Levitical priestly service that
of our Lord is universal.   The blessings of the Levitical
system were confined to Israel.   No stranger, unless
first naturalised, could share in them.   Human feeling
could flow only in the narrowest groove, and the effect
produced upon the mass of the people, however inconsistent with the economy under which they lived, found
expression in the words, " Thou shalt love thy neighbour, and hate thy enemy." [1]   With the Lord Jesus
Christ as the Priest of the better covenant all differences between races and classes disappear.   He is not
like Aaron the son of Israel: He is the Son of man.
" In Him there can be neither Jew nor Greek, there
can be neither bond nor free, there can be no male and
female." [2]   Not indeed that the distinctions lying in
nature and providence are in Him obliterated, or that
His Church will be like a large garden, full it may be
of luxuriance, but of luxuriance produced only by many
thousand specimens of the same flower.   In one sense
all the old varieties will continue to exist, and the
Greek, the Jew, the bond, the free, the male and female
will still be marked by those peculiarities of position or
of character which may show to what great division of
the human race they belong.   But all are saved in the
same way.   The fancied righteousness of the Jew does
not profit him.   The long-continued alienation of the
Gentile does not injure him.   The learned and the
ignorant, the powerful and the weak, the rich and the
poor, meet in a brotherhood of equal privilege and

[1] Matt. v. 43.   [2] Gal. iii. 28.

gratitude and love. The same foundation is laid for all. The same preparation in kind, although it may be different in degree, is bestowed on all. Beneath every distinction there is a common bond in which all are taught to feel for, to sympathise with, and to help one another, for all are "one man in Christ Jesus." Well might St. Paul exclaim that this universalism of the Christian faith, which proceeds directly from the universalism of Him in whom, as the High-priest of humanity, it is summed up, was the mystery which "in other generations was not made known unto the sons of men." [1] It was a "mystery" in St. Paul's days. It is hardly less a mystery in ours. Earth is longing for its fuller manifestation. The poor and the miserable are crying for it. The very wildness of effort often made to reach it is a testimony to the belief in its existence somewhere. And it does exist. But it exists as a revelation ; and as a revelation only given in the heavenly High-priest.

Nor is the Priesthood of Christ less universal when thought of in relation to the infinitely varied wants of individuals than when viewed in connexion with the different races of men. As the great High-priest of humanity the exalted Lord feels for every want, and is ready to pour the balm of His consolation into every wound from which the humblest of His people suffers. We go to a mother, a sister, a brother, with whatever grieves us, trifling though it may be: the Redeemer stretched forth His hand towards His disciples and said,

[1] Eph. iii. 5, 6.

"Whosoever shall do the will of my Father which is in heaven, he is My brother, and sister, and mother." [1]

Finally, as contrasted with the Levitical priestly service that of our Lord is everlasting. The priests of Aaron's line were made "after the law of a fleshy commandment"; our High-priest was made "after the power of an indissoluble life." [2] The contrast is striking, for the word "fleshy" is not the same as "carnal," and its use forbids the thought that any moral weakness of the Levitical priesthood was in the writer's mind. The members of that priesthood were simply of the dust, and they returned to dust again. Our High-priest has as His own peculiar prerogative a life in the possession of which He lives His priestly life for ever; not only throughout the years or ages of the present Christian economy but throughout eternity. Perhaps it might be thought that when the completed number of the elect has been gathered in to the safe protection of that heavenly home into which nothing that defileth enters, there will be no need either of priesthood or of priest. But such is not the teaching of the New Testament. We are rather taught there that in our Lord as Priest we shall always stand accepted before God, and that whatever progress towards perfection awaits us in the heavenly state must be made in Him. [3] We can never either stand or advance in our own strength. We can never forget to whom we owe the continu-

---

[1] Matt. xii. 49, 50.

[2] Heb. vii. 16.

[3] Expiati jam indigebunt con-summari per Jesum Christum a quo gloria eorum dependet.—Thomas Aquin. Migne's Ed. iv. 222, col. 1.

ance, as well as the first bestowal, of our blessedness. Throughout eternity the love of the Father must flow forth to us "in the name" of Jesus, as much as it flows forth to us in that name now. He has made known to us the Father's name, and He will also continue to make it known "that the love wherewith the Father had loved Him may be in us, and He in us."[1]   Therefore does the Seer of Patmos behold the glorified Lord in heaven clad in priestly robes; and in similar robes, in garments made white in the blood of the Lamb, His redeemed there either surround Him with their songs of praise or follow Him whithersoever He goeth.

4. The end which our Lord's Priesthood accomplishes is the end of all priesthood,—the bringing sinful creatures nigh to God and preserving them in constant fellowship with Him.   No truth is more deeply impressed upon the Epistle to the Hebrews than this, that to secure for us a confident and joyful access into the immediate presence of the Almighty is the ultimate issue of the work of Christ on our behalf. "As a forerunner [2] Jesus Himself entered for us within the veil." That they may in like manner draw nigh is "the better hope" of Christians and the most essential characteristic of their privileges.   Realising it their ideal state is reached.[3]   When most impressed with the Majesty of Him who is from everlasting to everlasting, they can approach Him in the spirit of

---

[1] John xvii. 26.

[2] See the excellent remarks of Professor Bruce on this word in

Expositor, 3rd series, vol. x. p. 48.

[3] Heb. vii. 19; x. 22; iv. 16; xii. 22.

adoption crying, Abba, Father.   There is no veil, there is no separation of apartments in the heavenly taber-nacle ; and raised to an even higher dignity than that of Israel's greatest functionary, who could enter into the Most Holy Place only once a year, the humblest follower of Christ may dwell there, beholding the glory of God, and resting beneath the shadow of His wings. This is indeed the "perfection" so often spoken of in the Epistle to the Hebrews, both in our Lord's case and ours,—not mere glory after shame, repose after battle, or rest after the race of life is run, but man's nature and condition brought to their ideal end; God united to man and man to God, in perfect, uninterrupted, and joyful fellowship.

LECTURE III

" It is witnessed of Him, Thou art a Priest for ever after the order of Melchizedek."—Heb. vii. 17.

WE have considered the more general characteristics of the Priesthood of our Lord. We have seen that He never was a priest after the order of Aaron; that from His first entrance upon His Priesthood He belonged to a heavenly order typified by Melchizedek; and that His inauguration into His priestly office dates from the moment when, "lifted up on high out of the earth," He virtually bade farewell to the objects of sense and time, and felt that His reign of "Eternal Spirit" had begun. In His person our Lord was thus a new Priest, not a priest of an old order of things ripened, matured, and brought to perfection, but a new Priest of a new Order, a Priest of Heaven, in Heaven, and for Heaven. The consequences of all this, more especially as they affect our conception of the Christian system and our own relation to it, cannot fail to be of a very momentous kind. But we are not yet ready to consider them.

Before doing so we have to turn our thoughts to the Work of the heavenly High-priest, or to the different functions which He discharges in that capacity.

I. The first of these is that of Offering. It was the chief duty of the high-priest in Israel to offer, upon the great Day of Atonement, the appointed sacrifice for the sins of the people, and that offering is fulfilled in Christ. If, too, the representation given in the last lecture be correct, it was fulfilled in Him as the super-earthly, that is, as the heavenly High-priest, His High-priest-hood having begun with the time when He was lifted up out of this lower world, and before He died. Whether, however, this representation be accepted or not, there can be no doubt upon one point, that the death of the Redeemer upon Calvary was a true and proper sacrifice for sin. In this light it is always and everywhere presented to us in Scripture. In this light, with comparatively little exception, it has always been acknowledged and believed in by the Church. No other explanation of it has obtained more than partial accept-ance. No other has been able to give peace to the troubled conscience, or to convey to us the assurance that a new and living way of access to the loving Father of their spirits had been opened for sinful creatures. The death upon the cross was no mere testimony to the faithfulness of an obedience which would not waver even in the utmost extremity of human suffering. It was no mere illustration of a heroic faith in God remaining steadfast even unto death. It was no mere surrender to wicked men, in the spirit of a glorious martyrdom, of a life which had been lived for

God, and which from its earliest to its latest moment
had been spent in the conviction that, not outward
honour but truth, uttered, maintained, and vindicated,
makes men kings. It was a sacrifice, an offering for
sin. Christ "bore our sins in His own body on the
tree"; "He gave Himself for us, the just for the unjust,
that He might bring us unto God"; He died that we
might live.

Again, not only was our Lord's death in its initial
stage an offering. That offering was still further carried
on towards its completion when, after His Resurrection
and Ascension, our Lord entered into the Holiest of all,
in order that He might be our Forerunner into that
blessed communion and fellowship with God which was
the great end and purpose of redemption.

Upon these two points it seems unnecessary to
enlarge, so generally is the one, so widely at least is the
other, admitted by Christian men.[1] It may be well,
therefore, to devote the time at our command to another
and more difficult question. Does the ascended and
glorified Lord even now present to His Father in
heaven anything that may with propriety be called
an offering? Or are His heavenly functions summed
up in the idea of Intercession? The latter view is that
generally taken. Our Lord's work of offering is supposed to have been finished when He died. In the
shedding of His precious blood it was accomplished;

[1] The author may be permitted to refer to his work on *The Resurrection of our Lord*, parti- cularly to note 56 in the later editions.

---

and, after His Ascension, He had only to present that sacrifice to the Father that, on the ground of its acceptance, He might thenceforward be an all-prevailing Intercessor on our behalf. It is not indeed denied upon this view that, after our Lord ascended, one thing remained for Him to do in order to complete His sacrifice. He had to place before the Father either the very blood which He had shed, or the ideas involved in that sacrificial act. But this is supposed to have been done only once and for ever. Having done this, the glorified Redeemer entered upon an entirely different part of His priestly work; and Intercession, not offering, is the function in which He always has been and still is engaged in the Heavenly Sanctuary.[1] Is the view thus taken to be accepted as complete? Are we to confine the thought of "offering" on the part of our Lord to His sacrificial death? Or are we so to extend the thought as to include in it a present and eternal offering to God of His life in heaven? The question is one in which there is no small danger of being misled by the ambiguity of words. But, if this danger can be avoided, it is a question of the utmost practical importance for our whole conception of Christianity, and for our own Christian faith and life. The following considerations may prepare the way for the answer to it:—

1. The true idea of offering is not to be sought in death. It is a mistake to imagine that in the act of offering there is always and necessarily involved the

---

[1] Comp. Wardlaw, *Systematic Theology*, ii. 632, and the dogmatic theologians generally. Comp. also Westcott on Hebrews viii. 3.

death of what is offered.   So far is this from being the
case that in the highest conception of offering death
has no place.[1] Had man never fallen it would still
have been his duty to offer himself, together with all
that he possessed, to the God in whom he lived, and
moved, and had his being; and the highest conception
of a redeemed life, when sin has been pardoned and
" the mercies of God," appropriated in faith, have become
its ruling principle, is set before us by the Apostle in
the words, " to present your bodies a living sacrifice,
holy, acceptable to God, which is your reasonable (or
spiritual) service." [2]   The relation which the Almighty
intended to exist between Himself and His intelligent
creatures was that of constant and loving fellowship;
no obstacle to the full outpouring of love upon His side,
or to the confident and free return of love upon theirs.
Communion of this kind, however, cannot be maintained
between parties of whom the one is absolutely dependent on the other, unless the dependence be acknowledged and the obligations implied in it fulfilled.
Offering, therefore, on the part of the creature to his

---

[1] " The idea of sacrifice does
not necessarily involve the shedding of blood."—Bishop Webb's
Priesthood of the Laity, p. 12.
Compare *Lux Mundi*, p. 279.
" Sacrifice, in fact, in the most
general form, belongs to the life
of man, and, in the truest sense,
expresses the life of man. It is
essentially the response of love to
love, of the son to the Father,
the rendering to God in grateful
use of that which has been received
from Him.   Language cannot
offer a more expressive example
of moral degeneration in words,
than the popular connexion of
thoughts of loss and suffering
with that which is a divine
service."—Westcott on Hebrews,
p. 281.

[2] Rom. xii. 1. Compare Prayer
after Communion in Book of
Common Prayer.

Creator, Preserver, and Benefactor is the law of man's nature; but not necessarily the offering of death. The slaughter of a victim is not always needed. Man may offer the fruits of his field or his other substance in token that he is offering himself to God• while he may yet continue to live. The presentation of an offering without death was even familiar to the Jews in the ritual of their own law. The *Mincha* or Meat offering, which consisted simply of vegetable produce prepared according to special directions, was not less than the sacrifices of blood an "offering," and it is known in the Septuagint version of the Old Testament by the same term.[1] It is indeed the offering spoken of by the prophet as that which shall be made in the glorious kingdom of the future, "from the rising of the sun even unto the going down of the same";[2] and already in the "Teaching of the twelve Apostles," to say nothing of the early Christian fathers, that passage is quoted as prophetic of the Christian Eucharist.[3] No doubt without previous sacrifices of blood the *Mincha* could not have been accepted: but the simple fact that an offering without blood without death, was in certain circumstances well-pleasing to God, is enough to show that to the idea of offering death is not essential. That which in the case of man, as he is, makes death enter into any sacrifice, is sin. Not by arbitrary appointment, but by the eternal necessities of right and righteousness, " the wages

[1] θυσία. Comp. Kurtz, *Sacrificial Worship of the Old Testament*, Clark's Translation, p. 281. On an apparent, but only apparent, exception, comp. Kurtz, p. 125.

[2] Mal. i. 11.

[3] Didache, xiv.

of sin is death." It is not less, therefore, an eternal law that "apart from shedding of blood there is no remission."[1] When, on the other hand, sin has not been committed, or when the covenant with God has not been broken, there is in the thought of "offering" no place for death. Even when there has been sin, and when in consequence there must be death, that death, however imperatively required, cannot fill up the whole thought of offering. It is only a part of it, a transition step to another stage not less important or imperative than itself. How indeed is it possible to imagine the Almighty satisfied with death? If one thing was more impressed upon the Old Testament economy than another, it was the gulf between God and death. God was made known to Israel as The Living God, and not only as living Himself, but as desirous that all His creatures should live also.[2] Were death the essence of sacrifice it ought to be permanent; and the simple circumstance that in sacrifice, an animal could be substituted for man, shows that the aim of sacrifice was not to destroy man's life but to preserve it, bringing it at the same time into a new relation with God, so that man might be, more or less thereafter, "a living sacrifice." Sacrifice thus implies as its main end not death, but life; and, however in a sacrifice of blood death may first strike the eye, it is not the thing chiefly contemplated either by Him who receives or by him who makes the offering. Within, if we may so speak, or beyond the death there is the thought of life.

[1] Heb. ix. 22.   [2] Jer. x. 10; Ezek. xviii. 23.

2. The idea of offering is associated in Scripture with our Lord's work in heaven.   To refer only to one, but that perhaps the leading passage on the point, we read in the Epistle to the Hebrews, "For every high-priest is appointed to offer both gifts and sacrifices : wherefore it is necessary that this High-priest should have somewhat also to offer."[1]   It is, indeed, contended that the past tense of the verb "offer," here used by the sacred writer,[2] is a proof that he is dealing with the past alone, and that his mind is occupied with the thought of our Lord's one sufficient offering made upon the cross.   Were this idea to be accepted, the words could certainly not refer to any offering of our Lord in heaven.   The shedding of His blood on Calvary would be the one act contemplated by the writer, and in no strict acceptance of the term could that blood be said to be "offered" now.   It could be thought of only as the means by which our Lord entered into the Divine presence, and purified the heavenly things and the people.[3]   Is this view then correct ?

One thing at least is evident,—that the person spoken of as "this High-priest" is the person described in the immediately preceding verses as "such an High-priest who sat down on the right hand of the throne of the Majesty in the heavens, a minister of the holy things and of the true tabernacle, which the Lord pitched, not man," so that the reference of the passage to the Lord as ascended and glorified cannot be mistaken. The only question is, Do the words " that He also have

---

[1] Heb. viii. 3.   [2] προσενέγκῃ.   [3] Westcott on Hebrews viii. 3.

somewhat to offer " take us back to the cross, and to
the cross alone ?   Or are they applicable to our Lord
at the moment when they were written ?   And, on the
supposition that they are so, do they describe Him as
ministering continuously with the presentation of Himself as an offering in heaven ?

The tense of the verb used in the original is insufficient to determine this, and both here and in many
similar circumstances the appeal of the interpreter
must be to the context in which the tense occurs, and
to the scope of the passage as a whole.[1]   When such an
appeal is made in the case before us, it would seem to
be impossible to understand the " somewhat " to be
offered of anything only done by our Lord when He was
on earth, in the power of which He had now entered
heaven.   The purpose of the writer is to describe present not past priestly acts, a ministry at that moment
going on, and not even in the particular referred to
finished.   He desires to illustrate the glory and fitness
of the High-priest of the Christian faith by showing,
not what He had done in the days of His flesh alone,
but what He continued to do after He sat down at the
right hand of the Majesty on high.   Nor can it be said
that that glory and fitness are sufficiently brought
out by the Intercession of the heavenly High-priest.
Intercession is not enough.   The comparison made
between the functionaries of the old and the new
Covenants has relation not simply to intercession, but

[1] Compare Westcott on Hebrews x. 5, p. 310 ; comp. also ix.
24, νῦν.

to the whole work which they severally discharged. The Jewish high-priest is seen entering the most sacred part of the Tabernacle in the wilderness. What is he about? Intercession is not the sole work in which he engages there; he offers the gifts and sacrifices upon which either his intercession rests, or in which it is involved. "This High-priest," the High-priest of the Christian dispensation, has in like manner entered into the heavenly Tabernacle. What is He about? He is not simply interceding on the strength of a past gift or sacrifice. He is presenting an offering on which His intercession is based, and in which it is involved. The idea of offering, therefore, cannot be separated from the action of our Lord after His Ascension, unless we also separate the thought of offering from what was done by the high-priest of Israel in the innermost sanctuary of his people. Such a separation the ceremonial of the law does not permit. The Jewish high-priest minis- tered in that sanctuary with more than the recollection or the merit of an offering already made. He had to sprinkle on the mercy-seat and before the veil the blood which he carried in along with him; he had to complete the reconciliation of Israel to God; he had to lay his people upon God's altar that they might thence- forward be a holy nation in union with Him who claimed them for Himself. And all this was a part of the offering, not merely something done after the offer- ing was ended. Had it been otherwise, we should be compelled to conclude that, in the supreme moment of his ministry, the high-priest did not engage in that "offering of both gifts and sacrifices," which was his most characteristic act; and we should certainly have expected that intercession for Israel, rather than continued procedure with the blood, would have been distinctly spoken of as his chief function in the most holy place. As, therefore, the Jewish priest continued his work of offering after he had gone within the veil, so, in similar circumstances, we must connect with Him in whom the economy of Judaism is fulfilled the idea of offering. Our Lord, even in His exalted and glorified state, must have "somewhat to offer."

The force of what has now been said will indeed be greatly weakened if we accept the opinion recently expressed by one whose conclusions on any such point can be spoken of with nothing but the utmost deference. According to that opinion, "The blood was not properly 'offered in the Holy of Holies on the Day of Atonement. It was used as the means of entrance and purification. Even so Christ entered into the Divine Presence 'through ($\delta\iota\acute{a}$) His own Blood ' . . . but we do not read that He 'offered' it"; and again, "This sprinkling of the blood is regarded in a wider sense as an 'offering.'"[1] But the meaning of the preposition thus referred to, so far from excluding the idea of offering, implies it. The preposition is used in no local sense, as if the Lord had passed into the inmost sanctuary through His own blood. It is used rather to introduce the mention of the circumstances and relations under which the thing spoken of was done,[2] and it thus leads directly to the

---

[1] Westcott on Hebrews viii. 3; ix. 7.   [2] Moulton's *Winer*, p. 474.

thought of an offering with which, as well as in the power of which, the great High-priest entered heaven. Nor can it be said that the blood was not strictly offered by the Jewish high-priest when he went into the Holy of Holies, but was only used to purify the sanctuary. The words of another passage in the same Epistle, where we are told that the copies of the things in the heavens were to be cleansed with these, but the heavenly things themselves with better sacrifices than these,[1] prove clearly, when we note the following context, that the blood cleansed because it was offered,[2] and that had it not been an offering when taken within the veil it would not have possessed its purifying power. In addition to this, it is also to be observed that the distinction drawn in the words quoted between a strict and a " wider " or " not proper " meaning of the word " offering " is unknown to the law, and that it really eliminates altogether from the advanced stage of which it speaks the idea of offering. It brings us into contact at that stage with the presentation of an offering already made, and not with an offering itself. This, however, is contrary to the ritual of the law, in which the sprinkling of the blood was the culminating point of the high-priest's action. Not till he reached this point was his offering, in its strictest and most proper sense, complete. The action of the high-priest, moreover, upon the great Day of Atonement—his action both without and within the Tabernacle—is surely to be regarded as a unity. But if a complex act, which

---

[1] Heb. ix. 23.   [2] Comp. ver. 25.

supposes a longer or shorter space of time for its accomplishment, is to be looked at in this light, the ideas belonging to the initial must be found in the final stage, or we shall have no common thought binding the two stages into one.

Returning, therefore, to the words of the sacred writer, " Wherefore it is necessary that this High-priest also have somewhat to offer," it would seem that we are not entitled either to limit the offering spoken of to the offering on the cross, or to understand the word " offer " in a loose rather than a strict sense, because we may be compelled to connect it with a point of time after our Lord's entrance into heaven. When our Lord died on Calvary He presents to us the idea of offering. When He entered heaven the same idea penetrates and pervades His first presentation of Himself to the Father there.

3. It is impossible, however, to pause at the point that we have reached, and the further question arises, Whether the idea of offering is to be connected not only with the moment when our Lord presented Himself to His Father, but with His continued, His never-ending life in Heaven ? The thought of much that accompanied His offering on the cross must indeed be here laid aside. There is no more the humiliation, the sorrow, or the pain in which He submitted to the curse of the law. There is no more a valley of the shadow of death to be passed through in which every step taken forces from Him the prayer, "if it be possible, let this cup pass from Me." He is no more surrounded by an out-

ward darkness, the symbol of the awful mystery which had, in that " hour," been brought about by " the power of darkness." [1] There is no more death. But it is *behind* these things, and not *in* them, that the true conception of the offering on the cross is to be sought. It is in the willing acceptance of them, in the voluntary submission to them, that its essence is to be found. And this essence, we appear to be taught, is continuous and unceasing. At the moment when the sacred writer says that "This High-priest must also have somewhat to offer," he is speaking of a time long subsequent to our Lord's entrance into Heaven; and yet, as we have seen, he speaks of the " somewhat " as a present thing. If it was then present, no one will deny that it must be always present. What our Lord was after He sat down at the right hand of the Heavenly Majesty He can never cease to be. The idea of a continuous application of redemption, resting upon what had been done in the past, cannot exhaust the work of the unchangeable and everlasting High-priest. What He had done must penetrate what He always does ; and the thought of Offering cannot give place to that of Intercession. The first is the foundation of the second, but the second is pervaded by the conception and spirit of the first. If we rightly interpret the words, Offering and Intercession imply one another. There is even a sense in which Intercession is Offering, and Offering Intercession. Let it also be allowed (and no other conclusion seems possible) that, as our High-priest is Himself " heavenly," His

[1] Luke xxii. 53.

work must be of the same character, and it will necessarily follow that the idea of His Offering is likewise
heavenly, and, as heavenly, eternal.

4. One other point must be noticed. It is a fundamental lesson of the New Testament that our Lord's
offering of Himself for sinful men cannot be repeated.
No truth is more distinctly impressed upon us by the
sacred writers than that, in contrast with the offerings
of the law, Christ's offering was made not once only but
" once for all." The legal victims died; their life-blood
ebbed away; their efficacy was only for the moment;
the offering of them needed to be constantly renewed.
Not so with the death endured for us by Him who is
Victim as well as Priest. The distinguishing feature of
His sacrifice is, that it is " one sacrifice for sins for
ever." [1] " Christ being raised from the dead dieth no
more; death no more hath dominion over Him." [2]

In these circumstances it is natural to ask whether
there is any view of our Lord's sacrificial work which
shall combine in one the ideas of the different stages of
that work,—His death upon the cross and a continued
offering by Him as the risen and living Redeemer. If
this question can be answered in the affirmative we
shall be compelled to allow that our High-priest not
only offered Himself in the moment of His death, but
that, when after His Resurrection He passed within the
veil, He had still " somewhat to offer"; and we shall be
prepared for a further unfolding of the nature of that
" somewhat."

[1] Heb. x. 12.   [2] Rom. vi. 9.

Turning, therefore, to this part of our inquiry, it would appear as if the fundamental conception of that offering of our Lord by which the breach of the broken covenant is healed, and man is restored to the Divine favour, is not death but life.   The place held by death in the process of restoration will have to be spoken of immediately.   In the meantime it is enough to say that life, not death, is the essence of atonement, is that by which sin is covered.

Our thoughts upon this subject are apt to be confused by the fact that the associations of the present day with the word " blood " are so widely different from those with which that word was connected in the Hebrew mind.[1]   Every reader of the New Testament has observed that redemption is continually spoken of by its various writers as due to the " blood " as well as to the " death " of Christ: " Take heed unto yourselves, to feed the Church of God which He hath purchased with His own blood "; " The Beloved in whom we have redemption through His blood "; " But now in Christ Jesus ye that were once far off are made nigh in the blood of Christ "; " And through Him to reconcile all things unto Himself, having made peace through the blood of His cross "; " Knowing that ye were redeemed, not with corruptible things, with silver or gold, but with precious blood, as of a lamb without blemish and without spot, even the blood of Christ "; " The blood of

[1] The writer must again refer to the much fuller discussion of this subject in his book on *The Resurrection of our Lord*, p. 140, with note 56 and its appendix. It is introduced here with the view of establishing a different point.

Jesus His Son cleanseth us from all sin"; "And they sing a new song saying, Worthy art Thou to take the book, and to open the seals thereof; for Thou wast slain, and didst purchase unto God with Thy blood men of every tribe, and tongue, and people, and nation."[1]

Reading passages such as these, we almost inevitably understand the word "blood" to have the same meaning as the word "death"; and hence, not only in popular but in scientific theology, the whole work of our atonement is supposed to have been consummated in the death which the Saviour died upon the cross. There, it is urged, the only-begotten and well-beloved Son of God bore, as our Substitute, the penalty of our transgressions. There He made a full, perfect, and sufficient oblation for the sins of the whole world. Travel back in thought to Calvary; see the love that flows from His streaming wounds; believe that He died in thy room and stead; and, from the remembrance of His finished work, draw those powerful considerations which will lead thee to live henceforward to One who died for thee.

This is no unfair or exaggerated representation of Christian sentiment widely entertained in every age of the Church's history. The minds of men have been directed to the cross, and to the cross alone. The sacrifice of Christ has been regarded as nothing more than the penalty of violated law; while some have even spoken of it as if, when presented in this light, it

[1] Acts xx. 28 ; Eph. i. 7, ii. 13 ; Col. i. 20; 1 Peter i. 18, 19 ; 1 John i. 7 ; Rev. v. 9.

shocked our natural susceptibilities and invited us to
enter again into "the shambles of heathenism." Of
such a mode of speaking as this last little need be said.
Justice to the view so travestied demands rather the
grateful admission that, partial and one-sided as it is,
it has yet proved itself powerful for good in the hearts
and lives of men. How has it deepened in many a
follower of Christ that sense of sin without which there
can be no true faith! To what sighs of contrition, to
what tears of penitence, to what searchings of heart
over faults and shortcomings has it often led! What
separation from the evil of the world, what saintly
lives, what love and self-sacrifice, what deeds of heroic
virtue, has it not unfrequently produced! We know
but a small part of these things. They seldom come
before us in the heat and bustle of our daily life. But
every one who has opened his eyes has beheld enough
to let him know how innumerable are the quiet and
gentle and loving spirits that, nourished by such aspects
of Christ's atonement, have drawn as near as human
frailty would permit to Him who was lowly of heart,
and whose very presence, without our speculating regarding Him, gives rest to the soul. And these aspects
of Christ's work have effected this by means of the
truth, not the error, which they contained. They have
answered the cry of the awakened conscience. They
have dispelled the alarm of the troubled heart. Let
the Church cease to proclaim them, and her strength to
execute her mission will be gone. Notwithstanding
this, however, the view thus taken of the plan of our

redemption is in a high degree imperfect; and, though
in exceptional cases, it may not have hindered the
manifestation of the fairest forms of Christian living,
it has unquestionably tended to divert the thoughts
of the Church as a whole from the supreme importance
of that sacrifice of herself in which alone either
her worship of God or her service of man can be
accomplished.

The imperfection now referred to will become manifest, and the work of the heavenly High-priest will be
better understood, if for a moment we recall to mind
more fully than we have yet done the ritual of the
Jewish law. For, according to that law, the death of
the animal selected for sacrifice did not atone for sin.
Sin was not thereby "covered." The offerer had no
doubt identified himself with his victim. Its life had
been set before God as a representation of his life; and
in the shedding of its blood, so that the victim died, the
offerer had acknowledged in symbolic act that death
was the meet reward of the transgressions with which
he himself was chargeable. Another step, however, had
to be taken before atonement was made. The blood
obtained by slaughtering was given either upon
ordinary occasions to the priest, who smeared it upon
the horns of the altar; or upon the great Day of
Atonement to the high-priest, who sprinkled it upon
the Mercy-seat, that he might thus bring it into the
closest contact with God. Not till this was done was
the atonement perfected, sin covered, and the broken
covenant restored. Atonement, in short, was found,

not in death for sin, but in the use afterwards made of the blood thus shed in death.[1]

In all this process it is to be kept steadily in view that the blood was the life. Even when shed it did not cease to be so. It was indeed the life under a peculiar aspect, for it was life which had passed through that death which is the wages of sin. But it was still the life; and as life, not as death, it was brought into fellowship with the living God, and made one with Him. Such was, briefly, the ritual of the law; and the law, designed as it was to shadow forth the fundamental ideas of the Gospel, may often help us to understand the more spiritual form in which the Gospel states them.

When accordingly we turn to the manner in which the ritual now spoken of was "fulfilled" in our Lord, this conception of the meaning of the word "blood" must be retained. As "the blood always includes the thought of the life preserved and active beyond death,"[2] so the blood of Christ is the life of Christ. When it was shed for us on Calvary it was His life

---

[1] On the point here spoken of Professor Robertson Smith's lectures on *The Religion of the Semites* are highly instructive. The conclusion is there established by a wide induction of particulars that among the Semites the blood was the life, and that the main idea in the application of the blood to the altar and the worshipper was to make a life-bond between the god and men. The deepest thought involved in sacrifice was not the expiation of sin by death, but the establishing of an act of communion in which the god and his worshippers partook together of a sacred victim, and which acted as an atonement by wiping out all memory of previous estrangement.

[2] Westcott, additional note on 1 John i. 7.

given for us in another and a deeper sense than that in
which we use the expression "to give one's life," that is,
to die. His life was what He gave to God *as life*,
although it was a life which then and there, as demanded by eternal considerations connected with the
relations between God and man, passed through death.
The same blood then, or, in other words, the same life,
is next presented to the Father within the sanctuary;
and the only difference between what it was before
Christ died and what it was after He died is this, that
it has now its new character fully impressed upon it,—
the character given it by that death which has been
freely accepted in obedience to the Father's will, and in
love to the Father and to men. Thus we obtain a view
of our Lord's work by which its two great stages, that
of His dying upon the cross and that of His presenting
Himself to His heavenly Father in the Most Holy
Place, are united under one conception—the conception
of offering.

In the considerations now adduced we have the
answer to the question with which we started. The
thought of "offering" on the part of our Lord is not
to be confined to His sacrificial death: it is so to be
extended as to include in it a present and eternal offering to God of Himself in heaven. What He offered on
the cross, what He offers now, is His life, a life unchangeable not only in its general character as life, but
in the particular character given it by the experience
through which it passed. The difference between these
two views of offering, as death or life, is important

Death is an act accomplished in a moment. If any claim is to be founded upon it, it must be recalled as a past act in order that the claim may be allowed. Life is a condition or state. At every instant of its course it may bear the stamp imprinted upon it at its beginning, and it will be judged of by what it is, not by what it was. We may offer ourselves to death in a manner pleasing to God; and, rising again, we may entreat Him to remember the manner in which we died. But if, instead of death, we offer Him in the moment of death life passing through death, and to which that transition gives a special colouring, then our life, when it has passed through death, cannot fail to retain that element of offering which led to its surrender. It was thus with Christ. In dying He did not merely perform an act. He did not offer to the Father a life extinguished in death and afterwards to be recalled in thought. "He offered Himself as living in death,"[1] and as possessed of the life which never ends. How can we separate the idea of "living" from that of "offering"? As the life is imperishable, and that too in its new capacity, so also the thought of offering connected with it lasts and must last for ever.

Other considerations lead directly to the same conclusion. To refer in the first place to one or two passages of Scripture, our Lord Himself, in words already quoted for another purpose, connects the thought of offering in the closest manner with that of His future triumphant life. "And I, if I be lifted up on high out

of the earth, will draw all men unto Myself." [1] The use
of the preposition " out of" here demands special notice,
if we would enter into all that is embraced in these
remarkable words. The same preposition meets us in
our Lord's High-priestly prayer, when He says, " I pray
not that Thou shouldest take them out of the world, but
that Thou shouldest keep them out of the evil one." [2]
In both cases the force of the preposition is to be particularly marked. In both it is the very hinge upon
which the meaning of the language turns. When therefore, as immediately afterwards interpreted by the
Evangelist,[3] our Lord speaks of His crucifixion as a
being lifted up on high " out of the earth," and as the
means by which He will draw all men to Him (not to
His memory, but to Himself, to the ever-living " Me "),
He shows us that the element of offering undeniably
involved in it is to be taken forward to His future
glory. What when lifted up upon the cross He will be
in His redeeming power, He will always be.

The Epistle to the Hebrews is hardly less instructive
when it describes our Lord as saying in words of the
Psalmist, " Sacrifice and offering Thou wouldest not, but
a body didst Thou prepare for Me; in whole burnt
offerings and sacrifices for sin Thou hadst no pleasure :
Then said I, Lo, I am come (in the roll of the book it is
written of Me) to do Thy will, O God. . . . He taketh
away the first, that He may establish the second." [4]
These words cannot be understood to mean no more

---

[1] John xii. 32.   [2] John xvii. 15.   [3] John xii. 33.
[4] Heb. x. 5-9.

than this, that our Lord came to do God's will by con-
senting to die. Such submission was but a part, although
it may have been the most striking part, of the manifestation of the spirit which exclaims, " I am come to do
Thy will, O God." Yet that spirit includes more than
submission to death. The perfect and continuous fulfilling of God's will, including death, is substituted by
the Priest and Victim of the New Covenant for the
offerings of the Old. In other words, the spirit which
does God's will in everything is the essential element
of what Christ was as the one great offering for man.
The spirit of so doing was immanent in Him and in His
redeeming work ; and, because it was so, it belongs to
His heavenly not less than to His earthly life.

Once more, that vision of the glorified Lord in the
Revelation of St. John, which may in one sense be said
to be the leading vision of the book, teaches the same
lesson. When the glorified Lord is beheld in it as the
Lamb that had, or rather that hath, been slaughtered,
it is obvious that the marks of His wounds are still upon
Him. It is with the tokens of His offering telling not
of the past only, but of the present, that the Lord reigns.

In the second place, we have to remember the bearing
upon the point now before us of the constitution of our
Lord's Person. In heaven He is not less truly than He
was on earth, Son of man as well as Son of God. He
possesses there not only the Divinity which belongs to
Him as the Eternal Word, but the humanity by which
He is fitted to represent the children whom God has
given Him. His continued life in heaven, therefore,

being still the life of humanity though glorified, must be
brought under the conception of offering.   Not only at
first, but always, it must ascend before God as the
" savour of a sweet smell."   In the very nature of things
it must be a life of obedience, submission, and dependence, a life finding its highest satisfaction in occupying
this relation to the Father.   In other words, it must be
an offering.

In the third place, the same conclusion follows from
the thought of that relation in which the glorified Lord
and His glorified saints stand to one another.   It will
at once be admitted that, whatever may be said of Christ
in glory, the redeemed in glory have always to present
themselves to the Father as an offering.   In no other
way, however, can they do this than in Him who is their
life.   Whatever they are must be first in Him ; whatever they do must be first done by Him.   According to
His own teaching their relation to Him corresponds
exactly to His relation to the Father : " As the living
Father sent Me, and I live because of the Father ; so he
that eateth Me, he also shall live because of Me." [1]   Thus,
whatever idea is fulfilled in them must first exist in
Him.   They do not live simply in the power of something which He bestows on them as a gift, apart from
what He is.   They live " because of " Himself in them.
Their life is His life and the spirit in which they serve
is the spirit which, existing in Him, is transferred
to them.   If they therefore present themselves as an
offering to the Father, He in whom they do so must

[1] John vi. 57.

Himself be an offering to the Father. "By one offering He hath perfected for ever them that are sanctified ";[1] or, in other words, He hath perfected "all who from time to time realise progressively in fact that which has been potentially obtained for them."[2]   Do saints in heaven realise this in a past or in a present Lord ? Not "by," let it be observed, but "in"[3] the will of the Son, as He perfectly does the will of the Father, and is thus an offering to the Father, have they been sanctified, and that will must be for ever operative if they are for ever to experience its effects.   It must for ever supply the sphere in which their sanctification is accomplished.

In the light of what has been said we are now prepared to form a distinct idea of what is to be understood by the "offering" of our heavenly High-priest.   That offering began with the cross, with the moment when, separated from all that was material, local, or limited, the Lord who died was able to enter upon a spiritual, universal, and everlasting priesthood, and to present to the God against whom His people had sinned, His spiritual, universal, and everlasting offering.   Then, as One bearing the sins of all who had committed, or should afterwards commit, themselves to Him in faith, He yielded up His own life, and theirs in His, as the penalty due to sin.   For Himself and for the members of His Body He accepted the sentence, "The soul that sinneth shall die," while at the same time He bowed Himself to the law so mysteriously

---

[1] ἁγιαζομένους : note the tense.
[2] Westcott on Hebrews x. 14.   [3] Heb. x. 10 ; comp. R. V. margin.

linked with that sentence, that, as things are in a present world, it is only through death that we can conquer death and find the path to life. Thus He submitted to the punishment of a violated law, acknowledging that the law was holy and righteous, and just and good. On the cross He gave Himself for us, the just for the unjust, so that when we identify ourselves with Him as the Victim upon which our help is laid, we behold in Him the law vindicated, our sins expiated, and our admission to the Divine presence and favour secured.

This, however, is no more than the first part of the one great step taken for us by our heavenly Highpriest. A second part followed. As the blood, or, in other words, the life, of an animal was liberated in death in order that by the sprinkling a union might be effected between the offerer and God, so the blood, or, in other words, the life, of Christ was liberated on the cross in order that our life in His might be united to the Father in the closest communion and fellowship, and that the broken covenant might be replaced by one that should last for ever.

A third part still remained, depending upon these two, naturally resulting from them, and necessary to the completion of the issue to which they were designed to lead. The life thus united to God was actually surrendered to Him in a perpetual service of love and praise. It may indeed be said that our Lord had always occupied this latter relation to His Father. True, but not in the midst of the same conditions as those in which He occupied it after He had accomplished His Mediatorial work. Before His Incarnation He had been only the Eternal Son who in the beginning was with God and was God; and had the word " Me " in His High-priestly prayer, " And now, O Father, glorify Thou Me," [1] expressed only the Eternal Sonship, it would have shown that He was about to return to that original state. But it expressed more, and the " glory " for which He prayed, though essentially the same as ever, was also different, in so far as He was different. He had taken our humanity into union with His Divinity, and the life which He carried with Him into the heavenly Sanctuary was the life, not simply of God, but of the man Christ Jesus. This was the " living sacrifice " which, with His people in Him, He presented to the Father, in union with whom not only reconciliation but Divine life is found.

As, too, Christ retains His humanity for ever, so His people are for ever in Him. As they were identified with Him in the earlier, they are also identified with Him in the later steps of His offering. In no part of His work does the Redeemer stand alone. He never ceases to be the Mediator between God and Man, the Head of the Body, the Representative of the whole line of His spiritual descendants. Even in heaven He presents Himself to the Father saying, " Behold, I, and the children which God hath given Me," " In the midst of the congregation will I sing Thy praise." [2] When all this is done our Lord's offering is complete. The end

---

[1] John xvii. 5.   [2] Heb. ii. 12, 13.

of the Christian Covenant is attained, and in the
members of His Body it is ideally, if not yet actually,
realised.

Such then is the offering of our heavenly High-
priest ; and if the view now taken of it be correct, it
follows that we are not to confine it to the death upon
the cross, but that we are to include in it a present and
eternal offering of His life in heaven.

The important truth only stated before may now
also be more fully and clearly seen,—that the offering
of our Lord cannot be repeated, and that, not only
according to the teaching of the Epistle to the Hebrews
but of St. Paul, His death was " once for all "—" For in
that He died, He died unto sin once for all." [1]   That
only which comes to an end can be repeated, not that
which is in its own nature continuous, unchangeable,
and everlasting.   Its repetition is then impossible, not
simply because of the excellency of the offering when
first made, but because it never ceases, or can cease, to
be before God in the very same light as that in which
upon the cross it was acceptable to Him.   Its one
perfect sufficiency, so far from being disparaged, is thus
enhanced, and we obtain a foundation of increased
security upon which to rest that truth.   An act may be
repeated, and, if not in a real, it may (as in the Roman
Catholic Church) be repeated in an unreal form.   A state,
a condition which knows no end, cannot be repeated.
That is the case here.   In surrendering His life for man
our Lord fulfilled the highest conception of a perfect

[1] Rom. vi. 10.

and everlasting offering which cannot in the nature
of things be followed by any other sacrifice for sin.
The penalty for sin once completely paid cannot be
paid again. Its stamp remains imperishably on the
life now lived by the Ascended Lord. In the presence
of His Father He is for ever the Lamb that was slain,
and no repetition of His offering can take place.

Before passing on it may be well, in a few sentences,
to consider that, in the light in which we have now
regarded the offering of our Lord, it most of all possesses those characteristics which make it the fulfilment
of the whole sacrificial system of the older covenant
and a perfect offering.

a. As an offering of life it possesses the power of a
present offering, not merely of an offering made and
accepted for us nineteen centuries ago, but of one which
ascends even now for us before God, as much an offering as
it ever was. It is this thought that seems to give to the
Roman Mass its powerful hold over so many minds. The
Redeemer to whom the partakers in that mysterious
solemnity are to cling is there, there on the altar before
their eyes, there as He is, a Victim dying for their sakes.
How shall they not cling to Him and hold Him fast?
The same strength and consolation may be ours without
the Mass, when we feel that one of the great elements
of Christ's sacrifice is, that it was not made only at
a special moment of the past, a sacrifice to be ever
afterwards remembered and pleaded; but that, as an
offering continually presented to the Father, it has a
present sacrificial efficacy as powerful always as it was

at the very first. The present becomes as the past in
vividness. The Mount on which the Redeemer died
can never be removed, and we are ourselves on Calvary.
St. Paul could say to the Galatian Christians, notwithstanding their distance from Jerusalem, that "before
their eyes Jesus Christ was openly set forth crucified."[1]
In like manner the Cross is before our eyes. We
occupy in reality the same position as that of those
who stood beside it on the day when it was raised.
By faith we behold the life there surrendered in death,
and in which the hope and life of every believer are
wrapped up, still ascending before God, who is well
pleased for His righteousness' sake. We ascend in it, and
there is given to the peace bestowed by it all the increased
intensity belonging to an offering on our behalf which
we see, as compared with one of which we are only told
that it was executed in the past. Everything connected
with the Christian dispensation then assumes at once
its Scriptural characteristic of being a present thing.
The offering is present, and the faith which casts itself
upon it, the love which it awakens, the hope which it
inspires, are also present.

b. As an offering of life, the offering of our Lord most
of all possesses its true unity and completeness. On
any other view it divides itself into two entirely distinct
and separate parts. These parts are not always indeed
conceived of in the same way. With some they are our
Lord's death upon the cross, together with the presentation of His blood to God, by which He atoned for sin

---

[1] Gal. iii. 1.

and "cleansed the heavenly archetypes of the earthly
sanctuary,"[1] followed by the imparting of a new life.
With others they are "the presentation of a past death,"
followed by "that of the elevation and energies of a
present Life, which includes the life of His people, who
have their life hid with Him, because they are in Him
as the members of His Body."[2] Whichever of these
statements we adopt, our Lord's work, as a whole, is
considered to be twofold—partly an offering of death,
partly one of life; partly an offering made on earth,
partly one made in heaven. Both statements, too, make
the relation of the believer to his Lord in the first stage
of His work different from what it is in the second. On
the cross Christ dies, and dies alone. Alone He offers
Himself as a Victim for His people. In heaven He lives,
but His people are now in Him, enjoying a share in His
heavenly life, implanted in them though not yet perfectly developed. There is thus a want of unity in the
conception we are invited to form of the most momentous portion of the Redeemer's work ; and we are even
in danger of so separating its parts as to imagine that
the offering up of ourselves to God is a consequence,
instead of an integral constituent, of redemption.

On the other hand, let us look at our Lord's offering
as one of life, of life passing through death upon the
cross, and afterwards "perfected" in heaven, and His
whole offering becomes one, and our part with Him also
one. One with Him, we die in Him, rise in Him, reign
in Him. We are *in* Him from the beginning to the end

---

[1] Westcott on Hebrews, p. 298.   [2] Sadler, *The One Offering*, p. 47.

of our spiritual experience. Our repentance, our cry for pardon, our acceptance of the penalty of sin, our new and higher life, are all *in* Him—involved in the very idea of receiving Him as He is—and not conclusions to which we are led by reasoning.

But the view now taken of our Lord's offering gives it completeness as well as unity. On any other view our death with Christ upon the cross appears to want that moral and religious element which, according to the sacred writers, is more than intimately associated with it, which is even wrought into its very texture. So far as concerns us it becomes a merely outward act, to be applied for our benefit in no other way than any Divine gift. It sets us free from the guilt and punishment of sin. It does not in itself involve deliverance from the power of sin. That deliverance follows only as a necessary result. There is incompleteness in this way of considering the matter. Pardon of sin and deliverance from its bondage—or, at all events, pardon of sin and the impartation of the principle which, as it acquires strength in the soul, will and must in ever-increasing measure deliver us—cannot be separated except in thought. The redemption which touches our legal position before God touches at the same moment our life and character. The necessities of the Protestant controversy with Rome have obscured this truth, but it does not cease on that account to be one of the most important truths of the New Testament. In Christ's death the believer beholds more than the ground upon which he is forgiven. In it he also dies to sin, as truly

and really and inwardly as in Christ's life he lives to
righteousness. All this, however, loses its immediateness of application to ourselves unless we think of our
Lord's offering as an offering of life, of life in death.
Then every step taken in carrying it out comes home to
our life, and has there its corresponding answer. Union
on our part to Christ in all His fortunes penetrates the
whole process of redemption; and our Lord's offering,
while He takes us into it and along with it from the
first, is complete as well as one.

c. As an offering of life our Lord's offering most of
all "fulfils" those various offerings of the law by which
it was foreshadowed. A general fulfilment or accomplishment of this kind must find a place in any true
conception of the Saviour's offering, for He came to
accomplish not one part only, but every part of the law
which had expressed the will of God to Israel. If,
however, we confine the offering of Christ to His death
on Calvary, the highest and most important sacrificial
rites of Israel have in Him no corresponding fulness.
We may speak of Jesus as the true Sin or Trespass
offering, but what of the Burnt and Peace offerings,
which belonged to a later and still more elevated region
of the religious life? Those, indeed, who see Christ's
Priesthood in His earthly ministry have not this difficulty to contend with, and they may behold Him as the
perfect Burnt-offering in the zeal for His Father's glory
which was always flaming up within His soul, in His
eagerness to work the work of Him that sent Him while
it was day, and in that calm serenity of spirit with which

He was able to exclaim, "I do always the things that please Him." In like manner they may behold the fulfilment of the Peace-offering in that peace and joy which filled the Redeemer's breast, even in the midst of the troubles by which He was surrounded. But this cannot avail us if we believe, in conformity with the whole tenor of Scripture, that the priestly work of Christ is mainly executed in heaven, and that the zeal for God, the eagerness for work, the never-failing obedience, the peace, the joy, the sense of filial relationship to His Heavenly Father, which He exhibited on earth, were rather the preparation for the priesthood than the manifestation of its functions. Able theologians accordingly have been constrained to say that " the service of the peace-offering bears respect more directly and properly to the people of Christ than to Christ Himself." [1] That cannot be. Whatever is to be fulfilled in the members of the Body must first be fulfilled in the Head. Besides which, the natural order of religious thought and act is overturned. The Burnt and Peace offerings must follow, not precede, the Sin and Trespass offerings ; and, if we are to seek for the fulfilment of the latter on the cross alone, there is no room for the fulfilment of the former. The conception of Christ's Priesthood as a heavenly Priesthood, and of the life that He now leads in heaven as the consummation of His offering, alone gives us the accomplishment, and that too in appropriate order, of everything that was involved in the separate offerings of the law. In the life *now* offered to the

---

[1] Fairbairn, *Typology of Scripture*, ii. p. 353.

Father we see not only the perfected Sin and Trespass, but the perfected Burnt and Peace offerings. There the life won through death is surrendered into the Father's hands. There it burns in the never-ceasing devotion of love and submission to the Father's will. There it is passed in the enjoyment of a fellowship with God undisturbed and glorified. And thence it descends to all the members of the Body; so that they find, in Him who gave and still gives Himself for them, reconciliation, union, nourishment for a heavenly service, and the comfort and joy of a heavenly feast.

d. As an offering of life our Lord's offering embraces in its efficacy the whole life of man. When as our High-priest and Representative Jesus offers His life to God, that life touches not only individual acts of our life, it covers it in every one of its departments. There is no portion of the life lived by us in which, by the fact that He had lived a human life, the Redeemer of the world had not shared. Must we labour? He had laboured. Must we suffer? He had suffered. Must we be tempted? He had been tempted. Must we at one time have solitary hours, at another move in social circles? He had spent hours alone upon the mountain top, and He had mingled with His disciples as companions and friends. Must we die? He had died. Must we rise from the grave? He had risen from it on the third morning. Must we appear before the Almighty as our Judge? He had appeared before Him who " sent " Him with the record of all that He had accomplished. Must we enter into eternity? He has entered it before us, and eternity is now passing

over Him.   More even than this has to be said.   For
our High-priest had not only moved in every one of
the scenes in which we move.   In each He had been a
conqueror, and that for us; so that, when He presents
His life to the Father, the conquest which He had gained
in each is included in His offering, and we may be of
good cheer because ˙He has overcome.   As the offering
which He makes is His perfected human life, our whole
human life is brought in Him within the scope of His
consecrating power, and every part of it is presented to
God as a trophy of His victory.[1]

II. The second part of our Lord's High-priestly work
in heaven is His Intercession.   This is generally supposed to refer to petitions which He offers up to His
Father for those members of His Body who are still
amidst the trials and temptations of their earthly pilgrimage.   Having made His own complete and everlasting offering of Himself upon the cross, and having
in the power of His blood there shed entered into the
immediate presence of God, and presented His offering
to Him as an atonement for sin, He now pleads the
cause of His people with all-prevailing intercession on
their behalf.   He applies to them the work which He
accomplished upon earth; and, as One whom the
Father heareth always, He obtains for them the
measure of grace which they require, until at last they
are perfected in glory.   It was not indeed imagined by
the fathers of the Church,[2] nor has the idea been enter-

---

[1] Comp. further on, the Offering of our Lord, Note **B.**
[2] Comp. Petavius, lib. xii. cap. 8, § 8.

tained by later theologians,[1] that this intercession necessarily takes the form of spoken words. In heaven our
Lord appears as "a Lamb standing as though it hath
been slaughtered";[2] and whether this means (a point
upon which opinions differ) that the marks of His sufferings are still to be seen in His glorified body, or that
the thought only of His past offering is before the
Father's mind, the conclusion is, that His very presence
in His humanity is enough to secure the hearing and
answering of His prayers. This view is accompanied
by the admission that, unlike His offering on the cross
or its completion in its presentation to the Father, the
prayers of our Lord are continuous and unceasing. His
offering was made once and for ever. His Intercession
continues so long as the humblest believer needs His
aid. Such is the view commonly entertained upon this
point; and it appears to be mainly founded upon the
impression that the proper and literal meaning of the
term used in the original to describe this part of our
Lord's work[3] is "to pray."

Such, however, is not the case. That expression
occurs only six times in the New Testament (one of the
six even being a compound form);[4] while a substantive
derived from it occurs only twice.[5] It is not found in
the Greek translation of the Old Testament canonical
books, although it is met with several times in the Old
Testament Apocrypha and in the early fathers. There

---

[1] Comp. Davidson and Westcott
on Hebrews vii. 25.

[2] Rev. v. 6.

[3] ἐντυγχάνειν.

[4] Acts xxv. 24; Rom. viii. 27,
34; xi. 2; Heb. vii. 25; Rom.
viii. 26.

[5] 1 Tim. ii. 1; iv. 5.

is some want, therefore, of the information we might
wish in order to reach a definite conclusion upon the
meaning of the phrase; but there is enough. By ex-
amining it in its different contexts it will at once
be seen that the verb does not mean simply to pray.
It means to deal or transact with one person in reference to another, either making a statement "concerning"
him upon which certain proceedings ought to follow, or
asking something "for" him or "against" him. Peti-
tion is indeed the general result of such action, and
hence the phrase passes easily into this meaning when
there is anything in the connexion to give it that particular force. When, however, it stands alone, without
anything to limit the interpretation, it ought to be
understood in a much wider sense, as including the
whole series of transactions in which one person may
engage with another on behalf of a third.

The disposition to limit the Intercession of our Lord
too exclusively to prayer has been in all probability
strengthened by the supposition that when, on the
great Day of Atonement, the high-priest went within
the veil it was to intercede for Israel, and this again has
seemed to derive support from what we are told of the
vision of Zacharias in the temple, when the angel an-
nounced to him that he should have a son. But the
prayer spoken of in connexion with Zacharias is that
of "the whole multitude of the people, who were praying without at the hour of incense," while of himself
it is only said that "according to the custom of the
priest's office, his lot was to enter into the temple of

the Lord and burn incense."[1]   The idea, indeed, that
the high-priest went within the veil to pray has no
clear foundation in Scripture.   The incense which he
carried within the veil was not so much to symbolise
his prayers as to be a cloud between him and that
glory of the Divine Presence upon which it was impossible for any one to look and live.   There is no
evidence that he there prayed.   He simply completed
the offering which he had begun immediately before ;
and, when the offering was complete, he came out to
perform the ceremony of the two goats, in which the
results of his offering were set forth.

In these circumstances it may be a matter of regret
that the English language seems to possess no better
word than "intercession" to express the action of our
High-priest in heaven after He had presented His
offering to the Father.[2]   For this, however, there is no
help, and all that can be done is to impress upon the
inquirer the fact that "Intercession" is a much wider
word than prayer.   That prayer is included under the
term is not for a moment to be denied, but we are not
to limit it to prayer.   We are to understand it of every
act by which the Son, in dependence on the Father, in
the Father's name, and with the perfect concurrence of
the Father, takes His own with Him into the Father's
presence, in order that whatever He Himself enjoys in
the communications of His Father's love may become
also theirs.

[1] Luke i. 9, 10.
[2] The gain would be great could
we speak of "interacting" and
"interaction," but it is impossible
to do so.

From this Intercession of the heavenly Lord, indeed, there is no reason why prayer—why even prayer in words—should be excluded. One thing only has to be remembered, that the glorified Redeemer does not pray to the Father in the sense in which the creature prays to the Creator. The fact has been often before, but cannot be too frequently noticed, that in the fourth Gospel our Lord never uses of His own approach to the Father the word expressive of the manner in which the creature approaches God. He goes to Him not as one between whom and God a gulf has to be bridged, or as if He were asking aid from an external source. He goes to Him in the full consciousness of mutual love; in that Divine fellowship in which He knows that the will of the Father is His will; and in which, therefore, He has only to utter the thoughts that belong in common to the ineffable unity of Their common life. But, so going, He prays.

The seventeenth chapter of the Gospel of St. John may cast light on the point now spoken of. That chapter constitutes the very centre of the fourth Gospel, the Holy of Holies of the sacred Tabernacle which is formed by the Gospel as a whole. With no feelings but those of even deeper than common reverence may its words be touched; but on that very account they require also to be considered with the utmost possible faithfulness, and every turn of expression ought to have its due weight assigned to it. This faithfulness has been exhibited in the Revised translation of the New Testament, and we need, therefore, have no scruple in using the Revised instead of the Authorised Version to illustrate the point before us.

Let us weigh, then, the import of the following verses when, in conformity with the original, the past is substituted in them for the perfect tense. "Even as Thou gavest (not, hast given) Him authority over all flesh." "Him whom Thou didst send, even Jesus Christ" (not, Jesus Christ, whom Thou hast sent). "I glorified Thee on the earth, having accomplished the work" (not, I have glorified Thee on the earth: I have finished the work). "I manifested Thy name unto the men whom Thou gavest Me out of the world" (not, I have manifested Thy name). "And they received them, and knew of a truth that I came forth from Thee, and they believed that Thou didst send Me" (not, and they have received them, and have known surely that I came out from Thee, and they have believed that Thou didst send Me). "And not one of them perished" (not, and none of them is lost). "And the world hated them" (not, and the world hath hated them). "As Thou didst send Me into the world" (not, as Thou hast sent Me). "That the world may believe that Thou didst send Me" (not, that Thou hast sent Me). "That the world may know that Thou didst send Me, and lovedst them, even as Thou lovedst Me" (not, that the world may know that Thou hast sent Me, and hast loved them, even as Thou hast loved Me). "O righteous Father, the world knew Thee not, but I knew Thee ; and these knew that Thou didst send Me" (not, O righteous Father, the world hath not known Thee: but I have known Thee, and

these have known that Thou hast sent Me). "And I made
known unto them Thy name, and will make it known;
that the love wherewith Thou lovedst Me may be in
them, and I in them" (not, and I have declared unto
them Thy name, and will declare it: that the love
wherewith Thou hast loved Me may be in them, and I
in them).[1]   We have enumerated all the changes of the
kind of which we speak, and the list is a remarkable
one.   Considered even in itself, it is sufficient to show
how deliberately the past tenses were chosen by our
Lord.   It is true that the Greek readings are occasionally uncertain.   Scribes seem to have been confused
by the frequent transitions from the perfect to the past,
and from the past to the perfect tense.   But, after
making all due allowance for this, the repetition of the
past so frequently, in circumstances where we should
expect the perfect, is sufficient to show that it was our
Lord's design to bring out some aspect of the truth
which would have failed to find utterance in any other
method of expression.   What that aspect is it may
require time for the Church, under the influence of the
new and more correct renderings now given, to discover.
Meanwhile it is enough to say that this at least is
evidently involved in them,—that our Lord is before
us, not in the position of One who, surrounded by the
sufferings of earth and in the immediate prospect of
death, is praying for His people, but in that of One who
prays for them as if He were already at the right hand
of the Father, in His heavenly abode.   At the moment

[1] John xvii. 2, 3, 4, 6, 8, 12, 14, 18, 21, 23, 25, 26.

when He utters this prayer He is less the humbled and
dying than the exalted and glorified Redeemer. He
has passed onward in thought to the accomplishment of
His work, and to the time when He shall be engaged in
the application of it to those for whom He died.   In
the other parts of the fourth Gospel and in the earlier
Gospels we follow Him amidst the sorrows of His
earthly state, and see Him drinking the "cup of trembling" which had been put into His hand.   Here we
are permitted to follow Him within the veil; and these
words of His are not so much words which He pours
forth while the shadow of the cross is resting upon
Himself and His disciples, as words which rise from
Him to the Father when, no more in the world,[1] He
prays for those who are left in the world to carry on
His work.   How true is the instinct which has always
led the Church to designate this prayer the High-
priestly prayer of Jesus! In heaven only is He perfect
High-priest, and the words of the prayer belong at
least in spirit to that upper sanctuary.   They are the
concentration of all the prayers of the heavenly
Intercessor, as He bore on earth, as He bears now, and
will bear for ever, the wants of His people before the
Father, who is both able and willing to supply them.

It is not, however, in prayer alone that the Intercession of the Church's High-priest in heaven is exercised.
We have seen that the word has a much wider meaning.
"I know thy works" is the language in which the
exalted Redeemer addresses each of the seven churches

[1] Ver. 11.

of Asia, as they successively represent one or other of the conditions in which believers shall be found from the beginning to the end of their struggle with the world, and He "knows" them in order that He may furnish them with the supplies of strength and guidance which their ever-varying circumstances require. Each church has its own promise, and each promise is adapted to the church's need. He that walks in the midst of the seven golden candlesticks keeps them, and trims them, and pours fresh oil into them, that they may burn with undimmed brightness in the sanctuary.

Many other passages of Scripture, by directing us to a constant activity of the glorified Lord on behalf of the members of His body, teach us the same lesson. Thus it is that He watches over every manifestation of love, however trifling, made by the believer in His name. No gift of meat to the hungry, or water to the thirsty, or hospitality to the stranger, or clothing to the naked, and no visit paid to the prisoner or the sick, is unnoticed by Him. Each is rather marked in His book of remembrance, and it shall not be forgotten in the Judgment.[1] Thus also it is that to whatever lands His disciples travel in the discharge of their commission, or whatever labour or trials they have to face, He conveys to them the assurance, "He that receiveth you receiveth Me," "Lo, I am with you alway, even unto the consummation of the age."[2] Thus it is that He sees their shortcomings and falls, and obtains for them ever new applications of the pardoning efficacy of His

[1] Matt. xxv. 35, 36.   [2] Matt. x. 40 ; xxviii. 20.

blood.[1]   And, yet again, it is thus that He gives us the
consolation of words spoken at the moment when His
departure was at hand, "I go to prepare a place for
you.   And if I go and prepare a place for you, I come
again, and will receive you unto Myself, that where I
am, there ye may be also." [2]

Rightly conceived, the work of Intercession on the
part of our heavenly High-priest seems to be that,
having restored the broken covenant and brought His
Israel into the most intimate union and communion
with God, He would now, amidst all their remaining
weaknesses, and the innumerable temptations that surround them, preserve them in it.   And He would do
this by keeping them in Himself; so that in Him they
shall stand in such unity of love to the Father that the
Father will love them as His own sons, will need no
one to remind Him that they are so, and will directly
pour out upon them, as very members of the Body of
the Eternal Son, every blessing first poured out upon
the Head.

In the light of what has now been said, a clear line
of distinction may be drawn between the Intercession
of our Lord and that ascribed in the New Testament to
the Holy Spirit.   Of the latter, we read in the promise
of Christ to His disciples, " And I will make request of
the Father, and He shall give you another Advocate,
that He may be with you for ever, even the Spirit of
the truth: whom the world cannot receive; for it
beholdeth Him not, neither knoweth Him: ye know

----

[1] 1 John ii. 1.   [2] John xiv. 3.

Him; for He abideth with you, and shall be in you"; [1] while the same truth is undoubtedly referred to by St. Paul when he says, in writing to the Romans, "And in like manner the Spirit also helpeth our infirmity : for we know not how to pray as we ought; but the Spirit Himself maketh intercession for us with groanings which cannot be uttered; and He that searcheth the hearts knoweth what is the mind of the Spirit, because He maketh intercession for the saints according to the will of God." [2]   There are thus two "Advocates" mentioned in the New Testament—the one by St. John, when he says that "we have an Advocate with the Father, Jesus Christ the righteous"; [3] the other by our Lord when, in His last discourse to His disciples, He promises "another Advocate, that He may be with them for ever." [4]   It is in the idea of representation that the two designations meet.   Jesus glorified represents us before the Father's throne; the Holy Spirit abiding with us represents in us Jesus gone to the Father.   The first Advocate is external, the second internal.   The first takes all our necessities to the Father, that, as Himself one with the Father, He may so "make request" [5] on our behalf that, out of the common love of the Father to the Son and the Son to the Father, these necessities may be supplied. The second brings the Redeemer in such a manner home into our hearts [6] that, in the innermost depths of our nature, we see and judge and feel with

---

[1] John xiv. 16, 17.
[2] Rom. viii. 26, 27.
[3] 1 John ii. 1.
[4] John xiv. 16.

[5] The proper rendering of ἐρωτήσω in John xiv. 16.
[6] "He that searcheth the hearts knoweth."—Rom. viii. 27.

Him; that His requests for us become our prayers for ourselves; and that the unity of Father, Son, and redeemed humanity is in Him completely realised.

Finally, it may be observed that the blessings of redemption thus applied to us through the Intercession of our Lord, in the wide sense in which we have been led to understand that word, are blessings that flow from His own continued offering. The Intercession and the Offering cannot be separated from each other. The offering is itself a continuous intercession; the continuous intercession implies the offering as a present thing. What the Redeemer gives us, in giving all, is Himself, and therefore Himself as He is now. This is the meaning of every promise made " to him that overcometh" in the seven Epistles addressed to the universal Church in the Revelation of St. John. The glorified Lord is the tree of life that is in the paradise of God. He is the victory over the second death. He is the hidden manna, and the white stone inscribed with the new name which no man knoweth but he that receiveth it. He is the morning star. His is the white raiment in which they who have not defiled their garments shall be clothed. His is the new name written upon those who are pillars in a house of God from which they go no more out. And, lastly, His is the throne upon which they sit down with Him, even as He sat down with the Father upon His throne.[1] The members of the mystical Body have nothing except what is given them in that Head who is the Alpha and the Omega

---

[1] Rev. ii. 7, 11, 17, 28 (comp. xxii. 16); iii. 5, 12, 21.

the beginning and the ending, the Author and the Finisher of their faith. If we ask for one conception that, more than any other, shall combine all the characteristics of a life to which such blessings belong, there is none so appropriate as that expressed by the words offering, oblation, sacrifice—a life yielded up to the Father of our Spirits in order to carry out the purposes of His love, and filled with Him. But such a life comes always and immediately from Christ as a living Lord. Without this thought Christ's unity with His people would not be so intimate or real or interpenetrating as it is, and His life in heaven must therefore embrace in it that idea of a continuous offering in which alone the members of His body can offer themselves continually, and experience all the blessings of an accepted sacrifice.

III. The third part of our Lord's High-priestly work in heaven is Benediction or Blessing. We have seen that this function was discharged by the priests of Israel, and we may expect, after all that has been in other respects revealed of the Work of the heavenly High-priest, that it will also be fulfilled by Him. Let it not be said that we can do without an authoritative and definite Benediction from on high, because we know that, in providence and in grace, in our persons and our families, in our work and in our suffering, " to them that love God all things work together for good, even to them that are called according to His purpose." [1] It is the Christian's strength, indeed, to be assured that

---

[1] Rom. viii. 28.

M

"every good act of giving and every perfect gift is from above, coming down from the Father of lights, with whom there can be no variation, neither shadow that is cast by turning." [1]   He believes that his Father in heaven desires to shower down blessings with a full hand upon all His creatures. But this is not enough. In the weakness of our nature we need to see the channel opened by which the blessing is conveyed, and to behold, as it were, the streams which actually convey it.   Thus it was that Joseph, assured as he was of his father's love to his children, brought his sons to Jacob, that the aged patriarch might lay his hands upon their heads, and might bless them before he died; and thus it is that it never fails to be a source of precious consolation to the members of the family of some departing saint, when they are permitted to gather around his bed, and, ere his lips close in death, to hear him bless them.   In all this nature speaks with her deepest and holiest tones; and the faith of Christ sanctifies and elevates, instead of destroying, such feelings.   The Apostolic Epistles, accordingly, almost invariably conclude with a Benediction, and the Church of Christ has never permitted any of her services to close without one.

Here again, therefore, the heavenly high-priest recognises and meets the longings of His people. From this point of view there is a peculiar force and tenderness in St. Luke's narrative of the Ascension, when he tells us that "Jesus led His disciples out until they were over against Bethany: and He lifted up His hands,

[1] James i. 17.

and blessed them. And it came to pass, while He
blessed them, He parted from them, and was carried up
into heaven." [1]

Nay, what is the whole New Testament dispensation but, in one respect at least, the fulfilling of the
words of that priestly Blessing which was wont of old
to raise the fallen and to comfort the mourner in Israel?
—" The Lord bless thee and keep thee; the Lord make
His face to shine upon thee, and be gracious unto thee;
the Lord lift up His countenance upon thee, and give
thee peace." "The Lord bless thee and keep thee,"—
and how many are the words of blessing which during
His life on earth fell, which now during His life in
heaven fall, from the lips of Him of whom it had been
prophesied by the Psalmist, "The Lord shall bless thee
out of Zion," [2]—the blessings of the Sermon on the Mount,
the blessing on them that hear the Word of God, the
blessing on them that have not seen and yet have
believed; [3] while it was part of His High-priestly prayer
on their behalf, "Holy Father, keep them in Thy name
which Thou hast given Me." [4] "The Lord make His face
to shine upon thee, and be gracious unto thee,"—and is
it not one of the privileges of the New Jerusalem of
which all saints are citizens, that "they see their Lord's
face, and that His name is on their foreheads"? [5] while
the beloved disciple tells us that "grace," as well as
truth, "came by Jesus Christ," and that "out of His

---

[1] Luke xxiv. 50, 51.   [2] Ps. cxxviii. 5.
[3] Matt. v. 1-11 ; Luke xi. 28 ; John xx. 29.   [4] John xvii. 11.
[5] Rev. xxii. 4.

fulness we all received, and grace for grace."[1] " The
Lord lift up His countenance upon thee, and give thee
peace,"—and is not our Lord the Prince of peace ? Was
not His legacy to His disciples, as He felt that the end
was near, given in the words, " Peace I leave with you ;
My peace I give unto you " ?[2] while " Peace be unto
you " was His first salutation to them when, on the day
of the Resurrection, He showed Himself out of His
glory.[3] Above all, though this must be reserved for the
next Lecture, the Benediction of the heavenly High-
priest is to be found in the gift of the Holy Spirit,
bestowed first upon His people, and then through them
upon all who will receive it.

Such, then, is the work of the heavenly High-priest.
It corresponds to what we saw in a previous Lecture to
be His qualifications for it ; and its effect is the restoration of His Israel to God, in joyful confidence and holy
devotion to His service.

After the High-priest of old, on the Great Day of
Atonement, had finished his offering in the Tabernacle,
there followed his procedure with the scapegoat, when
he laid his hands upon its head, confessed over it all
the iniquities of the children of Israel, and all their
transgressions in all their sins, and then sent it away
by a fit man into the wilderness to perish there. That
act closed the more particular services of the day. Sin
was not only expiated, but banished. The covenant was
restored. The people were again united, however im-

[1] John i. 16, 17.   [2] John xiv. 27.
[3] John xx. 21.

perfectly, and only for a time, to God, and were ready for that feast of Tabernacles which commemorated the most signal deliverance of the past, which, as celebrated at least in later times, gave promise of the noblest blessings of the future, and of which, even more than of the other festival seasons of the Jewish year, it was said that he who did not know its joy knew not what joy was. Yet this was only the shadow of that more perfect blessedness which comes to the Christian Church through the work of her heavenly High-priest, for in Him she has sin pardoned; she is loosed from sin; grace and peace are multiplied to her as she enters upon and pursues her heavenly path—"elect according to the foreknowledge of God the Father, in sanctification of the Spirit, unto obedience and sprinkling of the blood of Jesus Christ."[1] The sprinkling seals for her an everlasting covenant. Her festival of highest and purest joy has come. The voice of ancient prophecy, as it foretold that she should "keep her feast of Tabernacles,"[2] is fulfilled. And, having offered the first-fruits of her increase, she enters upon a free, joyous, independent life, breathing that invigorating and quickening air of the wilderness which strengthens her amidst all the trials of her homeward march.

---

[1] 1 Pet. i. 1, 2.   [2] Zech. xiv. 16.

LECTURE IV

"If any man hath not the Spirit of Christ, he is none of His."
Rom. viii. 9.

TOWARDS the close of the last Lecture the remark was made that the chief blessing bestowed by our Lord as High-priest of His people is the gift of the Spirit. The subject was too important to be considered at the time, and we turn to it now.

Every reader of the New Testament is familiar with the fact that the gift of the Spirit is spoken of by the sacred writers with remarkable frequency and emphasis, that it is referred to as the great gift of that dispensation under which Christians live, and that it is described as embracing in itself alone everything that the believer needs. The thought of a written word does not there occupy the place assigned to it in the later ages of the Church, in which it has to a large extent practically excluded the work of the Spirit as a living agent from the minds of many. It was not a written gospel, but a message and a power to come from the inspiration of the Spirit, that the Saviour had in view when, after His Resurrection, He instructed the Apostles whom He had chosen to " wait for the promise of the Father, which,

said He, ye heard from Me."[1]   On the day of Pentecost
the Church was planted by means not of writings, but
of the Holy Spirit, who descended in tongues of fire
upon the heads of the disciples.   In the energy of the
same Spirit the Church continued to be propagated ;
and numerous passages of the Acts of the Apostles make
it clear that the first gift bestowed upon converts to the
faith of Christ, after they had been admitted into the
Church by Baptism—the gift which sealed them in
their new position and fitted them for their new duties
—was that of the Spirit, imparted by the laying on of
hands.   The fulness of blessing, also, everywhere connected with the gift of the Spirit, is not less remarkable
than the frequent mention of the gift itself.   Even in
the earlier Gospels, in which the teaching of our Lord
upon the point is less emphatic than in the fourth, we
read, "If ye then, being evil, know how to give good
gifts unto your children ; how much more shall your
heavenly Father give the Holy Spirit to them that
ask Him ? "[2]   There had been no reference to the Spirit
in any previous part of the discourse in which these
words occur.   In answer to the request of His disciples
our Lord had just taught them that prayer in which
the universal Church delights to recognise the expression of all her wants, when in a sudden and unexpected
turn of language He closes with the promise of this gift
of the Holy Spirit.   From that gift, then, we cannot
exclude the thought of provision for every want experi-
enced by us ; and in the parallel passage of St. Matthew

---

[1] Acts i. 4, 5.   [2] Luke xi. 13.

the one form of expression is even substituted for the other, "How much more shall your Father which is in heaven give good things to them that ask Him?"[1] The gift of "the Holy Spirit" and that of "good things" cover the same ground.

The truth thus indicated is brought out with still greater force in the last discourses of our Lord in the Gospel of St. John.[2] There the Paraclete or Advocate takes the place of all other gifts which the departing Redeemer might be expected to allude to in that trying hour. Two great lines of promise appear in these discourses—the first, that the disciples shall be fitted for their work; the second, that they shall be supported in performing it; and both lines are directly associated with the Advocate to be sent after Jesus had gone away. Of the first we read, "And I will pray the Father, and He shall give you another Advocate, that He may be with you for ever, even the Spirit of Truth"; "But the Advocate, even the Holy Spirit, whom the Father will send in My name, He shall teach you all things, and bring to your remembrance all that I said unto you."[3] Of the second we also read, "But when the Advocate is come, whom I will send unto you from the Father, even the Spirit of Truth which proceedeth from the Father, He shall bear witness of Me : and ye also bear witness, because ye have been with Me from the beginning"; "Nevertheless, I tell you the truth ; it is expedient for you that I go away : for if I go not away, the Advocate will not come unto you; but if I go, I will

[1] Matt. vii. 11.   [2] John xiv.-xvi.   [3] John xiv 16, 17, 26.

send Him unto you." [1]   Nor is this all; for here too, as in the earlier Gospels, the specific promise of the Spirit immediately follows promises of the most general kind, as if to combine them into a simpler and more concrete form : " If ye shall ask anything in My name, that will I do "; " That whatsoever ye shall ask of the Father in My name, He may give it you." [2]   Then comes the promise of the Advocate, who is thus in Himself the fulfilment alike of the "anything" and of the "whatsoever" that we ask.

The same lesson is implied, if not so expressly taught, throughout the rest of the New Testament.   Every grant and privilege enjoyed by the disciple of Jesus is connected with the Spirit's work.   He is the Spirit of truth, and adoption, and freedom, and purity, and brotherly love. [3]   He is the soul of acceptable worship and the sustainer of effectual prayer. [4]   He reveals to us the deep things of God ; giving us the word both of wisdom and knowledge. [5]   He helps our infirmities, making intercession for us with groanings which cannot be uttered. [6]   He not only quickens us into spiritual life, but, after we are quickened, carries forward the work of Sanctification in our souls. [7]   Christians "live" by the Spirit, "walk" by the Spirit, are "led" by the Spirit, are a "habitation of God" in the Spirit, and are "filled" with the Spirit. [8]   In addition to all this the Spirit is also

---

[1] John xv. 26, 27 ; xvi. 7.

[2] John xiv. 14, xv. 16.

[3] John xiv. 17, xv. 26 ; Gal. iv. 6 ; 2 Cor. iii. 17 ; 1 Cor. vi. 19 ; 1 John iii. 24, iv. 12.

[4] Phil. iii. 3 ; Eph. vi. 18.

[5] 1 Cor. ii. 10, xii. 8 ; Eph. i. 17.

[6] Rom. viii. 26.

[7] John vi. 63 ; 2 Thess. ii. 13.

[8] Gal. v. 25 ; Rom. viii. 14 ; Eph. ii. 22, v. 18.

the earnest of our inheritance. He witnesses with our
spirits that we are the children of God. He seals us
unto the day of redemption ; and, when believers at
last rise from their graves on the morning of the
resurrection, their mortal bodies are quickened because
of the Spirit of Christ that dwelleth in them.[1]

Allusions so numerous as these and many others leave
no doubt upon the point that the gift of the Holy Spirit is
the leading and characteristic gift of the Christian dispensation; and that from His grace and power flow alike
the privileges which Christians enjoy, and the distinctive graces of their new and higher life.   There is not,
in short, one single office in the Church of Christ, not
one good work done, not one grace exhibited, by any of
its members that is not dependent upon the operation
of the Spirit.   There are diversities of gifts, of ministrations, and of workings, but each of these is part of what
St. Paul styles "the manifestation of the Spirit."[2]

Such is the language of the New Testament : and a
similar importance is attached to the gift of the Spirit
in the Old.   Nothing is more worthy of notice than
the fact that, amidst all the externalism often thought
to be her only mark, the Old Testament Church associated with this gift the chief glory of the Messianic
age.   One symbol, in particular, is constantly employed
by the prophets to denote the precious and abundant
blessings then to be poured out upon the Church; and

[1] Eph. i. 13 ; Rom. viii. 16 ;
Eph. iv. 30 ; Rom. viii. 11.
[2] 1 Cor. xii. 4-11, "The Holy
Spirit is the *Executive* of all the
works of God."—Smeaton, *Doctrine of the Holy Spirit*, p. 126.

it is so clearly interpreted both by them and by our
Lord Himself, that there can be no mistake as to its
meaning. That symbol is water. It is made use of in
every form—now as a fountain, now as showers of rain,
now as pools in the thirsty desert, and now again as a
river that brings life to the surrounding country, teems
with multitudes of fishes, and is covered with the ships
of the nations. Besides this frequent use of the symbol,
many passages also meet us in Old Testament Prophecy
in which the Spirit is expressly spoken of as the special
gift and glory of Messianic times. Of these the words
of Joel quoted by St. Peter on the day of Pentecost may
be taken as an example.[1] The feast of Tabernacles, too—
the crowning festival of Israel's sacred year—was understood, at least in later ages, to testify to the same great
truth. Nor can the ceremonial of drawing water from
the pool of Siloam on the eighth or great day of the
feast, and pouring it out upon the altar, while the
assembled multitudes shook their palm-branches and
made the temple resound with song, be explained except
by remembering Israel's hope that at that very moment
the Spirit would be given. St. John, indeed, has interpreted the ceremonial for us when, explaining the
Saviour's promise, he says, "This spake He of the
Spirit, which they that believed in Him were to receive."[2]
There can be no doubt, then, that the gift of the Holy
Spirit is the distinguishing gift of the New Testament
dispensation, or that it may even be regarded as the
sum and substance of all the blessings of the new and

---

[1] Joel ii. 28 ; Acts ii. 17, 18.   [2] John vii. 39.

better covenant. The present dispensation is indeed styled by St. Paul "The Ministration of the Spirit."[1] It is unnecessary to say more upon this point. Other questions connected with the subject demand consideration.

I. What is the special nature of the gift?

The idea commonly entertained is that the Spirit promised by our Lord is simply the Third Person of the Trinity, viewed in His absolute and eternal Being. He who had been from everlasting the bond between the Father and the Son, and the thought of whose distinct and separate Personality is necessary to any just conception of the Personality of God, is supposed to be communicated to us, and in some mysterious way to take up His abode within us. This, however, is hardly the teaching of the Bible. We seem rather to be taught there that the Spirit bestowed upon us by the glorified Lord is not the Third Person of the Trinity in the soleness of the Personality possessed by Him before the foundations of the world were laid; but rather that Person as He entered into, took possession of, consecrated and "perfected" the human nature of our Lord. We seem to be taught that the Spirit which, as believers, we receive is the Spirit of the Christ as Christ now is, and not as He was before He became flesh and tabernacled among us. The human nature of our Lord in His heavenly abode is filled with the Spirit. In that fulness it is now for ever united to the Divine nature of the Eternal Word; and out of this combined fulness

[1] 2 Cor. iii. 8.

of the Divine and human we receive, and grace for grace.[1]
So important is the point before us that it will be well
to pursue it a little further.[2]

1. Even during His life on earth our Lord possessed,
and He still possesses, the fulness of the Spirit. At
the very opening of His ministry in the synagogue at
Nazareth He applied to Himself the language of ancient
prophecy, "Spirit of the Lord is upon Me";[3] and, in
so applying it, He obviously intended to express the
character of His ministry as a whole.   According,
therefore, to His own claim thus distinctly made we are
called upon to think of Him as One who, from the
beginning to the close of His Messianic work, was dwelt
in, moulded, guided, encouraged, and strengthened by
the Spirit of God.   All the other statements of Scripture
upon the point lead to the same conclusion.

By the power of Holy Spirit His flesh was so formed
within the womb of the Virgin Mary that, while truly

[1] John i. 16.

[2] In his excellent practical
treatise, *Through the Eternal
Spirit*, Dr. Elder Cumming objects
to what he understands to be the
teaching of this lecture, and advocates the ordinary view, that "the
Holy Ghost dwells in the Christian
in His simple and absolute Deity."
The whole book is well worth the
reader's attention. But on one
point Dr. Cumming, speaking
simply from hearing and news-
paper reports, has not exactly
caught the meaning of what was
said. "Without denying," he
says, "that the positive side of
the view proposed has much to
recommend it, yet the indwelling
of the Spirit in the believer is not,
so far as I can judge, to be regarded only as one of the results
of the indwelling of Christ; it is
rather the indwelling of the Spirit
which makes Christ's indwelling
possible and real" (p. 99). It
will appear in the sequel of this
lecture that its writer not only
accepts, but attaches great importance to, what is said in the
latter part of Dr. Cumming's
statement.

[3] Luke iv. 18.

our flesh, with all its characteristic qualities and natural infirmities, it was yet free from that taint of sin which would have rendered it impossible for Him to become the new Head of a line of spiritual descendants, to the ideal conception of whom (a conception to be ultimately realised) no sin belongs. "Holy Spirit," said the angel to Mary, "shall come upon thee, and the power of the Most High shall overshadow thee : wherefore also that which is to be born shall be called Holy, the Son of God."[1] When at His Baptism He was solemnly in-augurated to the task assigned to Him, "the heavens were rent asunder, and the Spirit as a dove descended and abode upon Him,"—a visible symbol satisfying the highest expectations of the Baptist, who "saw and believed that this was the Son of God."[2] Immediately after His Baptism the Temptation in the wilderness followed, when He met and conquered in their intensest form specimens of all the trials He was to encounter in His future work ; and of that season in His history we are expressly told that "Jesus, full of Holy Spirit, returned from the Jordan, and was led in the Spirit in the wilder-ness during forty days, being tempted of the devil."[3] When the temptation was over and His ministry began, it is said that "He returned in the power of the Spirit into Galilee."[4] The accounts given us in the Gospels of the manner in which He carried on that ministry teach the same lesson. Throughout it all He was "anointed with Holy Spirit and with power,"[5] and of

[1] Luke i. 35.   [2] Mark i. 10 ; John i. 32-34.
[3] Luke iv. 1.   [4] Luke iv. 14.   [5] Acts x. 38.

some of the most important of His miracles, such as the casting out of demons, He tells us Himself that He did them "by Spirit of God." [1] Nor was it otherwise with the various characteristics of His inner life. We are never permitted to think of Him as of one who exhibited only a complete human development, or in whom there was nothing higher than a strong and harmonious growth of the different parts of man's complex nature. Beneath and pervading all there was a Divine presence, a heavenly power, the immediate influence of God Himself. The peace which He possessed was not simply that of a well-balanced mind when the winds of earthly passion have been hushed; it was peace of which He said, "Not as the world giveth, give I unto you." [2] His joy was not merely that of a happy disposition, able to separate the sweet from the bitter in the mixed cup of worldly fortune; at a moment when it is spoken of we are told that "He rejoiced in the Holy Spirit." [3] While His love was no mere tenderness or sympathy for brothers and sisters surrounded by the adversities of life; it was a Divine love passing knowledge, "the love wherewith the Father had loved Him." [4]

As it was thus throughout the course of our Lord's life, so the same manifestation was made at its close. When He sent forth His disciples to carry on the great purposes of His mission, it was through "Holy Spirit" that He gave them commandment; [5] and His last and highest gift, that in bestowing which He felt that He

---

[1] Matt. xii. 28.   [2] John xiv. 27.   [3] Luke x. 21.
     [4] John xvii. 26.   [5] Acts i. 2.

bestowed Himself, was the gift of the Spirit: "He breathed on them, and said unto them, Receive ye Holy Spirit." [1]

Statements such as these, so numerous and varied, are sufficient to show in how deep and true a sense our Lord, even during His earthly life, was animated and pervaded by the Spirit of God. Not that the Holy Spirit thus dwelling in Him took the place of His Divinity. The union of the Divine Son with the Divine Father could never be interrupted, whatever the self-limitations which the former, in becoming man, might, not apart from His Divinity but in the power of His Divinity, impose upon Himself. As from everlasting ages of the past, so through all the ages as they run their course, and to the everlasting ages of the future, the Three Persons of the Trinity must, while no doubt to be thought of separately, form such a unity that they shall be more than *beside*, that they shall be *in* each other, and that no one of them can ever have a place assigned to Him out of the Hypostatic union, in which some other existence might occupy the sphere He is supposed to have resigned. When, therefore, the Second Person of the Trinity took flesh and dwelt among us, He was not less *in* the Father than before, and at that great epoch the Holy Spirit was not less than formerly *in* both the Father and the Son. The Son did not by His Incarnation forfeit that Divine *Hypostasis* which He had always been, nor could He then receive what He had eternally possessed. He rather filled the manhood

[1] John xx. 22.

which he assumed with the power of the Divinity which He retained; and thus filled it at the same time with the Spirit which dwelt in that Divinity. In a similar manner the Divine and human natures of our Lord were also distinct; but again we are not to think of them as standing side by side in His one Personality, in the relation of two parallel lines. The Divine nature was more than parallel to the human; it penetrated and pervaded it. The human nature again penetrated and pervaded the Divine in all those moral and religious departments in which the two natures are akin, and the sphere of the Spirit was that in which this union was effected. Theologians have often endeavoured to solve difficulties of Scripture by separating the two natures, and ascribing words or acts of the Redeemer now to one of the two and now to another. The experiment has always failed. New difficulties have been created more serious than those which an effort had been made to escape. Christ, Divine and human, was one; and in the actings of each nature the other had a part, except in so far as we are compelled to suppose that His "emptying of Himself" was continued by Him throughout all His life below. When, therefore, we endeavour to conceive what Jesus was on earth, we must think of Him as filled with the Spirit in both the natures that are essential to His Personality. The two cannot be separated without destroying the unity of His Person. In Him they meet and mingle and interpenetrate each other.

If it was thus with our Lord when He was upon earth, it is not otherwise with Him now that He is in heaven.

The human nature which He there possesses is still penetrated and pervaded by the Spirit—the Spirit who was
eternally in the Son; and the difference in that respect
between His state on earth and His state in heaven
consists simply in this, that the dominion of the Spirit
in Him is now absolute, and free from every restraint
to which He had subjected Himself during the days of
His humiliation. In this sense St. Paul speaks of Him
as " Spirit " when he says of Christians that, " reflecting
as in a mirror the glory of the Lord, they are changed
into the same image from glory to glory, even as from
the Lord who is Spirit." [1] Not, indeed, that He is
wholly Spirit, like a formless ether diffused throughout
the immensity of space. The " Spirit " which He is, is
expressed in form. He has a body—the " spiritual body"
of which the same Apostle tells us in another passage; [2]
but that body is in complete subservience to the Spirit,
adapted to its requirements and obedient to its behests.
As the humanity of Christ is not less perfect now than
it was before He died, so its union with His Divinity is
now not less close than it was then. If parallelism in
the one state is no explanation of the union, neither is
it in the other. Nay, if it be possible, we must even
think of the Divine element as interpenetrating the
human, and the human the Divine, in the glorified
Redeemer more thoroughly and more completely than
before. " Let all the house of Israel know assuredly,
that God hath made Him both Lord and Christ—this
Jesus whom ye crucified." [3]

[1] 2 Cor. iii. 18.   [2] 1 Cor. xv. 44.   [3] Acts ii. 36.

Our Lord then possessed on earth, and possesses now in heaven, the fulness of the Spirit. Let it only further be observed that this possession is not to be thought of as a mere dwelling of the Spirit in Him, in a way similar to that in which a man may dwell in the house he occupies. It is not a dwelling so much as an indwelling, organic, permeative—an efficient source of being and action, as true and real an indwelling as is that of the soul in the body. Hence that remarkable later reading of the New Testament, where we are told that when St. Paul, on his second great missionary journey, would have carried his apostolic labours into Bithynia, "the Spirit of Jesus" (not simply, as in the Authorised Version, "the Spirit") "suffered him not."[1] The Holy Spirit had so penetrated and pervaded the human nature of the exalted Lord that He could be spoken of as "The Spirit of Jesus."

2. The Spirit bestowed by our Lord in His glorified condition is not merely the Spirit, but the Spirit with which He Himself is filled; or, in other words, His own Spirit. Thus it is that St. Paul exclaims, "And because ye are sons, God sent forth the Spirit of His Son into our hearts, crying, Abba, Father."[2] In the garden of Gethsemane Jesus cried, "Abba, Father."[3] We, in our turn, cry, "Abba, Father." The same Spirit cries in the Head and in the members. So, again, St. Paul exclaims, "For I know that this shall turn to my salvation, through your prayer and the supply of the Spirit of Jesus Christ";[4] where the words, "the Spirit

---

[1] Acts xvi. 7. [2] Gal. iv. 6. [3] Mark xiv. 36. [4] Phil. i. 19.

of Jesus Christ," mean more than a Spirit given us by
Jesus Christ, and more than a general spirit of life in
Him.   They describe the Spirit belonging to Jesus
Christ, belonging to the Son, at the moment when the
Apostle wrote.   It was of no past historical personality
that St. Paul was writing, nor was it merely of a blessing taken out of the treasures of the Lord's grace.   It
was of the Spirit of a present and living Lord.   That
very Spirit which had sustained the Redeemer amidst
His sorrows, and which was His Spirit as He lived in
heaven, was granted to His suffering servant, that he
as well as his Master might "glory in tribulations also."
The same thing appears in our Lord's use of such expressions as "My peace," "My joy"[1]—expressions to
which we fail to do justice if we regard them only as
meaning a peace, a joy, which He bestows.   They are
His own peace, His own joy, passing over into us, and
becoming our peace, our joy.   The very peace with
which our Lord rested Himself on earth, with which He
rests Himself in heaven, on His Father's breast, is to be
our peace.   The very joy which was and still is His,
as He dwells in His Father's love and contemplates the
results of His finished work, is to be our joy.   If it cannot be said that we experience them as He did, it is
because we are not yet perfected.   Our hearts are not
yet sufficiently enlarged to receive the fulness of the
blessing.   But they will be enlarged ; and as they are
enlarged we shall receive more.   Not to the Son alone,
but to all who believe in Him, does the promise belong,

[1] John xiv. 27 ; xv. 11.

" He giveth not the Spirit by measure." [1]   The Spirit promised in the New Testament to believers is the Spirit of Christ.

It is no sufficient reply to this to say that in other passages the Spirit is called the Spirit of God, and is said to be given us by God.   That statement is true. " If so be that the Spirit of God dwell in you"; " The Spirit of God dwelleth in you"; "The Holy Spirit whom God hath given to them that obey Him"; "He that anointed us is God, who also gave us the earnest of the Spirit in our hearts." [2]   But the thought of God underlying these statements is not that of the First Person of the Trinity in Himself: it is the thought of Him in relation to the Son.   Hence the word used by our Lord Himself, when He speaks of the source from which all blessings flow to the believer, appears to be pre-eminently not God but Father—" The Father," " My Father," " Your Father."   The two truths meet in the higher unity, that the Spirit proceeds from the Father as He reveals Himself in the Son, and from the Son as the revelation of the Father.   He comes from the Father; but God is the Father only in the Son. He comes from the Son, but the Son is the only-begotten which is in the bosom of the Father, and is the " way " to the Father.   Such, there is every reason to think, is the true meaning of the Western Church in that great declaration of her Creed which did so much to cause,

---

[1] John iii. 34.   The words of the A. V. in italics ought to be omitted.

[2] Rom. viii. 9 ; 1 Cor. iii. 16 ; Acts v. 32 ; 2 Cor. i. 22.

and which more than everything else perpetuates, the
schism between her and the Eastern Church—that the
Holy Spirit proceeds not from the Father only, but
from the Father and the Son. It was never intended
by that clause to assert that there are two distinct
sources from which, in exactly the same sense, what is
called the Procession of the Holy Spirit takes place.
The meaning only is, that it is contrary to Scripture
teaching to rest in one of these Divine Personalities
alone. The Spirit comes from the Father through the
Son, and through the Son as the Son of the Father; [1]
and, inasmuch as "the Son can do nothing of Himself,
but what He seeth the Father doing"; and as "What
things soever the Father doeth, these the Son also doeth
in like manner," [2] the Son's works being thus the Father's
works, it is clear that the Spirit bestowed upon believers, whether spoken of as the Spirit of God or the
Spirit of Christ, is the same gift. The particular mode
of speaking depends simply upon the order of our
thought,—whether we ascend through the Son to the
Father, or descend from the Father through the Son;
and St. Paul has combined both forms when, writing to
the Galatians, he says, "And because ye are sons, God
sent forth the Spirit of His Son into your hearts, crying,
Abba, Father." [3] The fact, therefore, that the Spirit
granted to us in Christ Jesus is often spoken of as the

---

[1] In *Lux Mundi*, p. 335, Gore
speaks of the formula "from the
Father and the Son" as "less
nicely discriminated language."
Comp. Browne on the Thirty-
nine Articles, Art. v.; comp. also
Gess, p. 264.

[2] John v. 19, 36.

[3] Gal. iv. 6.

Spirit of God is no objection to the truth, that that
Spirit is Christ's Spirit, the Spirit of One who is human
as well as Divine.

3. When the Spirit is bestowed upon us, He must
be made ours, not outwardly alone, but inwardly and
experimentally. It is not enough to regard the Spirit
as a precious blessing granted out of the abundant
treasures of Divine love, or as a gift like that of the
sunshine or the rain, in which we can rejoice, although
they have no real contact with what we are. Such a
conception falls far short of that of the closeness of union
which, as we have seen, existed between our Lord's
human nature and the Spirit by which that nature was
occupied and informed. Whatever Jesus was or is,
whatever He did or does, the Spirit was an active agent
in His being or doing it; and what the Spirit was to
our Lord's human nature He must be to our human
nature also. The simple fact that the Eternal Son of
God became man in order to carry out the work of our
redemption is a proof of this necessity ; while the principle underlying every practical precept of the New Testament—that the believer must pass through the same
experience as his Master—leads to the same conclusion.

Again, it lies in the essential conditions belonging
both to the Spirit who acts and to the human being who
is acted upon, that the union between the two must be
of an inward and penetrating kind. In dealing with
the work of the Spirit in man we deal not with dead
matter laid upon dead matter, but with life kindling
life. When spirit is brought home to spirit, the

Spirit of Christ to the spirit of man, the two cannot in the nature of things remain separate from each other. The one cannot be set within the other as a precious jewel may be set in gold, the jewel remaining the jewel, the gold the gold. They must rather mingle like two different atmospheres, each diffusing itself throughout the other, so that both shall be found in every particle of their united volumes. The Spirit is more than a guide or instructor of those in whom He dwells, and He does more than reveal to them the great example they are to imitate. He penetrates their being; He acts at the centre of their life. "He that is joined to the Lord is one Spirit." [1]

The truth now dwelt upon is confirmed by every analogy employed in Scripture to illustrate the relation between our Lord and us. Is He the Head and are we the members of the body? The Head not merely exercises authority over the members, and issues commandments as from a throne; it transmits its subtle influences through every nerve and tissue of the frame. Is He the vine and are we the branches? The branches are not merely attached to the stem; they have their smallest twig and most distant leaf nourished by the sap by which the stem also grows. Is He the foundation and are we the stones of the spiritual temple? The founda-

---

[1] 1 Cor. vi. 17. "We have to carry into all thoughts of the relation between the Spirit and the Christian the mysterious relation between the Spirit and Christ."—Moule's *Outlines*, p. 134.

Dr. Newman beautifully says: "He pervades them (Christians) as light pervades a dwelling, or a sweet perfume the folds of some honourable robe."—*Parochial and Plain Sermons.*

tion not only supports the stones, it is thought of as sending upwards through them a principle of life; so that they become "living stones," sharers in the very life in which the foundation lives. Is He the Shepherd and are we the sheep? The sheep do not merely follow the Shepherd and listen to His voice; they are united to Him in the experience of an inward fellowship: "I am the Good Shepherd and I know Mine own" (notice throughout the deep meaning of the word "know"); "and Mine own know Me, even as the Father knoweth Me and I know the Father."[1] Or, finally, is Christ the Bridegroom and are His people the Bride? Then are they no longer twain, but one. The same thing may be said of the various symbols in which our Lord sets forth what He is to those who accept Him in faith. He is the "Light," yet in such a sense that He shines not only around them, but in their *hearts*, giving them the light of the knowledge of the glory of God in the face of Jesus Christ.[2] He is the "true bread out of heaven," but only he that eateth Him shall live by Him.[3] He is the "living water," but only he that drinks of the water shall never thirst.[4] Lastly, we must eat His flesh and drink His blood if we would have eternal life.[5]

Hence the fact that, in speaking of redeemed men, Scripture always takes for granted in the boldest manner that, while they are dependent for every Christian virtue they possess upon the free grace of God, they are engaged in a work of saving themselves—in holding fast, strength-

[1] John x 14, 15.   [2] John viii. 12; 2 Cor. iv. 6.   [3] John vi. 32.
     [4] John iv. 10.   [5] John vi 54.

ening, and perfecting their own salvation. Not one
Christian grace is theirs if to them it is no more than
an outward gift. Each must spring up from within.
Each must be an exercise of their own willing and
doing, so that it shall not simply be God who worketh
in them both to will and to do, but they also who work,
working out his good pleasure.[1]

Nothing, indeed, is more worthy of our notice than
the manner in which our Lord in His teaching brings out
the individuality and self-movement of His people, and
their independent, if at the same time their dependent,
strength. Two methods of expression employed by Him
are in this respect of peculiar interest, and the more so
that we meet them even to a greater degree in the
fourth than in the other Gospels. The very Evangelist
who has done most to preserve words of Jesus giving
expression to our Lord's identification of Himself with
us, and of us with Him, is also the Evangelist who has
done most to transmit to us words of the same Divine
Master pointing to the necessity for the individual
action of his followers.

(i.) In no Gospel is so much importance attached to
the exercise of our own will for the performance of any
duty or the obtaining of any blessing. When Jesus
asked the impotent man at the pool of Bethesda whether
he desired to be made whole, He put His question in
the form, "Hast thou a will to be so?"[2] When He
reproved the Jews for being too easily satisfied with
the light which the Baptist was able to afford, He said

[1] Phil. ii. 13.   [2] John v. 6.

to them not that they were willing, but that they
" willed " to rejoice in his light; [1] and when He asked
the disciples whether they too were offended by His
words, He said, " Is it possible that ye also should will
to go away ? " [2]   In like manner He says, not if any man
is willing, but "if any man willeth to do His will, he
shall know of the teaching whether it be of God " ; [3] and
to take but one passage more, in which the Evangelist
himself speaks, we read not that the disciples, after the
storm on the sea of Galilee had been calmed, "were
willing," but that they "willed," to take Jesus into the
boat. [4]   In all these passages there appears to be an
emphasis upon the word " will," which it is of extreme
importance to observe.

(ii.) The same conclusion is still more forcibly impressed upon us by another form of expression distinguishing the fourth Gospel, and as yet too little
heeded.   The peculiarity has been missed in the Authorised, but will be found in the Revised Version.   On one
occasion our Lord says to " the Jews," " But I know you,
that ye have not the love of God in yourselves " (not
" in you," A. V.) [5]   Upon another occasion He says,
" Verily, verily, I say unto you, Except ye eat the flesh
and drink the blood of the Son of man, ye have not life
in yourselves " (not " in you," A. V.) [6]   The expression
thus used by Jesus is best illustrated by the manner in

---

[1] John v. 35.
[2] John vi. 67.
[3] John vii. 17.
[4] John vi. 21.
[5] John v. 42.

[6] John vi. 53.   Comp. also
John xv. 4, although the A. V.
there translates, " The branch
cannot bear fruit of itself." Comp.
also Matt. xiii. 21 ; Mark iv. 17.

which He describes His own relation to the Father: "For as the Father hath life in Himself, so gave He to the Son also to have life in Himself," [1]—words which can only mean that, while there is a certain subordination of the Son to the Father, the Son is possessed of life exactly similar and parallel to the Father's life ; so that He acts in that life as the Father acts, and is a Giver of life to others. Believers, in like manner, have not only life. Life has so entered into them that in the possession of it they are "themselves." Their appropriation of the life of Christ is so far from extinguishing their individuality, responsibility, and freedom, that it rather brings these prominently forward as characteristics especially distinguishing them. The Spirit is not bestowed upon them as a vague and mysterious general gift, in the possession of which, without knowing how, they have more than they previously had. It is a gift which enters as a principle of life into every department of their nature. It exerts a leavening and moulding influence upon all their powers, faculties, affections, emotions, tendencies, and aims. It makes all these new. It is a new life-blood in the system, a new sap in the branches. The Spirit does not rest upon the natural character of the believer as the throne of a king might rest upon a floor of clay. The relation between the floor and the throne is changed. The regal qualities of the throne penetrate the clay, so that both it and the throne have the same character, and form a homogeneous whole. "If the Son shall make you free, ye shall be free indeed." [2]

[1] John v. 26.   [2] John viii. 36.

Let us recall the three considerations that have been mentioned. First, that our Lord Himself in His Divine-human nature was on earth, and is now in heaven, possessed of the fulness of the Spirit, and this in such a manner that the Spirit entered into all He was in the one sphere, and enters into all He is in the other. Secondly, that the Spirit given us by our Lord in His glorified condition is *His own* Spirit in the most definite and particular meaning of the words. Thirdly, that when the Spirit is bestowed upon us He must be made inwardly and experimentally ours, entering into all that we are in a manner similar to that in which He entered into all that Jesus was and is. Let us fix these three points distinctly in our minds, and it will follow that the Spirit promised as the chief gift of the New Covenant is pervaded by human as well as Divine elements. As the Spirit of the exalted and glorified Lord, He is not the Third Person of the Trinity in His absolute and metaphysical existence, but that Person as He is mediated through the Son, who is human as well as Divine. It is on this particular aspect of His being that He diffuses Himself through the members of Christ's body, and abides in them. Only as human, entering into and coalescing with what is human, can He be also our Spirit dwelling in a living and real way within us.

One insuperable difficulty may be thought to attach to what has now been said. The effect, it may be objected, is to incarnate the Third as well as the Second Person of the Trinity. Not so. It is only to allow that there is a difference between the Third Person of the

Trinity in Himself, and in the form in which He is promised as the gift of the New Covenant. Incarnation implies the assumption by a Divine Being of both a human soul and a human body : "The Word became flesh, and tabernacled among us." There is no thought of such assumption here. The Spirit remains the Spirit. He is only modified by partaking of that element of the human Spirit which exists in the Church's exalted Head. " God is Spirit " (not " a Spirit "), " and they that worship Him must worship Him in Spirit." Some similarity of nature must exist between God and us, or we could not be asked to worship God in that frame of mind which, in its purest and most perfect form, is the essence of His being. There must, in fact, be a Divine side in man constituting the ground upon which the obligation of religion rests. We cannot ask the lower animals to be religious : they want the religious element in their nature. We ask man to be so, because thus alone can he do justice to that part of his nature which fits him for converse with the spiritual, the infinite, and the eternal. How is it possible, indeed, to think that the Incarnation of the Second Person of the Trinity should not affect the Trinity as a whole ? As the Son is not only Divine, but human, and as God is the Father of the not only Divine but human Son, it seems evident that the bond uniting the Father and the Son, and the Son and the Father, must partake of both the Divine and human elements, and that the Spirit cannot otherwise be given us as the Spirit of the Son. If it be part of a true

definition of the Spirit that "through the Spirit interpenetrating and embracing the Father and the Son,
there is a mutual co-inherence and eternal fellowship
between the Divine Persons,"[1] that co-inherence and
fellowship must have been effected by the changed
condition of the now and for ever Incarnate Son.[2]

The dogma of the Western Church on the Procession
of the Holy Spirit has in the course of this discussion
been mentioned and explained.   What has now been
said ought to illustrate its importance, and the necessity
of maintaining it with the utmost watchfulness.   It is
no mere question of metaphysical or theological refine-
ment that is involved in it.   It connects itself with
practical consequences of the utmost moment.[3]   The
Eastern Church has suffered greatly from its rejection.
More particularly we may trace to that cause much at
least of the immobility that has marked her through
so many centuries.   Great as in various respects her
services to Christianity have been, she has fallen far
behind her Western sister in activity of Christian

---

[1] Hutchings, *The Person and Work of the Holy Ghost*, p. 19.

[2] "Christ's absolutely perfected humanity is quite assumed
into the Logos, and, in so far, into
the life of the Trinity."—Dorner,
System of Christian Doctrine, iv.
139.   "The Holy Ghost," says
Archer Butler, "lives in the soul
under this Dispensation as the
Spirit of Christ.   We are not to
regard Him in the mere simplicity
of His infinite Deity, but as sent
forth by the God and Man, Christ
Jesus, as His ; nor is the abiding
preserver of this holy principle
less essentially Divine, because
bestowed and operative under
special conditions and in a special
aspect ; " and again the same
writer speaks of the Spirit's coming "with a superadded tincture
of celestialised humanity."—
Sermons, 3rd ed. pp. 313, 315.
Comp. also Bishop Webb on *The
Holy Spirit*, pp. 40, 41.

[3] Comp. Smeaton, *Doctrine of
the Holy Spirit*, p. 291.

speculation and life. Because in her view the Spirit has proceeded from God alone, without thought of the Son, human as well as Divine, along with Him, the fountain of human life in our Lord has been choked, and the Greek Church has become a stagnant pool instead of that abounding river which in the Latin Church has fertilised the West. The noblest hymns, too, celebrating the glory of the Spirit, such as the *Veni, Creator Spiritus* and the *Veni, Sancte Spiritus,* have been Latin hymns. The Greek Church has nothing to compare with them. Nor is it any reply to all this to urge that the Christian Church flourished for centuries without the dogma. To reject a doctrine once formulated is attended with far more serious consequences than to live without the clear perception of the doctrine before it has been formally defined. It was one thing for the early Church to live without the expression of this truth. It was quite another thing for the Eastern Church to set it deliberately aside. In the one case it might be implicitly understood, and, though not uttered, might be a valuable undercurrent of the Church's life. In the other case it cannot be lived by, because the flow of its waters has been stopped.[1]

[1] The late Dean Stanley, in his *Lectures on the Eastern Church,* refers to the controversy on the Procession of the Spirit as one of the extinct controversies of the Church (p. 62). Nothing can be further from the truth. On the repetition of the sentiment by others it is better to be silent ; but it is somewhat surprising that so eminent a historian of the Church as Professor Schaff should, in an article separately published, on "The Revision of the Westminster Confession of Faith," have blamed the Western Church for the importance attached by her to the *filioque* clause.

It is impossible to pursue this investigation further, and enough has been said to supply an answer to the question, What is the special nature of the gift of the Spirit under the Christian dispensation? We have seen that the Spirit is not simply one of many gifts bestowed upon us by the glorified Redeemer, but that, as the expression and agent of Him who is at once the substance of our faith, the principle of our life, and our hope of glory, He is the sum of all gifts and influences needed to perfect the Divine-human life of Christ in the soul of man. We have seen also that He is not so much the Third Person of the Trinity in His original and absolute existence, as that Spirit in the effect produced upon Him by the economy of salvation; that Spirit as He is the Bond, not between God and the Eternal Word alone, but between the Father and the Incarnate Son; or that Spirit as He is the Spirit of the Christ from whom in His combined natures proceed all the blessings of the covenant of grace. Finally, we have seen that when this Spirit, as the Spirit of the Living Lord, penetrating and filling all the properties of that human nature which the Living Lord possesses, is received by us, He must be so received as to penetrate and pervade our whole nature. He is not a mighty influence working upon us from without; He works upon us from within. He cannot be used at one moment and laid aside at another. As we cannot put away our natural life and live, so our spiritual life is more than weakened, it is extinguished, if the Spirit be dispensed with. He is the nourishment proceeding from the root of our higher being. He is the water of its central fountain, sending forth continually fresh streams into every department of what we are, unto eternal life.[1] He is, in short, Christ's own Spirit become our own spirit. When He dwells in us we are "ourselves."

These considerations go far to supply an answer to a second question which we have now to ask in connexion with this subject.

II. What is the function or work of the Spirit in man ? The remarks just made upon the special nature of the gift ought to furnish an answer to this question. If the Spirit that we receive be not simply a gift from Christ, but the spirit, the breath, the life of Christ Himself ; and if it is implied in our receiving Him that He enters into and identifies Himself with every part of our nature, it follows that His chief work must be to form the Living Christ within us. The spirit of parents is inherited by their children, the spirit of an ancient and honourable house by its descendants; and in both cases the effect may be traced in the likeness of the later to the earlier born. The same thing must take place here. Christ's own Spirit, the Spirit by which His humanity has been moulded into what it is, passes into His people, so passing into them as to pervade every part of what they are. What can the effect be but the revelation and formation of Christ himself within them ? Our instruction on many subordinate or preparatory points is no doubt also due to the operation of the Spirit. He convinces us of sin and misery ; so that

[1] John iv. 14.

we are led to long for One who may guide us to holiness and happiness. He enlightens our minds in the knowledge of Christ; so that we behold a Divine glory shining beneath His lowly form and tragic fate. He renews our wills; so that, instead of choosing the evil or the false, we may say to the holy One and the true, " Lord, to whom can we go but unto Thee?" All these operations, however, are only preliminary to the execution of the great work committed to Him. They lead to the goal, but they are not the goal. That goal is Christ offered to us in the Gospel.

It is hardly necessary to say that this was the teaching of our Lord Himself when He was in the world. " Come unto *Me,* all ye that labour and are heavy laden; and *I* will give you rest. Take *My* yoke upon you, and learn of *Me;* for *I* am meek and lowly in heart : and ye shall find rest unto your souls "; " Ye will not come unto *Me,* that ye may have life " ; " If any man thirst, let him come unto *Me,* and drink " ; " *I* am the Way, and the Truth, and the Life : no man cometh unto the Father, but by *Me* "; " This is eternal life, that they should know (that is, experimentally know) Thee the only True God, and Him whom Thou didst send, even Jesus Christ." [1]

But it was not the teaching of our Lord only when He was on earth; it is not less His teaching by His Apostles now that He is in heaven. With them the entrance of Christ in His glorified humanity into us, and communion on our part with it, constitute the

---

[1] Matt. xi. 28, 29 ; John v. 40, vii. 37, xiv. 6, xvii. 3.

Christian standing and form the Christian character.   In their eyes Christianity is always the
impartation of a new life in Christ, not the improvement of an old life.   Believers receive "the right to
become children (not sons) of God";[1] and by abiding
in Christ their life, thus given, is maintained.[2] They
are new creatures not merely "by" but "in" their
Lord; and they grow up in all things unto Him which
is the Head, even Christ.[3]   As with their individual, so
also with their social life.   By living in the risen and
glorified Lord as their Head, they are made members of
His Body, and "it is the life of Christ which is the
bond of unity."[4]   Hence that remarkable double series
of expressions describing the relation between Christians and their Lord, not only as He may be before
them in the memories of the past, but as He is now.
On the one hand, they are "in" Christ, in the living and
present Lord : "If any man be in Christ, he is a new
creature"; "Who hath blessed us with every spiritual
blessing in the heavenly places in Christ: even as He
chose us in Him before the foundation of the world";
"That I may gain Christ, and be found in Him"; "In
whom we have our redemption, the forgiveness of our
sins"; "As therefore ye received Christ Jesus the Lord,
so walk in Him, rooted and builded up in Him";
"Your good manner of life in Christ."[5]   On the other
hand, Christ is "in" them : "If Christ be in us"; "The

---

[1] John i. 12.   [2] John xv. 4.   [5] 2 Cor. v. 17 ; Eph. i. 3, 4 ;
[3] Eph. iv. 15.   Phil. iii. 9 ; Col. i. 14, ii. 6, 7 ;
[4] Andrews, *God's Revelation of*   1 Pet. iii. 16.
Himself to Men, p. 269.

law of the Spirit of life in Christ Jesus hath made me free from the law of sin and of death"; "Let Christ dwell in your hearts through faith"; "Know ye not as to your own selves, that Jesus Christ is in you? unless indeed ye be reprobate"; "Christ in you, the hope of glory."[1]

Language of this kind cannot be read without conveying to us the distinct impression that personal identification and union with Christ is the fundamental and regulating conception of our state as Christians. We are "in" Christ Jesus ; that is, as a man who is in the world lives and moves and has his being in it, so we live and move and have our being in Christ ; encompassed by Him as in our natural condition we are encompassed by the atmosphere; His gracious influences pervading everything around us, and flowing into us, in order to preserve our souls in health and vigour. Again, Christ is "in" us. He stirs, moves, and acts in us, so that, except in so far as we are troubled by sin and weakness, His thoughts are our thoughts, His words our words, His acts our acts. The two modes of expression, when taken together, bring out the closest and most intimate idea of union which it is possible to form. The members are in the Head, and the Head is in the members. The branches are in the Vine, and the Vine is in the branches. There is a constant play of influences between them, and in that play of influences they are one. And all this is effected by the Spirit; so that in one passage of St. Paul the two expressions "to be in Christ" and "to have the Spirit of Christ"

[1] Rom. viii. 10, viii. 2 ; Eph. iii. 17 ; 2 Cor. xiii. 5 ; Col. i. 27.

alternate with each other as equivalent in meaning, showing that if Christ be in us it is only by the Spirit.[1]

Not only so. It would seem to be the lesson of Scripture that Christian men have to repeat in the world, though of course they can do it only in an imperfect form, the life of the Redeemer; and that, in a deeper sense than is implied by the mere cultivation of His spirit or the imitation of His example. The distinctiveness and reality of the Christian life ought, indeed, most of all to appear in this, that, in its aims and efforts, in its toils and sufferings, it shall present to the world the life of Jesus. The fact that in our day Christians may not be placed in exactly the same circumstances as their Lord ; that they may live at ease, without toil or suffering or the cross, makes no difference in what the Christian faith really is. Our immunity from persecution and other outward ills ought rather to lead to the inquiry, not so much whether our lot is cast in happier times than our great Master's, as whether our Christianity is of precisely the same type. No view of the Christian revelation can be conceived more utterly at variance with its essential nature than that which leads many to imagine that their Lord toiled in order to free them from toil, and suffered that they might escape suffering. Were that Lord to show Himself on the earth at this moment, not less true to His Father in heaven, to the thought of a spiritual world, or to the value of the eternal in comparison with the temporal, than when He spoke in Jerusalem and Galilee ; were

---

[1] Rom. viii. 9, 10 ; Grétillat, *Théologie Systématique*, iv. p. 449.

He to treat the pretences and superficialities of an outward religiousness, the vain shows of wealth, or the self-
indulgent luxury of so large a portion of the professing
Church, as He treated such things before ; were He to
denounce every form of sin, in the high as well as the
low places of the land, with the faithful and plain speaking with which He once denounced it, who will venture
to say that His reception would be very different from
what it was ? But, if so, how shall His people in their
living action exhibit Him except by repeating Him ?
except by being and doing and suffering what He, had
He been still in the midst of us, would have been and
done and suffered ? This identification of Christ's people
with their Lord, this carrying forth of the life of Christ
in the world, is the idea lying at the root of the Revelation of St. John, and is one of the keys to the interpretation of that mysterious book.[1] No intellectual knowledge of the Redeemer, no *Imitatio Christi,* no effort to
comply with His demands as those of an authority which
it is our duty and interest to obey, no zeal in the
observance of His ordinances, no hope of the fulfilment
of His promises, is sufficient to make us His in the full
and proper sense of the term. He must Himself dwell
in us and walk in us ; must Himself be the spring of
our new and higher being ; must be one with us, and
we one with Him ; so that all that He was and is may
be "fulfilled" in us, before the great end of salvation is
accomplished for us.

---

[1] Comp. Milligan, *The Revelation of St. John* (Macmillan), 3rd
edition, p. 59, etc.

To reveal the Incarnate and glorified Lord in us is
therefore the function of the Spirit, and each of the two
parts of this proposition is to be kept steadily in view.

On the one hand, the Spirit is not an independent
authority, taking the place of Him who has gone to the
Father, and leading us into new fields of truth and
holiness. At the moment when our Lord promised the
Spirit to His disciples, He did it in the words, " Howbeit when He, the Spirit of truth, is come, He shall
guide you into all the truth: for He shall not speak
from Himself; but what things soever He shall hear,
these shall He speak : and He shall declare unto you
the things that are to come. He shall glorify Me : for
He shall take of Mine, and shall declare it unto you.
All things whatsoever the Father hath are Mine : therefore said I, that He taketh of Mine, and shall declare it
unto you." [1] In these words our Lord undoubtedly
speaks of the Spirit's guiding the disciples into " all the
truth," and showing them the " things that are to come."
But it is of the utmost importance to observe that the
truths thus referred to are not really new. They are
old truths made new, expanded, unfolded, illuminated by
history,—when history is read in the spirit of Christian
insight, trust, and hope. There will not be in them one
revelation, strictly so called, that was not in the person
or the teaching of Jesus Himself; but their ever greater
depths will be seen as the relations of the Church and
the world become more complex. It has been so in the
past; it will be so in the future. The treasure in the

---

[1] John xvi. 13-15.

words of Christ will never be exhausted. According to
the seeming paradox of the Apostle, it contains what we
are " to know," although it " passeth knowledge." [1] But
no revelation given by the Spirit may go beyond the
revelation given us in Christ, or supersede the necessity
of our seeing that its contents are involved in what He
was or is. The Spirit which we receive is the Spirit of
Christ, bestowed by Him, descending upon us from Him,
and so flowing as a new life-blood, but still the blood of
Christ, through the veins and arteries of our spiritual
frame, that we shall be "new creatures," yet new creatures
not in the Spirit, but "in Christ Jesus." [2] To look at
the matter in any other light not only opens the door
to the follies and fanaticisms which, in connexion with
the doctrine of the Spirit, have defaced the history
of the Christian Church, but overturns the rational
character of the Christian faith, eliminates the immediateness of that human element in the application of
redemption which is essential to real mediation between
God and man, leads to an undervaluing of those instru-
mentalities—the word, the sacraments, and the ministry
—which have been appointed by Divine wisdom for our
edification and comfort, and deprives the Christian life
of that stability by which alone the aberrations of
individual zeal can be corrected. Nay, more. To
separate the function of the Spirit from the historical
Redeemer is nothing else than " to substitute the Holy

---

[1] Eph. iii. 19.
[2] Comp. Hutchings, *Person, etc., of the Holy Ghost*, p. 68 ; Webb on
The Holy Spirit, p. 71.

Ghost in the place of the Son ; or rather to maintain
that, whereas the work of man's government and salvation was at one time discharged by God under the name
of Christ, at a later period there was a new title
adopted, and the same Being reappeared under the
name of the Holy Ghost." [1]   The fundamental principle
of the New Testament, that the whole Trinity—Father,
Son, and Holy Spirit—co-operate in the work of our
redemption, thus disappears, and the doctrine of the
Trinity itself is in danger of becoming a metaphysical
speculation, without any practical bearing upon our life
and character.   It seems only necessary to add that, in
speaking of the historical Christ, we are not to think
simply of our Lord as He was on earth.   It is the
glorified Christ whom it is the peculiar function of the
Spirit—that is, of the Spirit of Christ as glorified—to
reveal within us.   To Himself as glorified our Lord
obviously refers when, speaking of the aspect of the
Spirit's work now before us, He says, in words already
quoted, "What He shall *hear*, that shall He speak";
"He shall glorify *Me*."

If the first truth involved in the general proposition,
that it is the function of the Spirit to reveal the glorified
Lord, be thus important, on the other hand, the second
truth involved in it, that the glorified Lord in His
Divine-human personality acts only through His Spirit,
and not directly, upon His people, is not less so.   Words
of St. Paul, writing to the Romans, as given in the
Authorised Version, may indeed seem to lead to an

---

[1] Wilberforce on the *Incarnation*, p. 196.

opposite conclusion : " If the Spirit of Him that raised
up Jesus from the dead dwelleth in you, He that raised
up Christ Jesus from the dead shall quicken also your
mortal bodies through His Spirit that dwelleth in
you." [1]   But the word " through " here, though still
found in the text of the Revised Version, ought in all
probability to give way to the reading " because of "
suggested in the margin.   So read, the language of the
Apostle ceases to imply any material force by which
the Spirit acts, and we are left to the general teaching
of Scripture, that only by His Spirit does the glorified
Lord carry on His work in man.   That Spirit may,
indeed, in ways to which human life affords clear
analogies, produce an effect even upon our material
frames, but there is no reason to believe that He does
so directly or by bodily impact.   He works upon us
spiritually, and only through His spiritual operation is
Christ revealed in us.   This aspect of the truth is not
without great importance in our day.   Many powerful
influences of modern life favour the materialising of our
Lord's relation to us, and there is even a mysticism to
be sometimes met with in deeply religious minds which
falls into the same error.   The invisible Lord is thought
to manifest His presence by the bodily sensations which
that presence awakens, and an immediate communion
is supposed to be held with Him through the bodily
organs.[2]   Scripture lends no encouragement to such
thoughts.   St. Paul has rather said, with a force of
expression which it is impossible to misunderstand,

[1] Rom. viii. 11.   [2] Comp. note C.

"Wherefore, henceforth know we no man after the flesh; yea, though we have known Christ after the flesh, yet now henceforth know we Him so no more."[1] By the Spirit, and the Spirit alone, does the glorified Redeemer carry on His work; and a thorough conviction of this truth is necessary to guard us against dangers as fatal to Christian progress as forgetfulness of the fact that the Spirit in revealing cannot go beyond what Christ was and is.

Two paths of error thus stretch before us, into either of which we may easily diverge—that of a fantastic spiritualism on the one hand, and that of a too materialistic conception of Christ and Christianity on the other. The path of safety lies between them, in the truth that to reveal the Incarnate and glorified Lord within us is the function of the Spirit.

III. A third question connected with the mission of the Spirit meets us, When was the Spirit in the New Testament sense of the word bestowed? There can be no hesitation as to the answer. But, before giving it, it may be well to look for a moment at two different methods of expression found in the New Testament with regard to the Spirit, to the distinction between which sufficient attention has hardly as yet been paid. These are "The Holy Spirit" and "Holy Spirit," the definite article being employed in the one case, but in the other not. Unless there be the strongest arguments to the contrary, it is against all legitimate interpretation to imagine that the two have the same

[1] 2 Cor. v. 16.

meaning; nor can there be much hesitation in accepting the explanation usually adopted when the distinction is allowed—that the words "The Holy Spirit" refer to the Spirit in Himself, in His Personality, in the place occupied by Him in the Godhead; while the words "Holy Spirit" lead to the thought of His operation, and more particularly to His operation as manifested in its full power and magnitude in the Christian age. Keeping this distinction in view, therefore, we have now to ask, When was "Holy Spirit" first bestowed in this fulness of His power? and, How was the mission of the Spirit then distinguished from what it had previously been?

To the first of these questions St. John supplies the answer. Referring to the remarkable appearance of our Lord at the Feast of Tabernacles, and to His promise there given of the "rivers of living water," that Evangelist adds, "But this spake He of the Spirit, which they that believed in Him were to receive: for Spirit was not yet; because Jesus was not yet glorified." [1] On different occasions our Lord Himself speaks in an equally definite manner. Again and again, especially in His last discourses, He instructs His disciples in the truth that before the Spirit could be given He must Himself have gone to the Father; while in the lessons taught by Him between His Resurrection and Ascen-

---

[1] John vii. 37-39. There can be little doubt that the true reading here is simply οὔπω γὰρ ἦν πνεῦμα, see Westcott and Hort's *Gr. Test.* ii. p. 82. δεδομένον ought to have no place in the text. The Revisers adopted the true reading, but with a curious inconsistency read (though in italics) in English the word "given," which they had just rejected in Greek.

sion He informs them that they shall be "baptized in Holy Spirit not many days hence."[1] The fulfilment of the promise confirms and illustrates its meaning. The day of Pentecost came; the Spirit descended upon the disciples; and St. Peter declared, "This Jesus . . . being therefore by the right hand of God exalted, and having received of the Father the promise of the Holy Spirit, He hath poured forth this, which ye see and hear."[2] There can be no doubt, therefore, as to the time with which the gift of the Spirit spoken of in the New Testament is connected. Only after our Lord's Resurrection and Ascension was "Holy Spirit" given.

Not, indeed, that the Holy Spirit then for the first time acted either in the world or on man. At the Creation He had "moved upon the face of the waters."[3] In Providence He had been sent forth to "renew the face of the earth."[4] He had "striven with men" when they walked in their own evil counsels;[5] while, on the other hand, every Divine excellence or beauty of character exhibited by Old Testament saints is to be traced to His influence. From Him proceeded all that was good either in Israel or among the Gentiles. We are told that the Spirit rested upon Moses,[6] upon Joshua,[7] upon the Judges,[8] upon Elijah and Elisha,[9] upon David,[10] and upon Saul;[11] while of Bezaleel, to whom

---

[1] Acts i. 4, 5.
[2] Acts ii. 32, 33.
[3] Gen. i. 2.
[4] Ps. civ. 30.
[5] Gen. vi. 3.
[6] Num. xi. 17.

[7] Deut. xxxiv. 9.
[8] Judges vi. 34; xi. 29; xiv. 19.
[9] 2 Kings ii. 9-15.
[10] 1 Sam. xvi. 13.
[11] 1 Sam. xix. 23.

the construction of the Tabernacle was entrusted, it is said, " I have filled him with the Spirit of God." [1] David prayed, " Take not Thy holy Spirit from me : uphold me with Thy free Spirit." [2]   By the Spirit of God the prophets spoke ; [3] and the whole revelation of the Divine will then enjoyed was meditated through Him. [4]   Nor was the light bestowed by Him confined to Israel. [5]   Of the pre-incarnate Logos we read that " the life was the light of men " ; and, if so, the analogy of Scripture entitles us to say that it must have been by the mediation of the Spirit.   From the moment, indeed, when the Spirit of God is first spoken of in Scripture, down throughout the whole period of the Old Testament, He is referred to as the Agent by whom intercourse between the Almighty and man was effected and maintained.

Nor can it have been otherwise during the earthly ministry of our Lord.   To suppose that He then sus- pended His operations would involve the whole subject in confusion.   Yet we are expressly taught that " Holy Spirit was not yet ; because Jesus was not yet glorified." Although, in short, " The Holy Spirit" had acted throughout the whole previous history of the world and of man, it was only after the Ascension and glorification of our Lord that He was given in that form, or amidst those conditions, which especially distinguish the Chris- tian dispensation, and to which the term " Holy Spirit " is applied by the Sacred writers.

[1] Ex. xxxi. 3 ; comp. xxxv. 31.   [2] Ps. li. 11, 12.   [3] 2 Pet. i. 21.
    [4] Isa. lxiii. 10, 11 ; 1 Pet. i. 11.   [5] John i. 4 ; comp. x. 16.

How, then, is the mission of the Spirit after the
Ascension to be distinguished from what it previously
was? The question has been often asked, and one or
two replies to it may be briefly noticed.

It has been said that, whereas under the Old Testament dispensation the Holy Spirit was only an efflu-
ence or Divine communication to the saints, He is now
to the children of God a personal presence; that He
dwells among us and within us—a real person, knowing, loving, aiding us, and co-operating with Jesus in
our salvation.[1] But the actions of the Spirit in pre-
Christian ages were not less personal than they are
now; and to speak of two real persons dwelling in us
and co-operating for our salvation is to depart from the
general strain of New Testament language. Again, it
has been said that, whereas individuals of the ancient
theocracy enjoyed the gift of the Spirit, they received
Him only for particular and well-defined purposes; that,
even while they were enabled by His inspiration to
fulfil their mission, He did not pervade their whole
being; that He came to them fitfully, and was not a
central fountain in the heart. The idea is so far correct, but the contrast which it suggests does not
explain the peculiar nature of the New Testament gift,
which is bestowed not merely for the general consecration of the man, but to be the strength of the particular
energies distinguishing the members of the Christian
Church from one another.[2] Once more, it has been

---

[1] Hutchings, *The Person and Work of the Holy Ghost*, pp. 57, 59.
[2] 1 Cor. xii. 4.

urged that the difference lies in the measure of influence now exercised by the Spirit ; that it is less of kind
than of degree; and that, while the lives of the Old
Testament saints were in reality the same in principle
as ours, they had only a smaller impartation of the
heavenly grace.[1] In this idea as in the last there is
also a certain measure of truth. The Old Testament
saints were in a weaker condition than those of Gospel
times, and they knew their weakness. They mourned
over their want of the Spirit in His power, and they
looked forward to the Messianic age as a season when
He should be bestowed with a fulness of which they
had no experience.[2] Yet this merely quantitative
differentiation of the two gifts fails to explain the
unique importance attached to the gift of the Spirit in
the New Testament, while at the same time it only
takes the question a stage further back, without showing us why the difference should exist. These explanations, therefore, are insufficient for their purpose ; and
the true grounds why the Spirit could not be given as
" Holy Spirit " until our Lord was glorified are to be
sought in the internal necessities of the case, in the
essential characteristics of His Person and Work.

1. Before the Incarnation of our Lord the Spirit to
be given had not assumed that special form which He
was to possess in New Testament times. Had the gift
been merely outward, such as a Divine Person may

---

[1] Moule, *Outlines of Christian Doctrine*, pp. 145, 146.

26, 27 ; xxxvii. 13, 14 ; comp. Acts ii. 16-18.

[2] Isa. xliv. 3 ; Ezek. xxxvi.

bestow in the plenitude of His grace; or had it been
only the gift of the Third Person of the Trinity, viewed
in His Eternal existence and Divine attributes, it would
be difficult, if not impossible, to understand why the
Spirit should not have been granted in the same sense,
though perhaps not in the same degree, to the saints of
the Old Testament as to those of the New Testament
age. But we have already seen that, as the Spirit interpenetrates our Lord in His human as well as His Divine
nature, so our Lord in His human as well as His Divine
nature interpenetrates the Spirit. The Spirit bestowed
upon us as the fulfilment of the promise of the New
Covenant is the Spirit of Christ as He is now. With,
by, and in this Spirit we receive Christ Himself, together
with all that He is as the Redeemer of men. By faith
we become really and inwardly one with Him, and the
energies of His life pass over into our life. These may
be stronger or weaker, fuller or less full, according to
the capacities of the vessel receiving them. But in
character and essence they must be the same to every
believer. All Christian men are members of the Divine-
human Body of which Christ is the Head. They are
branches of the Vine of which He is the Stem. They
are in organic connexion with the Stem; and our Lord
Himself says, "Apart from Me" (not "without Me")
"ye can do nothing."[1] The beloved disciple, who records
these words of Jesus, has taught us the same lesson:
"Ye have an anointing (not the act, but the result of
the act) from the Holy One"; and "the anointing

[1] John xv. 5.

which ye received from Him abideth in you."[1]   In
other words, as He who was anointed with the Holy
Spirit is the Anointed One, so are ye in like manner
anointed ones ; and His Spirit is not given you only
outwardly, it abideth in you.   This, however, implies in
the nature of the Spirit an adaptation to human nature,
a possibility of His interpenetrating human nature,
which can only be reached by means of His possessing
a human element ; and that human element could not
enter into the Spirit of the Christ before the Christ
assumed humanity.

2. Before His Ascension our Lord was not in a position
to bestow the gift of "Holy Spirit."   It was only then
that He Himself was "perfected."   Until that time He
had been confined by the limitations and sinless infirmities of His pre-resurrection state.   During His life on
earth He had, by a constant exercise of His own will,
maintained that condition of humiliation which St. Paul
describes as an "emptying of Himself."   He had constantly exerted a self-restraining power.   He had not
reached that complete development of His own Person
which, in the economy of redemption, was the appointed
end and issue of all He was to do.   He had not become
essentially "Spirit" (although it must never be forgotten
that the "Spirit" which He became expressed itself
in the form of the "spiritual body"), and the Spirit
could not proceed in all His fulness from a fountain
which presented any obstacle to the outflow of its
waters.

[1] 1 John ii. 20, 27.

Upon these two conditions, then, rested, it would seem, the great truth which we are now considering, that "Spirit" (or "Holy Spirit") was not yet ; because Jesus was not yet glorified. Not that "the Holy Spirit" had no existence before that time, an idea which it is unnecessary to controvert. Not that the Holy Spirit had not been previously "given," for we know that He had been given. But "Spirit" in the peculiar sense in which the New Testament uses the word—that is, the Holy Spirit as the Spirit of the glorified Lord, and in the full exercise and manifestation of His power—had not yet begun to operate upon the minds of men. Then only could He do so when our Lord Himself entered on that stage of His Being to which St. Paul applies the term "quickening or life-giving Spirit," and when He could bestow the Spirit in fulness from the ever springing fountain of His own Spirit-life.

From that moment, accordingly, it is that the whole glory of the New Testament dispensation spreads itself out before our eyes. The dispensation then introduced is emphatically the dispensation of the Spirit, the last of the three great eras into which the history of the Church has been divided, the first being that of the Father, and the second that of the Son.[1] In this third and crowning dispensation of God's grace there is not merely a gift of the Spirit added to gifts that had been previously enjoyed, or a larger measure of the Spirit

---

[1] The saying is attributed to Joachim, Abbot of Floris, in the kingdom of Naples ; comp. Cheyne, *Hallowing of Criticism,* and Milner's *Latin Christianity* v. 254, etc.

bestowed than the Church had previously received. The promise of the older Covenants has rather been accomplished in a new and more perfect form. Freed from every restraint, and adapted in the most intimate manner to the spirit of man, the " Spirit of Jesus " has been sent forth to secure the illimitable issues of the Divine plan. With the beginning of the new dispensation not merely was the work of the Lord Jesus Christ the Saviour of the world finished, the redemption so dearly purchased completed, and the way opened by which the end of all human thought and longing may be attained in a perfect union between God and man. More was effected. These results are involved in the preliminary truth that the Spirit given to the Church is the Spirit of One who had successfully executed His Mission. The glory of the dispensation under which it is our privilege to live consists still further in the provision made for the application of redemption; so that the work of the glorified Lord may be intertwined with the inmost fibres of our being, and His Kingdom established as an actual reality in our hearts and lives. All holy thoughts, all heavenly aspirations, all works of faith and hope and love; all that was in Him who on earth could say, " I and My Father are One "; all that is in Him now glorified, may be ours. There is no hindrance on the Divine side to the communication of whatever is necessary to the progress and perfection of the world.

The history of the ancient Church illustrates what has been said. In the Old Testament there is not

seldom an incongruity, a want of harmony, between the
Spirit of God and the persons brought under His
influence. He came upon Balaam, yet the prophet
remained the unwilling and self-seeking servant of the
Almighty at the very time when he delivered the
Divine message to Balak. He came upon Saul, yet the
ungovernable passions of that king were not restrained.
He certainly dwelt largely in Elijah and Elisha, yet
some of the actions of these two prophets are difficult
to explain, so much do they seem to have gone beyond
even that measure of sternness which the law required.
Under the Old Testament, in short, there was no sufficient
provision for the complete reduction of our human
nature to order. There were high thoughts and noble
deeds, but there was then an inconsistency in the best
of human lives which makes us often wonder how those
who led them can be described as under the influence
of the Spirit, or as " men after God's own heart." The
truth seems to be that the Spirit, while Divine, was not
sufficiently human to penetrate with calm persistent
force into the human heart, or to " abide " there. Now
it is otherwise; and when the Spirit of Christ, human
as well as Divine, enters into our spirits, He takes complete possession of them, like a deep flood-tide

> Too full for sound or foam.

No doubt there are still in the believer inconsistencies,
shortcomings, and sins; but these are felt to be what
they are. They are seen to be at variance with the
Spirit's aims, and they are gradually left behind in the

soul's upward path. The least in the kingdom of heaven enjoys in this respect higher privileges, and has a more glorious career in prospect than even the greatest of the prophets before Jesus came.[1]

The same considerations may also help to explain the fact that, in various passages of the New Testament, so much emphasis is laid upon bringing the *body* into subjection to the Divine will, when we would rather expect a reference to the soul. Thus we find St. Paul writing to the Romans, " We ourselves also, which have the firstfruits of the Spirit, even we ourselves groan within ourselves, waiting for our adoption, to wit, the redemption of our body ";[2] and we ask, What is the relation between the firstfruits of the Spirit here spoken of and the redemption of the *body?* Why should the redemption of the *body,* not the soul, be regarded as synonymous with " our adoption "? Again, in another part of the same Epistle, we read, " I beseech you therefore, brethren, by the mercies of God, that ye present your *bodies* a living sacrifice, holy, acceptable unto God, which is your reasonable service."[3] Why is mention made here of *bodies* instead of souls? And, once more, the same Apostle, writing to the Corinthians, says, " Glorify God therefore in your *body* ";[4] and we are tempted to repeat the question, Why not the soul?[5] In answer to such questions it is not enough to reply that the body is an important part of man, or the

---

[1] Matt. xi. 11.
[2] Rom. viii. 23.
[3] Rom. xii. 1.   [4] 1 Cor. vi. 20.

[5] The reading of the T. R. strikingly illustrates the strength of this feeling.

instrument with which his spirit works, and that its sanctification is too frequently undervalued. The passages quoted might almost seem to regard it as the chief part of man; and we know that it is not. The answer seems rather to be that, although not the chief part, it is that to which the Christian, realising the ideal of his faith, has need chiefly to direct his thoughts, because it is not yet redeemed to the same extent as his spirit. The Spirit of the Lord has already taken possession of the Christian's spirit, has established His throne there, and has only to be allowed a more perfect control of every department of the spirit-life. The same work has not yet been accomplished in the *body*. Yet it has to be accomplished, and not till then will the whole process of our salvation be complete. While the spirits of believers even at present live, however imperfectly they may breathe it, in the atmosphere of a perfected spiritual existence, offering a full supply for every want of the soul's spiritual life, they wait for the application of a similar Divine ·power to the body Only then, when that hour arrives, when the corruptible body puts on incorruption and the mortal body immortality, shall they be presented, both soul and body, in one harmonious whole, to Him who in heaven is not only Spirit, but is clothed with "the body of His glory."

IV. A fourth point in connexion with the mission of the Spirit remains to be spoken of. On whom is the gift bestowed? We have seen that the Spirit promised in the New Testament is our Lord's own Spirit, the Spirit

as it penetrated and pervaded Him. We have further
seen that the Spirit can only be said to have been
received by us when it penetrates and pervades our
nature and diffuses throughout us the breath of a new life.
And, once more, we have seen that the function of the
Spirit is to lead the believer on to the perfection that
is in Christ Jesus, each glorious attribute of the Lord
finding its answer in him, enlisting his sympathy, attract-
ing his love, and drawing out the longings of his soul to
have the same attribute formed in himself. From all
this it follows as a necessary consequence that the
Spirit of Christ can be given in His fulness to the
members of Christ's Body alone. That there is an
initial work of the Holy Spirit upon the unregenerate,
by which they are awakened and converted, is not,
indeed, for a moment to be denied. But this work is
general and preparatory. It is the work implied in those
startling passages of the writings of St. John in which our
Lord and His Apostle speak of the acceptance or rejection
of the Gospel as dependent on a still earlier discipline of
the soul than that of listening to the word then spoken :
" He that is *of God* heareth the words of God : for this
cause ye hear them not, because ye are not *of God* " ;
" But ye believe not, because ye are not of *My sheep* " ;
" Every one that is *of the truth* heareth My voice " ;
" They are *of the world :* therefore speak they as of the
world, and the world heareth them. We are *of God :*
he that knoweth God heareth us ; he who is not *of God*
heareth us not." [1] In these and similar passages the

---

[1] John viii. 47, x. 26, xviii. 37 ; 1 John iv. 5, 6.

spiritual history of man is taken up at a different point
from that at which the eye rests only on the natural
disinclination of all to godliness. There has been subsequent to that, although previous to the Gospel call, a
discipline by which the heart was tested ; and that
discipline has been carried on by the Holy Spirit as, in
applying the lessons both of Providence and grace, He
has sought to awaken the moral susceptibilities of man.
Only, however, when these have been awakened, and
when man begins to display a tendency towards the
truth and God, so that he may now be said to be "of
the truth" or "of God," is he in a condition to receive
those further communications of the grace and love of
Christ which are implied in the promise of His Spirit.
Then, drawn to Christ in faith, he is by faith united to
Him and, in that union, is made capable of receiving
those influences of His Spirit which, by the very necessities of our nature when we yield ourselves to another,
demand sympathy on our part with Him from whom
they come.

Hence, accordingly, the words of our Lord, "And I
will make request of the Father, and He will give you
. . . the Spirit of the truth: whom the world cannot
receive; because it beholdeth Him not, neither learneth
to know Him :[1] ye learn to know Him; because He
abideth with you, and is in you."[2] The Spirit, the
Advocate, the Spirit of the truth, the world *cannot*
receive, because it has no perception of the things with

---

[1] Observe the force of the verb here.
[2] John xiv. 16, 17 ; comp. Godet and Westcott *in loc.*

which He deals, no relish for them, or adaptation to
them.   As it cannot " hear God's voice, because it is not
of God," [1] so it cannot receive the Spirit in the more
inward and effective communications of His power,
because it has no eye for spiritual things.   The Spirit
in His first and preliminary actings comes to the world
and would stay with it; but the world will not have
Him for a guest, and it never attains to that experimental knowledge of Him which alone is worthy to be
called knowledge.   But the disciples are " of the truth ";
they welcome the heavenly Guest; He "abides" with
them ; He "is" in them; and they advance to a continually deepening knowledge of what He is.   Hence
also the words of our Lord's High-priestly prayer, " I
make not request concerning the world, but concerning
them which Thou hast given Me." [2]   Not because He
would leave the world unsaved does our Lord so speak,
but because it is impossible in the nature of things that
the world should receive what He now asks for His own.
He is thinking of the deepest and richest blessings of
the Divine love.   How can He ask them for a world
which refuses to apprehend them ?   It may perhaps be
replied that other words of our Lord in His last discourse
to His disciples are inconsistent with this view.   In
promising the Advocate who should come after His
departure, did He not say, " And He, when He is come,
will convict the world in respect of sin, and of righteousness, and of judgment : of sin, because they believe
not on Me ; of righteousness, because I go to the

_____

[1] John viii. 47.   [2] John xvii. 9.

Father, and ye behold Me no more; of judgment, because the prince of this world hath been judged"?[1]
and in saying so did He not promise that through
His disciples there should be a work of the Advocate
on the world which shall lead it onward to the loftiest
heights of Christian truth? But an attentive consideration of the passage will show that, instead of being
occupied with the conversion, it refers to the condemnation, of the world. The word "convict" has not the
meaning of convert, and it is more than either to
reprove or to convince. It implies that answer of conscience to the reproving, convincing voice by which a
man condemns himself. The word "in respect of,"[2]
too, is wholly different from the word "of." No work
of conversion is, therefore, here alluded to, though it is
not said that conversion may not follow. What the
disciples are assured of is, that by their work that very
world which was to scorn and persecute and kill them
shall eventually be silenced and self-condemned, be
overwhelmed with shame and confusion of face. The
apparently conquered shall in the final issue be the
conquerors. Rightly interpreted, therefore, these verses
lead to no such thought as that of a *gift* of Christ's
Spirit to the world.[3]

[1] John xvi. 9-11.   [2] περί.

[3] The following words of Riehm may be quoted in confirmation of the general view expressed in the text. Referring to Heb. x. 13, Riehm says, "In speaking of the subjection of His enemies under the Lord's feet, the writer of the Epistle certainly did not think of their subjection through the *spiritual* power of the Gospel, or of conversion and a *voluntary* recognition of the royal rule of Christ effected by means of re-pentance and faith" (p. 355, note).

We return to the only answer that can be given to the question before us. The gift of " Holy Spirit," in its New Testament sense as the Spirit of the glorified Lord, belongs to none but the members of Christ's Body. In the Church of Christ alone can the perfections of the King in His beauty be displayed. The Divine seed may be scattered broadcast in the world, but the plant that springs from it must be nourished in the communion and fellowship of the saints. It must grow in the atmosphere of a well-diffused Christian life. It must be strengthened by the faith and hope and love of others growing beside it and helping it to grow. " There is one body, and one Spirit, even as we were called in one hope of our calling ";[1] and the peace of God which is to rule in our hearts is a peace to which we are called "in one body."[2] And this is the case, not because the Church is substituted for Christ by the sacred writers but because, in her, men are brought into contact with Christ in the very seat of His power, in the very centre of His enlightening, quickening, and comforting grace. The Church can no more be a substitute for Christ than Christ for the Father. Christ is "the way" to the Father, and the Church is the way to Him, if not always in the first stirrings of the awakened conscience, yet in that further progress by which we press forward to the end of our Christian calling. " It is necessary to receive the life of Christ, that the Holy Spirit may make us His home ; and when that life is ours He dwells in us for ever."[3]

[1] Eph. iv. 4.   [2] Col. iii. 15.   [3] Comp. Dale on Ephesians, p. 125.

The full truth, therefore, is not expressed by the formula, Christ first, the Church afterwards. If we rightly honour our Lord by preserving the idea of the Church as His body ; if we realise the fact as clearly as we ought that in the Church He actually dwells, and that through her He bestows His choicest blessings, we shall rather say that He and His Church act together in meeting the wants of men. He is in the Church, and the Church, if not always as a whole, yet always in a faithful remnant, is in Him. According to His own word, "He that receiveth you receiveth Me." Christ, indeed, is always first, prior alike to the Church and the individual convert. But it is through His Church and His power working in her that he perfects those who come to Him in faith. Nor has the Church failed from the earliest times to bear witness to this truth. In the Apostles' Creed the Articles, "I believe in the holy Catholic Church" and in "the communion of saints" immediately follow the Article, "I believe in the Holy Ghost," taking precedence of those that are occupied with the application of redemption to the individual soul; and the meaning is that in the holy Catholic Church and in the communion of saints is to be found, according to God's plan, everything that ministers to redemption in its fullest sense—"the forgiveness of sins, the resurrection of the body, and the life ever-lasting."

There is no proof that the highest influences of the Spirit are given except to those, and therefore through those, whom the Redeemer has called to a saving know-

ledge of Himself. The Christian Church is His Spirit-
bearing Body. She is the channel by which He com-
municates the Spirit in His power, the "vessel" with
the lamp out of which He maintains His light ever
burning in the world. Upon the Church of Christ
rests the responsibility of every advance that is to be
made either in the power or the beauty of holiness
upon earth, and that responsibility she dare not throw
upon her Lord in heaven, as if it were exercised by
Him directly, and not through her.

Let the Church then beware of finding an explanation of her weakness, of her shortcomings, of her failure
to convert and renew the world, in the thought of the
world's obstinacy, of the difficulties of her own position,
or of the mysteriousness of God's ways. Let her seek
the explanation where it will be found—in herself.
As a Body how often has she been no better than the
world! How often has she yielded to difficulties instead of looking upon them as a discipline by which
to gain strength! How often, to excuse herself, has she
drawn a veil of mystery over what God has made plain!
She has been unwilling to accept the full privileges of
the Gospel or the perfect heavenly life; and she has
thus choked the channels by which the all-conquering
Spirit of God goes forth to victory. Let her frankly
acknowledge the fact that the Spirit in His power
belongs to her alone, and that only through her can
they who sit in darkness receive the light of life.

Before closing what has to be said upon this subject,
one or two general remarks may be made. It is un-

questionable that the Church has not been sufficiently alive to its importance.   There are symptoms of improvement in this respect, but much remains to be done before we can hope to reach consistent and clear views upon the Person and Work of the Spirit under the New Testament dispensation.   It may be difficult to explain why it should be so.   But in all probability the chief explanation is our failure to recognise with sufficient distinctness that that "Spirit," or "Holy Spirit," to which the Church's vitality must be always due is the Spirit of Christ, the ever-living human as well as Divine Lord, and that He has been too exclusively thought of as the Third Person of the Trinity in His metaphysical existence.   We know that to the Lord Jesus Christ the redemption of man is owing, and that He is as much the Finisher as the Author of our faith.   When, accordingly, we hear of another work not less essential, but which seems to be carried out less by Him than by an independent Person, our minds become confused, and we are tempted to dismiss the subject.   On the other hand, let us feel that the Spirit given by the exalted Redeemer is His own Spirit, the Spirit by whom He forms Himself within us, and the different parts of the plan of our salvation will blend into one.

Nor can it well be doubted that the thought of a human element in the Spirit by whom the glorified Redeemer works would lend to the Church fresh power.   Men are crying for the human to heal them, and who that is human can refuse his sympathy?

There is need for the Divine. We have yet to see that
more fully. In the meantime let the necessity for the
human occupy a moment's thought. The Incarnation
has for ever sanctified and confirmed that necessity.
The human is in a certain sense Divine, and to suppose
that the heart of man will ever be really touched by
what does not possess in it a human element is to forget alike the philosophy of our nature and the lessons
of religious and civil history. There can be no more
profound mistake in religion, and there has been none
more fatal, than to hope to elevate the Divine by
sacrificing the human. The human to be used must,
indeed, be an ever-living human, not the human of an
earlier age forced upon a later, but the ever-living or, in
other words, the Divine human, always true to man at
the moment when we appeal to him, and thus to the
most distant age as new as was He who at the
beginning of the Christian era gave an old world new
life. But, when it is so, then in this lies the greatest
element of the Church's power. No fresh schemes of
benevolent exertion, added to thousands that have gone
before and perished, will meet our wants. Not the
world only, but the Church, is weary with the multitude of interests by which she is stimulated.[1] Simply
to increase the number of these completes the weariness,
and makes men long for rest from disappointment and
perplexity in the grave. We need a more inspiring

[1] Compare a striking article on "The Spiritual Fatigue of the World" in the *Spectator* for 1st June 1889. What is here said, though applied to the particular point in hand, is in substance derived from it.

view than we commonly possess of the influence of Christian truth, a more powerful impression of the strength which Christ supplies for Christian life, a brighter and more hopeful colour to be spread over every department of Christian labour. We need to recover the buoyancy, the generosity, the passion of youth ; and we can only obtain these by becoming young again in the ever-fresh aspirations of a humanity which, from season to season, fills its branches with a new spirit of life, and clothes them with new leaves and flowers. What, in short, the Church needs is not to extinguish humanity under the pressure of a too limited conception of the Divine, but to bring the two into the closest possible connexion. All her great doctrines must be associated with what is human if they are to tell on human things. This has been abundantly done with the doctrine of the Person and Work of our Lord, not sufficiently with the doctrine of the Person and Work of the Spirit. Only when it is done; when we feel that the Spirit dwelling in us comes from One as human as He is Divine, shall we have not simply "life," but "life abundantly."[1] Only then, in communion with Him who amidst all change is unchangeable, and amidst all decay everlasting, shall we have within us a spring of eternal youth, shall we run and not be weary, walk and not faint.[2]

[1] John x. 10.   [2] Isa. xl. 31.

LECTURE V

"As Thou didst send Me into the world, even so sent I them into the world."—JOHN xvii. 18.

WE have followed the work of our Lord in heaven until, in the High-priestly office which He discharges there, we have seen Him sending down His Spirit into the members of His Body ; while that Spirit, as the Spirit of His own glorified humanity, enters into the closest possible connexion with what they are, and becomes the pervading element of every department of their life. The work of our Lord, however, is not yet done. It is true that He left the world and went to the Father ; that, when the prospect of His departure was immediately before Him, He told His disciples that He would "make request of the Father, and He would give them another Advocate, that He might be with them for ever" ;[1] and that, according to His promise, this Advocate now leads them into all the truth, fits them for every duty, and brings to them the enjoyment of every privilege. But in and with the Advocate He Himself also comes. "I will not leave you orphans," He says ; "I come unto you," [2]—words in which the use

---

[1] John xiv. 16. [2] John xiv. 18.

of the present tense, "I come," is a sufficient proof that He refers, not to the close of the present dispensation, but to His continuous coming, in the Advocate, thenceforward to the end of time.   From the instant of His departure He would come to them, although in a manner not perceptible to the senses; and His coming to wind up the history of the world would rather be the "manifestation of His Presence,"[1] His visible return, when the Church should put off the garments of her widowhood, and clothe herself in nuptial robes to meet the Bridegroom.   In the meantime she waits, and lays out for her Lord whatever talents He has committed to her care.   In what capacity does she wait or work?   In what light are we to regard her during her present pilgrimage?

The answer to these questions depends mainly upon what was said in the last Lecture.   The Church exists by means of our Lord's communication to her of that Spirit which is His own Spirit.   It follows that what He is His people, according to the measure of their capabilities, must also be.   This principle is, indeed, a simple corollary from the fundamental conception of the Church as the Body of Christ, for the Body lives in such close communion with the Head that whatever the Head wills the Body must do.   "I am the Vine, ye are the branches,"[2] is the declaration by our Lord of His people's position in the world; "Abide in Me, and I in you,"[3] is His authoritative command; while other words spoken in the same discourse to a similar

---

[1] 2 Thess. ii. 8 ; Titus ii. 13.   [2] John xv. 5.   [3] John xv. 4.

effect, and directly connected with what was to follow
His departure, show that in all such passages He thinks
of Himself as glorified : *"In that day* ye shall know that
I am in My Father, and ye in Me, and I in you." [1]
With the knowledge of ever-deepening experience
the disciples shall know that the Son of man whose
"going away" seemed to be a separation between Himself and them is still really present with them in His
power, and that they are glorified in Him, and He in
them.   Thus the end of the economy of grace will be
attained—the perfect union, in a glory now given
though only partially realised, of Father, Son, and
all believers in one uninterrupted, unchanging, eternal
unity.   The true idea of the Church on earth is, therefore, not that of a Body starting from earth and
reaching onwards to a heavenly condition to be perfectly attained hereafter.   It is rather the idea of a
Body starting from heaven, and so exhibiting, amidst
the inhabitants and things of time, the graces and
privileges already ideally bestowed upon it, that it may
lead the world either to come to the light or to condemn itself because it loves the darkness rather than
the light, its deeds being evil.   It will also follow that
the community thus constituted must be the visible
Representative of our Lord while He is Himself invisible, and that to it must be committed the work which
in personal presence with us He can no longer do.   Not,
indeed, that we may ever lose sight of the subordination
of the members to the Head.   To whatever extent the

[1] John xiv. 20.

glorified Lord identifies Himself with those to whom He has given His glory,[1] and however close may be the resemblance between Him and them, He retains His absolute and unequalled pre-eminence.   He must always be what He is, "the beginning, the first-born from the dead."   He is not glorified with us, but we with Him; He does not grow up in all things into us, but we into Him; and the consummation of our joy is to behold *His* glory which God has given Him.[2]   With Him is the fountain of life, and it is the water which *He* bestows that becomes in us a fountain of springing water, unto eternal life.[3]

Let us notice very briefly the argument of the fourth Evangelist upon the point.   According to the first chapter of his Gospel, the Light of the World, which "was with God, and was God," had from the instant of creation never ceased to shine.   More particularly, so shining, it had been "the life of *men*."   It had lightened not only God's ancient people in their divinely provided fold, but those "other sheep" which, as we learn at a later point in the same Gospel, were yet to be brought into the one flock of the one Shepherd.[4]   Thus had it been up to the time of the Christian era.   Then there was a great development.   The light, no longer shining merely as a spiritual influence in the minds of men, reached its culminating point, and assumed its concrete and most powerful reality in the

[1] John xvii. 22.
[2] Rom. viii. 17 ; Eph. iv.
15 ; John xvii. 24. Grétillat,

Théologie   Systématique, iv. p.
250.
[3] John iv. 14.   [4] John x. 16.

Son. That Word who had hitherto been only an unseen light "became flesh, and tabernacled among us
(and we beheld His glory, glory as of an only begotten
from a father), full of grace and truth." [1] The effect of
this Incarnation was that, whereas no man had seen
God at any time, "The only begotten, which was in the
bosom of the Father, He declared Him"; [2] that is, He
came not simply as a spiritual influence from God, but
to set Him forth to the eyes of men. Then the Father
was "seen" in the Son, and to this manifestation of the
Father in Himself our Lord constantly appeals in all
His discourses with "The Jews," as the ground upon
which they were bound to acknowledge His claims and
to believe in Him. [3]

The same principle must continue to operate The
Father of the spirits of all flesh desires still to make
Himself known for our salvation ; and, if human nature
in its deepest aspects is always the same, He must
effect this end in essentially the same way. The special
"declaration" of God, however, made by the Divine Word
at the time when He became Incarnate could be made
by Him to none but the men of His own generation.
A record of it might be preserved. Books might be
written regarding it. A full and detailed description
of what Jesus was while upon earth might be given to
mankind. But not in books alone could all that is
involved in communion with the Father be so presented
to the world as to attract it also into that blessed
fellowship. The world needed to see what such fellow-

---

[1] John i. 14.   [2] Ver. 18.   [3] Comp. Grétillat, iv. p. 457.

ship implied; how it elevated and consecrated and beautified human life; and, in the only sense in which the word ought to be used, brought to it "salvation." This mission, therefore, our Lord entrusted to His Church. "As Thou," He said in His High-priestly prayer, "didst send Me into the world, even so sent I them into the world"; "And the glory which Thou gavest Me I have given unto them; that they may be one, even as we are one; I in them, and Thou in Me, that they may be perfected into one; that the world may know that Thou didst send Me, and lovedst them, even as Thou lovedst Me."[1]   Hence the words of the disciple whom Jesus loved: "The life was manifested, and we have seen, and bear witness, and declare unto you the life, the eternal life, which was with the Father, and was manifested unto us; that which we have seen and heard declare we unto you also, that ye also may have fellowship with us: yea, and our fellowship is with the Father, and with His Son Jesus Christ."[2] And hence the promise to the Apostles, accompanying their great commission, "Verily, verily, I say unto you, He that receiveth whomsoever I send receiveth Me; and he that receiveth Me receiveth Him that sent Me."[3] The Body of our Lord, therefore, must represent Himself.

No doubt the Church can never during the days of her pilgrimage execute such a commission to the full. She has not yet realised the ideal perfection which belongs to her. Sin is too often found where there

---

[1] John xvii. 18, 22, 23.   [2] 1 John i. 2. 3.   [3] John xiii. 20.

ought to be holiness; disunion where there ought to be unity; weakness where there ought to be strength; and, however exalted the spiritual life of the members of the Church may be, they must bear about with them their body of humiliation, until He who is now waited for comes again and fashions it anew, that it may be conformed to the body of His glory.[1] Nevertheless the Church's ideal state supplies to her the standard of her duty, and to approach nearer to it ought to be her constant effort. From Him in whom it is already perfected she draws her measure of that state, to the extent to which she is able at any moment to exhibit it; and, when she is true to the gift bestowed upon her this measure cannot fail to be a growing one. The fountain to which she is invited is not some small spring opened on the mountain side. It is rather that great gathering of the waters above the firmament, the volume of which can never be diminished, though drawn upon for every want and through every age of the Church's history. Of these waters she first drinks for the nourishment of her own life; and then, as she passes onward in her course, they are to issue forth from her, in ever more abounding streams, for the fertilisation of widening lands and the refreshment of multiplying peoples. The true conception of the Church, in short, is that she begins in heaven and, in possession of the Spirit of her glorified Head, descends to earth. She does not begin on earth and work her way to heaven.

The principles involved in what has now been said

---

[1] Phil. iii. 20, 21.

so far from being unreasonable, are in strict conformity with the nature of man and the general providence of God.   For, in the first place, it is only natural to think that men will be most successfully appealed to when regard is had to both sides of their nature and not to one side only.   He who framed us with bodies as well as souls, with an outward as well as an inward aspect of our being, may be expected to act in religion as He acts in every other sphere of His relations to His creatures.   He may therefore be expected to address us by what is visible as well as by what is invisible, by what speaks to the senses as well as by what speaks only to the inner spirit.   This principle has been for ever consecrated by the Incarnation, the simple fact that the Father of all deemed the Incarnation of the Son necessary for the redemption of men being itself a sufficient reply to any opposing argument.   In the second place, we thus secure the thought of perpetual intervention of God in the religious training of the race similar to that perpetuity of action which marks His dealings in creation and providence.   He not only called the world into existence, He constantly intervenes in its behalf.   "He commandeth the sun, and it riseth not; and sealeth up the stars"; "He causeth the grass to grow for the cattle, and herb for the service of man."[1]   Is it not likely that He will proceed in the same manner in the plan of His grace; and that if, at the beginning of the Christian era, "Holy Spirit" was employed to prepare the Holy Child for birth, the same "Holy Spirit" will be unceasingly

[1] Job ix. 7; Ps. civ. 14.

employed on the same principle, though it may be in
another way, in carrying out what was then begun ?
Nor can it be urged that, even if men stand in need of
this visible declaration of the Father, a visible, as distinguished from an invisible, Church is incapable of
making it.   By the mere fact of its visibility the visible
is not despiritualised.   Were it so the Incarnation of
the Eternal Son would have been impossible.   Holy
thoughts and devout affections, when embodied in living
personalities, are as visible as the countenances of those
through whom they exert their power.   Without the
embodiment they would be lost upon the world, and
would fail to fulfil their mission for its good.

Upon these principles, then—principles to be read
not only in revelation, but in nature and in man—rests
the plea for a visible Church and ordinances, by means
of which there shall be continued in the world from age
to age both a representation of what Christ as the
manifestation of the Father is, and a channel for the
conveyance of His grace.   As an able though anonymous
writer has said—

The origin and cause of all that is done in the Christian
Church is the Incarnation of our Lord Jesus Christ.   God is a
Spirit, essentially invisible.   In Him is all life, and grace, and
power to bless ; He is visible in the God-man Christ Jesus ; and
only from, and by, and through that God-man, all that is in God
for us can come to us ; and except through Him that is visible,
we can receive nothing from Him who is the invisible.   Jesus
Christ is the image of the invisible God, the symbol of Him who
is invisible ; the channel, the means, through which all spiritual
grace and power come.   But for the time being, and during the

period between His first and second advents, He also is invisible
to us.   He, therefore, has instituted certain images, or symbols,
which represent Him in some character or office, or ministry, or
act, or operation, or some fact concerning Him.   And by means
of these Christ ordinarily ministers to His people the grace,
power, and blessing of those offices, acts, and operations which
they respectively symbolise; and, by the use of them in the
manner He has appointed, the faithful obtain that grace and
blessing.   The material part of our Lord's human nature, in and
by which God is imaged and symbolised to us, and through
which all grace is ministered to us, is taken from the substance
of this earth; and all those symbolic things of which we speak
must be of the substance of, and appertaining to, this material
creation. . . . The Church cannot omit any of them, cannot
change any, cannot substitute anything else in their places; she
cannot add to, she cannot take from, any of them, without
suffering consequent detriment and loss.[1]

From these considerations it follows that whatever
function is discharged by our Lord in heaven must be
also discharged by His Church on earth.   Is he, as
glorified, a Prophet?   The prophetical office must belong
to her.   It may, for the sake of order, be distributed
through appropriate members; but primarily it belongs
to the Church as a whole, the life of Christ in His prophetical office being first her life, and her life then
pervading and animating any particular persons through
whom the work of prophesying is performed.   In like
manner is the glorified Redeemer a King?   The kingly
office must also belong to the Church; and, if it is to be
represented in any particular members rather than in
the Body as a whole, her life must so penetrate and

---

[1] *Creation and Redemption*, p. 30.

pervade them that they may be kingly. If it be thus with our Lord's offices as Prophet and King, it cannot be otherwise with that priestly office which is the foundation of both of these. All who allow that our Lord is a Priest in heaven must, upon the principles now laid down, acknowledge the priestliness of the Church on earth.

What has been said might of itself be sufficient to determine the priestly character of the visible Church. But the point is at once so essential to the conception of the Church of Christ, and the object of so much suspicion and dislike, that it may be well to consider the matter from another and more strictly historical side.

No truth is more readily or more universally accepted than that the Old Testament was preparatory to the New, and that the ideas embodied in it, instead of being destroyed by the entrance of the higher dispensation, were taken up, confirmed, extended, heightened, and for ever perfected. Our Lord's own words are decisive on the point: "Think not that I came to destroy the law or the prophets: I came not to destroy, but to fulfil." [1] It is unnecessary to spend time in showing either that the Old Testament dispensation as a whole is here referred to, or that the "law" spoken of includes the law in all its parts—moral, ceremonial, and civil. Upon neither of these points is there any difference of opinion worthy of mention, and we may rest with the most perfect confidence in the assurance that whatever can

[1] Matt. v. 17.

be shown to be a principle of the Old Testament dispensation is accomplished or fulfilled in the dispensation
which took its place.

The question, however, still arises, How is the one
dispensation accomplished in the other ? Is it by the
appointment of Christian ordinances, arrangements, and
institutions corresponding to those of Israel ? or are all
the parts of the Jewish economy in the first instance
fulfilled in Christ ? and only, as fulfilled in Him, and
deducible from a consideration of His Person and Work,
do the principles embodied in them become binding
upon us ? The answer to these questions is not difficult. The Jewish dispensation is accomplished in
Christ Himself, and its ideas have authority over Christian men, as coming direct from Him, not from Israel.

Thus it is that St. Paul, when treating the subject
in its most general form, exclaims, " Christ is the end
of the law unto righteousness to every one that believeth "; that, again, he says, " The law hath been our
tutor to bring us unto Christ, that we might be justified by faith. But now that faith is come, we are no
longer under a tutor. For ye are all sons of God,
through faith, in Christ Jesus "; and that, once more,
he explains his own experience in the words, " I
through the law died unto the law, that I might live
unto God." [1] In these passages, and others of a similar
kind, the Apostle's assertion is, that the whole legal
dispensation has passed away, not because it has been
fulfilled in new and higher institutions, but because it

[1] Rom. x. 4 ; Gal. iii. 24, ii. 19.

has been fulfilled in Christ. The lesson thus taught in its general form is elsewhere taught by the same Apostle with reference to particular rites of Judaism; as when, writing to the Corinthians, he says, "Wherefore let us keep the feast (or festival) . . . with the unleavened bread of sincerity and truth."[1] The figure lying at the bottom of his words is that of the Passover, but it is neither to the Jewish Passover nor to the Christian Eucharist that he refers in the word "feast" or "festival." He speaks of the whole Christian life. Because the Lamb slain for believers is, not once a year only but for ever, in the presence of the Father, the Christian life also is not confined to stated seasons, but goes on from year to year, from day to day, from hour to hour. Over the whole of it a festival light is thrown. The Christian passover never ends. We learn what it is, not from Judaism, but from the fulfilment of Judaism in our Lord.

A similar lesson is not less strikingly taught us by the Gospel of St. John. One of the main thoughts pervading that Gospel, and illustrating the truth stated in the Prologue, that "The law was given through Moses; the grace and the truth came through Jesus Christ," is that in Christ Himself we have the fulfilment of all the institutions of the Old Testament. It can hardly be denied that such is the light in which we are to read the miracle of the multiplying of the bread, with the discourses accompanying it, in chap. vi.—there Christ is the fulfilment of the Passover; or that we are to

[1] 1 Cor. v. 8.

read in the same spirit the narrative of our Lord's
action in the temple at Jerusalem, at the feast of
Tabernacles, given in chap. vii.—there He is the fulfilment of that closing festival of the Jewish year. Let
us pass from these, and take another and still greater
institution of Israel, the Sabbath. No Jewish ordinance has either in itself a deeper interest, or can be
more plausibly appealed to in order to establish a conclusion different from that now contended for. It
appears most natural to think that the Sabbath of
the Jewish is fulfilled in the Lord's Day of the Chris-.
tian Church. Yet that is not the teaching of the
fourth Evangelist. He leads us rather to believe that
the Sabbath is fulfilled in something wider, deeper, and
more glorious than any single day, or any succession,
at intervals, of single days. It is fulfilled, like the Passover and Tabernacles, in Christ. The teaching of the incident at the pool of Bethesda, related in the fifth chapter
of the Gospel, is conclusive upon this point. He who
there heals the impotent man upon the Sabbath, and by
doing so rouses in a greater than ordinary degree the
opposition of His enemies, presents Himself to us in His
conversation with the Jews as Himself the accomplishment of the sacred institution. To the complaint that
" He did these things on the Sabbath " He replies, " My
Father worketh even until now, and I work "—as much
as to say, " Behold in My Father and in Me the right idea
of that Sabbath-rest which you show so much eagerness
to preserve. My Father's work of love to man and My
work of love in Him never know one moment's pause.

By day and by night, through the years, and through
the ages, We work on, seeking alike in providence and
in grace to heal the wounds inflicted by the children
of men upon themselves. In one sense, therefore, We
never rest. Yet in another sense We always rest; for
Our work is not like your work; and, in the end which
We contemplate, and in the spirit in which We accomplish it, We find that uninterrupted rest of which you
have only the shadow in the commandment you would
now honour and obey. So far from being a violation of
that commandment, the works done by Me in My Father's
name are its fulfilment. I am always working: I am
always resting: My work is rest: My rest is work:
and you may behold both the works and the rest in
Me."

These illustrations of the principle now contended
for must suffice. Every sacred institution of Israel
might be adduced for the same purpose; and, whether
we had to speak of Pentecost or the Day of Atonement,
of the Sabbatic year or the year of Jubilee, of the
Tabernacle or the Altar of incense, or the Shew-bread,
or the Golden Candlestick, it might be shown that
their "accomplishment" is to be sought in no single
Christian ordinance. All of them are shadows of something higher than any ordinance, even of Him who is
the substance of all the ordinances and the life of all
the institutions of His people; of Him who is the
Author and the Finisher of their faith; and whose own
and whose people's life are one. If the principle now
spoken of be not admitted, it will hardly be possible to

R

avoid charging the Church of Christ with remissness
and neglect of duty.   As a simple matter of fact there
are numerous institutions of the Old Testament economy,
to which, in her own arrangements, she has nothing
to correspond.   Nor can it be said that these were less
important than the others to which a closer analogy
is found in the Christian system.   All were equally
ordained of God; all expressed definite and distinct
ideas; and all were equally obligatory upon Israel.   If,
therefore, the New Testament Israel is to embody in
corresponding outward forms the ideas which, though
heightened and extended, have passed over to her from
the Ancient Church, she has no right to omit any institution upon which the seal of the Divine approbation
was once set.   Necessary for the religious life then, the
inference would be irresistible that they are not less
necessary now.   We are not entitled to select from
them those only that may gratify our own tastes or
suit our own purposes.   We must either adopt them
all, or be able to show that their "accomplishment" in
Christ involves the passing away of some along with
the retention of others.   This distinction cannot be
carried out; and, on the supposition therefore that the
institutions of Judaism are fulfilled in corresponding
Christian institutions, we ought to find, not an occasional, but a complete parallel between the types of the
Jewish Church and the separate fulfilment of these in
the Church as she is perfected in Christ.

On the other hand, what has been said does not
entitle us to infer either that there are no positive

institutions under the New Testament, or that there may not be a close resemblance between such as existed in Israel and those appointed by the Christian Church for the edification of her members. In point of fact we know that Christians have at least the divinely instituted Sacraments and the Ministry; and, when we remember that the principles of the religious life are in all ages essentially the same, we may expect that the Divine Spirit operating in the Church will guide her to arrangements similar in their nature to those once shaped directly by His hand. What is contended for is simply that the ordinances and institutions of the legal economy are not fulfilled in corresponding ordinances and institutions of the economy of grace. They are fulfilled in Christ. The idea of priesthood, therefore, as one of the most essential principles and fundamental institutions of the Old Testament did not pass away when Jesus came. It was fulfilled in Him, and no Christian denies that He at least abides a Priest for ever.

But if the idea of priesthood was thus fulfilled in Christ it must be fulfilled also in His Church. We cannot separate the Head from the members. The Christian Church does not simply live by Christ: she lives in Him, and He lives in her. By the constant communication of His Spirit she is what she is; and, as we have seen, the Spirit is not an outward gift which may be bestowed by the Giver while different in its nature from what the Giver is. The Spirit poured out upon the Church is that which so penetrates our

Lord's own being that He cannot give the Spirit without at the same time giving Himself, or give Himself
without giving the Spirit.   As, then, in the power of
that Spirit He is a Priest in heaven, the life lived on
earth by His Body, in the power of the same Spirit,
must be priestly.

Nothing, accordingly, can be more distinct than the
manner in which this lesson is impressed upon us in
Scripture.   At the moment when the Almighty was
entering into His most solemn covenant with Israel
He had declared that, if the people would obey His
commandments, they should be unto Him "a kingdom
of priests and a holy nation"; [1] and St. Peter, having
the fulfilment of that covenant in his eye,[2] speaks of
Christians as "a holy priesthood to offer up spiritual
sacrifices acceptable to God through Jesus Christ." [3]
Wherever also the priestly character of the Head of the
Church in heaven is treated of, there the priestly
character of His people upon earth appears.   Of the
extent to which this is the case in the central Old
Testament prophecy of the coming Priest after the
order of Melchizedek, it is unnecessary to say more than
has been said already.[4]   In the Epistle to the Hebrews
the same lesson meets us.   No sooner has the writer of
that Epistle set forth the glory of the Melchizedek
Priesthood, and of Jesus as a High-priest after that
order, than he makes the practical application: "Having,
therefore, brethren, boldness to enter into the holy
place, in the blood of Jesus, by the way which He

---

[1] Ex. xix. 6.   [2] 1 Pet. i. 2.   [3] 1 Pet. ii. 5.   [4] See Lect. ii.

dedicated for us, a new and living way, through the veil, that is to say, His flesh; and having a great Priest over the house of God; let us draw near with a true heart, in fulness of faith, having our hearts sprinkled from an evil conscience, and our body washed with pure water." [1]   The entering "into the holy place," spoken of in these words, at once suggests the light in which Christians are there thought of, for into it under the Old Testament economy priests alone could enter; and this conclusion is strengthened by the fact that the two participial sentences, marking out the mode in which we are to draw near, are grounded, the one on the sprinkling of blood which accompanied the consecration of Aaron and his sons to the priesthood,[2] the other on the command that, when the priests entered into the tabernacle of the congregation, they should wash with water, that they died not.[3]   As priests, then, the members of the Christian Church enjoy their privilege of immediate access to the presence of God.   Because they have an High-priest over the house of God they are priests in Him.   The same thing appears even more in the Revelation of St. John.   As in the fundamental vision of that book [4] we are taught that Christ exalted in glory is a Priest, wearing His priestly garments in the manner in which they were worn by the priests of Israel when engaged in active service,[5] so we are taught in the same book that in Him all His people are also priests.   They have been made "to be a kingdom, to be priests unto

---

[1] Heb. x. 19-22.   [2] Exod. xxix. 21.   [3] Exod. xxx. 20; Lev. viii. 6.
[4] Rev. i. 13-16.   [5] Ver. 13.

His God and Father,"[1] and the white robes which they wear throughout the book are the robes of priests. The idea of priestly function cannot be separated from the Christian Church. All the Lord's people are priests.

It is unnecessary to say more upon this point. What has been contended for will indeed be granted by most Christian men. They may dread the teaching of the Roman Church, which attempts to satisfy our need of a perpetual sacrifice by the doctrine of the Mass. They may shrink from the term Sacerdotalism or Priestliness as if it must involve an undue exaltation of the clergy and depreciation of the lay members of the Church. They may even fall into the mistake of totally misapprehending the meaning of the words which they condemn; and from one or other of these causes they may be led to urge that there is no priest on earth, that our Lord in heaven is the one sufficient and only Priest. But let Sacerdotalism be defined as our Lord defined it when He said: "The Son of man came not to be ministered unto, but to minister, and to give His life a ransom for many."[2] Let the priestliness of the whole Church, not that of any particular class within her, be brought prominently forward; let it appear that the very object of insisting upon the Church's priestliness is to restore to the Christian laity that sense of their responsibility and privilege of which Protestantism, hardly less than Romanism, has practically deprived them; and let the Church's priesthood be invariably represented as a continuation of our Lord's priestly

---

[1] Rev. i. 6.   [2] Matt. xx. 28.

office through her, not as something deputed to her ;—let all this be done, and prejudice against the doctrine would probably be removed. Yet it has been thought proper to dwell upon it at some length, because, to whatever extent theoretically accepted, there is need of a livelier apprehension of its power and consequences. It is not sufficiently felt that, in the strictest and fullest meaning of the words, the Church of the Lord Jesus Christ is a priestly Church, or that priestliness is even the prime element of her being, because it is the prime element in the being of her glorified Head.

What then, we have now to ask, is the Church's commission to the world? It is to represent her Lord, and, as the instrument through which He acts, to carry on His work. This representation may be considered under the four following particulars—her Life, her Work, her Worship, and her Confession. Let us advert to these.

I. The glorified Lord is to be made manifest in His people's Life. We have seen that the most characteristic part of our Lord's High-priestly work in heaven is Offering—that offering which is continually made in His presentation of Himself to the Father when, having accepted death as the penal consequence of sin, He yielded Himself to the Father in one perfect, free, loving, and undivided service. This is the service which St. Paul has in view when he says : "And when all things have been subjected unto him (the Son), then shall the Son also be subjected to Him that did subject all things unto Him, that God may be all in all." [1]   In thus sub-

---

[1] 1 Cor. xv. 28.

jecting Himself, however, our Lord does not stand alone. He never is or can be alone. Not even upon the Cross was He alone. His people were in Him when He died; they were in Him when He rose from the grave and ascended to "the heavenly places"; they are in Him as He loves and serves in heaven. He is the Second Adam, the Head of the new creation, the first-born among many brethren, who are His, not by an outward imputation merely, but by an inward appropriation of His righteousness. ".And for them," He says in His High-priestly prayer, "I consecrate Myself, that they themselves also may be consecrated in truth."[1] Every part of the statement is full of meaning. He might have said, as on a previous occasion, that He had been "consecrated and sent into the world by the Father";[2] but He speaks then of "*consecrating Himself*," because, as being everything that was truly human, He had laid all that He was upon the altar of God with perfect acquiescence and free will, and had thus gained that place which entitled Him to become the Head of a new line of spiritual descendants. The consecration of His disciples, it is also evident, was to be the exact counterpart of His own,—that "*they themselves also*" may be consecrated. While guided by the Spirit, they were to be so guided as to act in their turn a free and con-sciously willing part, devoting "themselves" in personal faith to the life in which they had been offered by their Lord. And all this was to be done "*in truth*," not simply truly, but in the sphere of "truth" in its most

[1] John xvii. 19.   [2] John x. 36.

absolute sense—truth given in that Son who is the
expression of the Father; truth as the eternal reality
of things in contrast with the merely outward and
phenomenal around us in all its unsubstantial, shadowy,
and transitory character.

In her whole process of sanctification, therefore, the
Church is only reaching onward in Christ to what
Christ is. She aims at no mere perfection of pagan
virtue, at no merely general idea of goodness, of obedience to the Divine commandments or submission to the
Divine appointments. Her aim is to be like her Lord,
and like Him in that character which distinguishes Him
as the heavenly High-priest, "holy, guileless, undefiled,
separated from sinners, and made higher than the
heavens." [1] Her sanctification is no mere *consequence* of
a redemptive act finished on the Cross. It is itself
salvation in its highest sense. It is that being "loosed
from our sins in the blood of Christ" which makes us
"to be a kingdom, to be priests unto His God and
Father." [2] To this result the Church, as one with her
Lord, has to press continually forward, yet not so much
by passing into new and hitherto untried spheres of the
religious life, as by realising in act what in principle
she already has, until the perfect consecration of the
Head becomes that also of the members of the Body.
As the glorified Lord, human as well as Divine, now
yields Himself in His heavenly Priesthood in eternal
submission to the Father, and in that submission enjoys
uninterrupted communion and fellowship with Him, so

[1] Heb. vii. 26.   [2] Rev. i. 5, 6. Note the later reading.

His people are to offer their life in His life, in a like perpetual service. Constrained by the mercies of God, they are to present themselves "a living sacrifice, holy and acceptable unto God." [1] In the joyful confidence of love they are to draw near continually, with full assurance of faith, into the inmost sanctuary of the Divine Presence, and there to obtain fresh quickening for the duties that would otherwise be too difficult for them, and for the temptations that they would be otherwise unable to overcome.

More particularly, there are three great elements forming the very power of our Lord's Priesthood, which the Church, during His absence, is in her priesthood to make manifest to the world.

1. There is the Divine element. We have already seen that this element must be found in the Priest, who, not by commission only but in His own nature, is to be the Mediator between God and man. It must, therefore, be found also in the Church. Nor is the necessity for its presence in a later age modified by any demonstration that it certainly did exist in the Church at the first, that it was borne witness to by signs and wonders and mighty deeds, and that nothing but the direct interposition of God will account for the rise and progress of the Christian faith in the earliest stages of its history. It is not enough to tell the world of a Divine Redeemer who tabernacled in the flesh nearly nineteen centuries ago, and who then left promises for ever valid. Much more is needed. The Church of

[1] Rom. xii. 1.

God has, in one way or another, even now to show that
a Lord of super-earthly power is in her midst ; that He
is working there ; that, in His Divine as well as human
personality, He is fashioning her to a higher sphere
than that of earth ; and that He is to her an influence
as present, real, and true as He was to the disciples
who followed Him when He was here below, heard His
voice, beheld His form, and received out of His fulness.
Thus it was that Jesus said to Judas (not Iscariot), " If
a man love Me, he will keep My words: and My
Father will love him, and We will come unto him, and
make Our abode with him." [1]   Thus it is that St. Paul
exclaimed, " We are a temple of the living God ; even as
God said, I will dwell in them, and walk in them ; and I
will be their God, and they shall be My people." [2]   And
thus it is that St. John, in the Apocalypse, "heard a great
voice out of the throne saying, Behold, the tabernacle
of God is with men, and He shall tabernacle with them,
and they shall be His people, and God Himself shall be
with them, and be their God." [3]   As truly, as really as
God dwelt in the Tabernacle of old and met Israel there,
must it appear that the glorified Redeemer dwells now
with His people, imparting to them an element of life as
positively Divine as was that element in His own life on
earth, as is that element in His life in heaven.

It is no answer to this to say that, if there be such
a Divine element in the Church, a continuous power to
work miracles is implied ; and that, without beholding
miracles, we can never know that it is there.   To such

[1] John xiv. 23.   [2] 2 Cor. vi. 16.   [3] Rev. xxi. 3.

statements it is enough to reply that no more mistaken position can be occupied, none more entirely contradictory to the teaching of the fourth Gospel, than that which only sees a manifestation of the Divine in what is commonly designated miraculous. Referring to His own works, our Lord on one occasion said, " Believe Me that I am in the Father, and the Father in Me: or else believe for the very works' sake. Verily, verily, I say unto you, He that believeth on Me, the works that I do shall he do also; and greater works than these shall he do; because I go unto the Father."[1] By the "greater works" here spoken of, our Lord cannot mean only what we call miracles. Greater miracles could not be wrought than those recorded in the very Gospel in which the words occur. The changing of water into wine; the healing of the nobleman's son; the multiplying of the bread; the opening of the eyes of the blind man; the raising of Lazarus—more stupendous miracles it is impossible even to conceive. Yet our Lord speaks of " greater works " than these; and He connects them in the closest manner with no special mission of apostle, saint, or prophet—" he that believeth " on Him shall do them. He cannot, therefore, refer to merely extraordinary or occasional manifestations by His people of a Divine power resting upon them. He can only have in view that power of the spiritual life in Him which should be exhibited by His disciples after, and because, He had gone to the Father; and this power was to be as convincing an evidence as miracles them-

---

[1] John xiv. 11, 12.

selves, if not even more convincing, that the living
Lord from whom it came was the revelation of the
Father to the age which witnessed it.

The history of the Church has taught us the same
lesson. In her earliest age she possessed those miraculous gifts of which St. Paul has given so striking a
description in his first Epistle to the Corinthians.[1]
Shall we say that, because of this, she was then at a
higher stage than she has since been or is now? It is
in grace as it is in nature. We can easily conceive
that on that morning when Noah and his family came
forth from the ark after the Deluge they would behold
such a burst of new life as they had never before seen.
After their long submersion trees would rush into leaf
and plants would spring up with a rapidity never before
witnessed. Everywhere life would display an intensity
of action unseen before or since. It would be a glorious
spectacle—renovated Nature's first offering to her God
—but not so glorious, not so calculated to exalt our
notions of the Divine presence, as when, season after
season, and morning after morning, Nature, at the Divine
bidding, puts forth her calmer powers—leaves gradually
decking the trees, the grass gradually becoming green,
one sustained quiet energy causing the earth through
successive ages to renew her youth with no agitation,
no noise, no excitement, but deep, undisturbed, irresistible, the power of Him Who, amidst all changes, is
Himself unchanged.

In like manner the highest idea of Christianity is

[1] 1 Cor. xii.-xiv.

not that where, under the mighty impulse of a first
outpouring of the Divine Spirit, miracles may be
wrought and, in the agitation of society, striking things
be done, but that where the agitation has subsided ;
where what was felt to be only supernatural and extraordinary has so identified itself with the heart and
life that it has become natural and ordinary; where
God is not less but more present than before—present
everywhere and in all things; and where He shows His
presence by the depth rather than the commotion of
the pious feelings which He awakens, by the calmness
rather than the agitation of that river of life the flood
of which in the soul He fills.

It is not, therefore, only in things to which we commonly confine the word miracle that the Divine appears.
It may appear not less in the whole tone and spirit of
the Church's life, in the varied Christian virtues of her
members, in the general character of their Christian
work, and in the grace received by them in the Christian Sacraments.   When that life is exhibited, as it
ought to be, in its distinctively heavenly character, it
bears witness to the presence of a power in Christian
men which no mere recollection of a past example, however heroic or beautiful, can supply.   The difficulties of
exhibiting and maintaining it are probably far greater
now than they were in the apostolic age; and as
nothing but a present Divine support can enable us to
overcome these, so, when they are overcome, a testimony
is given to the fact that God is with us.

It is not even enough to say this ; for the New

Testament teaches us that the heavenly, the Divine, element in the Christian life is its most essential characteristic, giving it both a new point of departure and a new spirit. The Christian life is not simply an advance on what went before, or a development of the past without any break in the continuity of human progress. At a moment when, as shown by the context, St. Paul's mind was filled with the thought of the glorified Redeemer, he thus describes it: " If any man be in Christ, he is a new creation : the old things are passed away ; behold, they are become new." [1] Twice in one verse he uses the word " new," and the word is not that which expresses the simple freshening of the old, but that which tells us that the object spoken of had been untried before.[2] The old things, indeed, are not destroyed ; they are only so transfigured that they may be spoken of as new. They remain, and we remain. But neither they nor we are any longer what we were. The animating principle of our life is new, and that principle makes all things new. The whole strain of the New Testament leads to the same conclusion. The Christian life is not grounded on or maintained by a Redeemer who was simply the purest and noblest of the human race. It is grounded on and maintained by One who entered this world by a miraculous birth ; who, after He had died, rose miraculously from the grave in which He had been buried ; who ascended in a miraculous manner to the right hand of the Majesty in the heavens ; and who, from His throne

[1] 2 Cor. v. 17.   [2] καινός.

there, sends His life-giving spirit to quicken miraculously into His own life the life of the members of His
Body.   All the most essential facts of Christianity are
directly and immediately Divine.   They may have
been contemplated, as we know that they were contemplated, from eternal ages.   They may have been
prepared for, as we know that they were prepared for,
by a world-wide training and discipline ; but, when
they occurred, it was by the interposition of God; and
the life founded upon them is also by His interposition.   It has a new beginning and a new spirit.
It is not the water of an old covenant cleansed
from the impurities that have become mingled with it
in the course of time.   It is wine, the new wine of our
Father's kingdom, so that Christians, while they are in
the world, are above the world, the springs of their
new being rising out of no earthly fountain, but out of
that fountain of perpetual life which is hid with Christ
in God.   There may be those who will reply to this,
Then there is no hope for the world ; the world will
never receive such teaching.   If it be so, there is no
help for it : the Church is not responsible for saving
the world ; she *is* responsible for holding up to the
world what is alone a real salvation ; if the world will
be ignorant, let it be ignorant.   Yet the reply may
be a mistake ; and, at all events the results of proceeding upon any other principle have not been
encouraging.

The Church of Christ, indeed, may well be warned
to hold fast the characteristic of her faith and life of

which we have been speaking. No error of the day is more subtle or pernicious in its effects than to suppose that our Lord may retain His value for humanity, and may constitute the Christian life in us, even when He has been divested of His Divine and super-earthly character, or that the life of His followers may be led without the constant inhabitation of His Divine as well as human Spirit. The logical conclusion from such views can only be that the sooner we get rid of Revelation and all the anxieties connected with it, the better. If by dealing with the human alone the highest ends of humanity may be reached, then let us deal with the human alone. We shall know where we are. We shall dismiss with a fresh enthusiasm the whole history of "the Christ" even upon earth as the product of superstition or fanaticism, and shall cast ourselves upon the history of the race and the laws of nature. It is true that the mystery of life will thus remain unsolved, that the hope of the future will perish, and that we shall be compelled to write folly, delusion, falsehood, and deceit upon everything that we have thought noblest and brightest, upon everything that has taught us how to live or suffer for others. But what will it matter? With no Divine around us and no eternity before us, there is but one other step to be taken; and then at last we shall be in the grave "where the wicked cease from troubling, and the weary are at rest."

From what has been said it will at once appear that under no circumstances whatever is the Church entitled to keep out of sight the Divine element of the Christian Revelation, in the hope that by presenting Christ merely in His human aspect she may gain an acceptance for Him that might otherwise be denied. Entrusted with a Gospel which has a glorified Lord for its central and characteristic fact, she is bound to proclaim a Divine Redeemer, and a present Divine life in Him. She is to " preach Christ Jesus as Lord." [1] She may not always, indeed, refuse her fellowship to good men who desire it, though they think themselves unable to receive all her testimony. The faith of such men is often deeper than it seems. But to one thing the Church is pledged, under the penalty of being regarded as faithless to her Lord. She must make clear to the world her own conviction that the Saviour whom she preaches and the kingdom which she establishes are Divine as well as human.

2. There is, secondly, the human element. The glorified Lord is human as well as Divine. Even at the right hand of God He is still the man Christ Jesus. The feelings, the emotions, the sympathies of His heart are exactly what they were when He welcomed the first symptoms of contrition in the woman who came to Him in Simon's house, or when He wept over the unbelief of Jerusalem. Even now He would leave no penitent uncheered, no mourner uncomforted, no friend unloved, no little child unblessed; and in all this He is the truly human as well as the Divine Priest of men.

But if it be so with the Head, it cannot be less so

[1] 2 Cor. iv. 5.

with those members of the Body whom the Head nourishes and guides. The Divine ought no more to obscure the human in them than the human the Divine; and, as the life of the glorified Lord, because the perfection of humanity, is the embodiment, not of the fantastically, but of the simply and naturally human, so the more the life of His people approaches perfection will it be simple and natural instead of constrained and unnatural. At the beginning of its course it may be otherwise. The armies of good and evil in the heart are then too equally balanced to give either the mastery, and there can be no truce between them. One must be expelled, and the expulsion is not yet effected. To the eye, therefore, which surveys the field it is no wonder that a strange and inconsistent scene presents itself; for now the one army is victorious, and now the other. Gradually, however, as the work of the Spirit goes on, the hosts of darkness are defeated, the Lord of Righteousness triumphs, and all is calm. With God Himself as the ruling principle in his nature, man is one. Then he becomes natural again.

Whatever is human also belongs to the Church of Christ, and is part of her inheritance. Scripture and history alike condemn the idea that Christianity narrows the thoughts of men, and that, under its sway, everything that adorns and beautifies human life— literature, poetry, painting, sculpture, architecture—is doomed to perish. So far is this from being the case that one of the first Beatitudes spoken by our Lord was, "Blessed are the meek: for they shall inherit *the earth* "; [1] and the last song of triumph sung by voices in heaven at the sounding of the seventh Trumpet is, "The kingdom of *the world* is become the kingdom of our Lord, and of His Christ." [2] It is, indeed, one of the greatest lessons of Scripture that in Christ Jesus "were all things created, in the heavens and upon the earth, things visible and invisible . . . all things were created through Him, and unto Him." [3] What, then, must be their relation to Him when they are redeemed, and when the creature is delivered from the bondage of corruption into the liberty of the glory of the children of God ? Can it be supposed that He by whom they have been brought into existence will be indifferent to any part of the work of His own hands, to any creature animate or inanimate, to any thought or vision, which has more or less partaken of the benefits of His redeeming work ? The teaching of history is not less conclusive. Not a few of the noblest conceptions of the human intellect belong pre-eminently to what are called the ages of faith ; and since that time the masterpieces of genius in every department of its labours have been penetrated by the influences which, in this respect, made these ages what they were. There is a fulness and richness in human life when it is connected with the thought of heaven and eternity which it cannot possess when confined to thoughts of earth and time. [4] And, if this is not always felt, it is in no small measure owing to those defective views of Christianity by which faith

---

[1] Matt. v. 5.   [2] Rev. xi. 15.   [3] Col. i. 16 ; comp. Lightfoot *in loc.*
[4] Comp. Bishop Webb, *The Tabernacle*, p. 35.

has been fixed too exclusively upon a past and humbled and dying, instead of being also fixed upon a present and exalted and living, Lord. The prayer of Jesus for His disciples was, " I pray not that Thou shouldest take them out of the world, but that Thou shouldest keep them out of the evil one." [1]

The Church of Christ, indeed, does not directly occupy herself with literature or science or art, and she would abjure her own special mission were she, in the hope of filling empty pews and stirring languid congregations, to change each house of God into a lecture-room, and each of her ministers into a lecturer on science popularised. It is no part of the charge entrusted to her that she shall discover, or that, having discovered, she shall proclaim, truths that can be reached by the natural force of the human mind. Whatever value she may attach, and she can hardly attach too much, to the smallest pebble gathered on the shore of truth's boundless and unfathomed sea, to gather pebbles of that kind is not her task. Enough for her that she has made men more fit for gathering them; that she has quickened their eyes to see and their ears to hear what might otherwise have been unseen and unheard in the universe around them; that she has taught men to consider every part of nature as the handiwork of God, so that they learn to feel that the leaf of a plant, or the wing of the smallest insect that lights upon it, is a study worthy of the highest powers and the most strenuous exertions. That is enough for the Church of Christ, and it is hers.

[1] John xvii. 15.

She has sent forth her sons into every field of nature, and she has welcomed them when they came back laden with spoils. Thus, then, it is that the heavenly life of Him in whom His people live elevates instead of destroying human things. Without it the inspiring thoughts which have found embodiment in word or form or colour, and which have filled generation after generation with awe and wonder, vanish away; and by the want of them life is not heightened but debased. Its silver becomes dross; its wine is mixed with water. If we wish to make it even a nobler possession than it is, there is nothing so fitted to effect this as to live under the practical conviction that our Lord in heaven desires his glorified humanity to be represented in the human lives of the members of His Body upon earth.

What has now been said is confirmed by one of the most striking declarations of our Lord Himself: "I came that they may have life, and may have abundance."[1] We have no right to limit the meaning of the word "life" in that declaration to spiritual or heavenly life. When Jesus uttered it the whole life of man as man was in His view. If the word "life" is often used in the fourth Gospel in a more limited sense, it is because other kinds and developments of life pass out of sight in the presence of that life on which the writer especially loves to dwell. The word itself has no such limitation of meaning; and, when used as here without anything to suggest limitation, it must be taken in its most comprehensive sense. In Christ was the

[1] John x. 10.

fountain of all life; and every form of life known or unknown, and every department of life, was only a drop of water from the stream which, gathered up in Him before, flowed forth at His command to people the universe of being with the endlessly multiplied and diversified existences that play their part in it.[1] When, therefore, our Lord exclaims that He came not only to give life, but to give abundance, we fail to do justice to His words unless we recognise in them a claim over everything that constitutes the life of man, over all learning and philosophy, over all literature and science, over every form of art, over every relation in which man stands in the family, the social circle, the community of the city or the state.[2] There is not one of these into which the breath of His life, Divine and human, is not to enter, which it is not to elevate and sanctify and bless.

3. A third element has still to be mentioned as pervading and animating the Church's life—that of self-sacrifice. Self-sacrifice is at once the result and the expression of that combination of the Divine and human elements which have just been spoken of. To empty oneself of Divine glory, and to assume and retain for ever the human lowliness, is itself self-sacrifice, which has thus a deeper place in the Christian system than we often permit ourselves to think. Why should there be self-sacrifice where there is no need for it? is an inquiry of many who keep

Heaven in their eye, and in their hand the keys.

---

[1] Comp. *Comm. on John* i. 3, 4, by Milligan and Moulton.

[2] Comp. Bishop Webb on *The Tabernacle*, p. 35.

Is it not to provoke the spirit of asceticism with all its wildest fruits ?   The Church's reply must be that without self-sacrifice she fails to enter into something so near to her Lord that it is involved in the very constitution of His Person.   To follow Him, to be like Him, to have the same mind in us that was in Him, is to learn to sacrifice ourselves for others, and without doing so we do not bear His cross.   No more need be said upon a point which has of late, and by so many voices of the prophets, been urged upon the Church.

Living, then, the life now spoken of, the Church of God is even in this world to repeat the life of her Head in another and a higher world. In one sense it is her own life, for in it the individuality and freedom of her members is preserved.   In another sense it is not her own ; it is her Lord's life in her, moulded upon what He is, imparted and sustained by Him, Divine because He is Divine, human because He is human, self-sacrificing because He sacrificed Himself; and these elements must be visible.   Men cannot be really touched by a life that is not seen to be human : they cannot be lifted above the world by a life that is not seen to be Divine.

This visible surrender of her life to God is the first duty of the Church, the first part of that representation of her Divine-human Head which she is to make.   In other words, it is the first part of her priestly offering to the Father, as she appropriates and reproduces the priestly offering of Him in whom she lives.   A priest

must of necessity have "somewhat to offer."[1] What
the Church offers is her life in her Lord's life.

These considerations ought to enable us to form a
clearer conception than we often have of the bond
between the thought of offering and the Eucharistic
Service of the Church. There can be no doubt that in
that service the idea of offering is more fully and forcibly
expressed than in any other Christian ordinance, or that
the Church has throughout all her history felt this to
be the case. With the exception of a comparatively
small number in recent times, her members have never
been able to rest in the idea that the Sacrament of the
Supper is simply a memorial of the death of Christ.
They have beheld in it, in one sense or another, an
offering which they make to God, as well as a remembrance of what God has done for them. They have felt,
to use the language of the Westminster Confession, that
it is an ordinance for "the further engagement of true
believers in and to all duties which they owe to the
Lord Jesus";[2] or that, in the words of the Larger
Catechism of the Presbyterian Church, "They that
worthily communicate, therein testify and renew their
engagement to God."[3] But the offering thus made in
the Eucharist is not an offering of death. That is
rather the Roman Mass, for the Mass is an "oblation
in which the thing offered is destroyed or otherwise
changed, in order to acknowledge the supreme dominion
of Almighty God over all His creatures, who, as He
made us out of nothing, can again destroy or change us

---

[1] Heb. viii. 3.   [2] Chap. xxix. 1.   [3] Qu. 168.

as He pleases." [1]   There is nothing of that kind here. The Eucharist is an oblation in which the offerer, offering himself, lives, having accepted death as the penalty of sin in Him who died upon the cross; but having now through death entered into life, the life of Him who died once, and dieth no more.   As our Lord's offering of Himself to His Heavenly Father never ends, or can end; so in that offering His people, organically united to Him, one with Him, must be offered, and must offer themselves; and this they do in the expressive and touching symbols of the Eucharist.   They do not simply remember what Jesus did on earth.   They bring to their remembrance as a present fact what He is doing in heaven.   They commemorate, they hold communion with, they accept, and at His Table are nourished by, a living Lord,—" in remembrance of *Me*," of Me, not as I was, but as I am, to the end of time.   Christ Himself, spiritually present with them, is the life of their souls; His body and blood there given them are the substance of their feast; and living in Him, and obtaining in Him pardon, peace, and strength, they transact here below what He is transacting in the heavenly Sanctuary.   In the Sacrament of the Supper, in short, they offer themselves in Him who is now and for ever an offering to the Father.

To return to our main line of thought.   So far as we have come little objection will probably be taken to anything that has been said.   But a most important aspect of the case here meets us, on which there may be

---

[1] Bishop Hay, *The Sincere Christian*, chap. xxii. 4.

more difference of opinion. The point seems to have
been hardly enough discussed in the Church; and what
is to be said ought to be regarded as rather suggesting
inquiry than as indicating positive or dogmatic conclusions.

The principle upon which we have proceeded is that
the offering of the Church on earth is the counterpart
of our Lord's offering of Himself in heaven. In that
offering, however, our Lord does not stand alone. He
does not simply surrender Himself to God in a life of
individual obedience, freedom, and joy. He surrenders
Himself for others, and with others in Him. He is the
Representative of His Church. He takes His Church
along with Him into His own blessed life. On the one
hand, as not less truly human than Divine, He carries out
the life of God in humanity to its utmost development
of glory and beauty. On the other hand, He has taken
His people into union with Himself. They are in Him.
They are partakers of His Spirit, and it is the aim of His
continued "Intercession" to make those who are already
ideally, more and more actually His; so that the Father
shall behold in them the many brethren of the elder
Brother. This, however, cannot be accomplished by a
merely legal act. Christ's people must offer themselves
in Him with a real and personal appropriation of such
a sacrifice as He made, of such labours and sufferings
as He endured, of such a death as that through which
He passed. Of this sacrifice, of these labours and
sufferings, of this death, the thought of enduring them
for others is an essential element; and there must,

therefore, be some sense in which a similar thought ought to have a place assigned to it in our conception of that Christian offering which is only Christian when it is made in Christ.

A little reflection, indeed, will be enough to satisfy us that we must suffer for others, if either salvation in any true sense of the word is to be ours, or if we are to produce that salutary effect on the world which ought to flow to it from the disciples of the Cross.

For, as regards the first of these two points, What, it may be asked, is salvation? Were it no more than pardon and heavenly happiness; or, even taking a higher view of it as likeness to the image of Christ, could that likeness be made really ours without a training or a discipline which can only gradually conform us to our ideal, self-sacrifice might not be needed. But salvation, as spoken of in Scripture, always implies deliverance from the power of evil, together with a re-creation within us of the Divine image; and this, according to the nature of man, cannot be effected without our passing experimentally through a process of dying unto sin and living unto God.[1] Now the root of sin is selfishness, and the essence of the Divine life is love. "God is love." Love is the fundamental conception of His being. It is that boundless crystal sea which contains within it all existence, and the privilege of being bathed in it is that which God desires to communicate to all His creatures. Love, moreover, cannot

---

[1] Even Christ "learned obedience by the things which He suffered" (Heb. v. 8).

be conceived of without the thought of others to share
what it has to bestow. We must therefore love others
if we are to know what "salvation" means; and in the
growing and perfecting of our love to others as well as
to God, our salvation grows and is perfected. Further,
when they to whom our love must flow forth, if we
have love at all, are sinful and rebellious against the
only true good; when they are ignorant of what their
real welfare is; or when, so far as they are dimly conscious of it, they are inclined to resist and to reject it;
when, too, they are involved, as is most frequently the
case, in misery that shocks our sensibilities, grieves our
hearts, and threatens to baffle all our efforts for its cure;
when their condition, in short, needs rectifying, and when
it cannot be rectified without pain, then love must assume the form of self-sacrifice. Without this it may be
a genuine pity or an empty sentiment, but it is not that
passion which is "strong as death," and which "many
waters cannot quench." To suffer for others is thus
not a burden laid in an arbitrary way upon the followers of Christ. Nor is it only a severe probation
through which they must pass that their affections may
be weaned from the present and directed to the future.
It is not even a mere duty imposed upon us by the
remembrance of Him who gave Himself for us, the just
for the unjust. That we shall suffer for others is implied in the very nature of a salvation adapted to man's
condition. It is part of the process. It is that experience in which our salvation is wrought out, that in
which we are brought nearest to the mind of God and

Christ; so that we may say with one who has recently written with great thoughtfulness upon pain and self-sacrifice, "If God would give us the last and greatest gift, that which above all others we might long for and aspire after, even though in despair, it is this that He must give us, the privilege He gave His son, to be used and sacrificed for the best and greatest end." [1]

Again, to look for a moment at the second of the two points spoken of above, self-sacrifice is not less necessary to those who would exert the salutary influence upon others that is both demanded and expected of the followers of Christ. Men must see suffering endured for their sakes if they are to own any power on the part of those who profess a desire to do them good. The spectacle of patient Christian suffering under ills directly inflicted by the hand of God may be a precious lesson to persons already within the pale of the Christian faith. It may be doubted whether it has much influence on the world. The world does not understand it. It may wonder, perhaps admire. Most probably it will treat the exhibition of such patience as something inexplicable, or as curiously illustrative of the delusions which men practise on themselves. If it is to acknowledge a right in the sufferers to speak to it, to warn it of error, or to demand its submission to views and ways different from its own, it must see more. To sacrifice ourselves for others, to bear for their sakes toil or want or privation or disappointment or sorrow, is, according to the laws of human nature, the necessary

[1] Hinton, *Mystery of Pain*, p. 17.

condition of touching their hearts and winning them to our side.

This necessity of suffering for others as our Lord suffered is taught in important passages of Scripture. How otherwise, for example, shall we explain the scene of the Foot-washing in the fourth Gospel? After that scene our Lord said to the disciples, "Know ye what I have done to you? Ye call me Master and Lord: and ye say well; for so I am. If I then, the Lord and the Master, have washed your feet; ye also ought to wash one another's feet. For I have given you an example, that ye also should do as I have done to you." [1] No one who has entered into the spirit of the fourth Gospel will for an instant suppose that we have here simply a lesson of humility and kindness. What had our Lord done to the disciples whom He was addressing? He had bathed them in His blood. He had taken them up into His own holy and blessed life. They were in Him; in Him their sins had been covered; they were united to Him, and in Him to God; they were "clean." But, clean though they were, they could not live in this world without soiling their feet. Sins and shortcomings would mark them every day, not, indeed, of so serious a kind as to destroy their interest in Christ, but enough to show that they stood in need of daily cleansing. In this their weakness, then, they were to offer for one another. In suffering and self-sacrifice they were to be victims for one another. The man strong to-day was to take up his weaker brother

[1] John xiii. 12-15.

into his life and to strengthen him. Weak himself to-morrow, he was to be taken up into the life of the man he had strengthened yesterday, and in him to obtain strength; until all, thus revived and completed by the communication of their brother's strength to make them strong, and of his life to make them live, were to be " clean every whit." This cleansing, then—not the ideal but the experimental cleansing; for Jesus had before said to them, " Ye are clean "[1]—was to be reached by offering, by self-sacrifice, by suffering for each other. Then the power of that sympathy and love, which were really Christ's Divine life flowing through them all, would change each other's sin into sinlessness, each other's imperfection into perfection, and each other's weakness into strength. To a similar effect is the language of St. Paul : " Now I rejoice in my sufferings for your sake, and fill up on my part that which is lacking of the afflictions of Christ in my flesh for His body's sake, which is the Church."[2] It is impossible to accept as satisfactory the explanations usually given of these words, for all of them are marked by the effort to distinguish between the sufferings of Christ and those of His people, whereas the obvious intention of the Apostle is, in one way or another, to identify them. St. Paul, indeed, would never have allowed that the suffer-ings of Christ lacked anything necessary to the full accomplishing of the purpose they were intended to effect. But that very purpose lay in this—that, as Christ Himself was perfected through suffering, so the

[1] Ver. 10.　　　　[2] Col. i. 24.

members of His Body might in Him be perfected, and might reach this perfection through suffering for their brethren's good. To introduce into the words of the Apostle a distinction between the sufferings of Christ as *satisfactoriae,* and in that sense *complete;* and as *aedificatoriae,* and in that sense *incomplete,* and needing to be supplemented,[1] is to introduce a thought which does not seem to have been in the Apostle's mind, and which is inconsistent with his desire to bring out a *similarity* between the sufferings of Christ and of His people. Even, indeed, when viewed as *satisfactoriae,* the sufferings of Christ may be said to be incomplete so long as His people are not associated with Him, for they were in Him when He suffered; and, had they not been in Him, His offering would have possessed only that character of a legal work—of a work to be outwardly imputed to man—which falls far short of the teaching of Scripture upon the point. The language of St. Paul, in the passage now before us, cannot be properly understood unless we behold in it the expression of the feeling that as the Head suffered for others, so also do the members of the Body. To idealise and consecrate for ever the law that "vicarious toil, pain, suffering, is the very warp of life"[2] was at least one great aim of the Redeemer in all that He did and suffered on our behalf; and as long, therefore, as there is sin or weakness for which to suffer—sin or weakness which can only be healed through the sufferings of

---

[1] Comp. Lightfoot on Col. i. 24.

[2] Westcott, *Victory of the Cross,* p. 24.

T

those who, in the spirit of their Master, try to heal it—the offering of Christ is not "filled up." Its final result is not attained, nor will it be attained until there shall be no more room for suffering on behalf of others; but both Head and members, penetrated by the same life, shall be presented to the Father in a perfected sanctification and in eternal joy.

Taking these considerations into account, we seem to be justified in asking whether the Church has not been too chary of allowing the idea of offering for others to be connected with her position and life. It is surely without sufficient cause that she has been afraid of encroaching on the one sacrifice of Christ, or of attributing to sinful men the possibility of making satisfaction for the sins of others. So long as the Church feels —what ceasing to feel she ceases to be the Church—that in her Lord alone is she accepted and complete, that her life is wholly in Him, and that she can do nothing except in the grace which He supplies, there can be no room in her mind for the thought of meritorious suffering. Such a thought can have no place when all that she does is her Lord's gift at first, and is afterwards maintained in Him, and in Him alone. Her suffering for others is simply the conveyance to them, through a life penetrated by the life of Christ, of the grace which flows from Him and leads to Him.

The life of the Church has been spoken of as pre-eminently the carrying forth on earth of the oblation-life of the heavenly High-priest. It may be added, in conclusion, that the weakness of the Church in our time is to be traced in no small measure to the fact that this conception of her position has been so faintly realised by her. For weak she is, and the endless statistical tables to which she appeals in evidence of her strength are not the least striking illustration of her weakness. When a man begins to count the pulses of his heart there is something wrong. So here. Christian activity may be great, but its root languishes. There is a want of the freshness, the buoyancy, the enthusiasm of earlier days. There is too much ease and self-indulgence in the Church's life. There is too little not of activity, but of that active ministry of love by which, in familiarity with suffering, the soul is trained to its highest moods and efforts. There is more than necessary thought of the earthly, less than necessary thought of the heavenly, good which the Church is both to seek for herself and to bestow on others. Even the conviction of thousands that Christianity offers a fairer tone of life than can be found elsewhere is not seldom rendered practically useless, because unaccompanied by the persuasion that it can only effect this end when it is seen to spring from a life beyond this life, from heaven and from God.

If it be so the remedy is clear. The Church must learn to give fuller scope to that ever new element of the Christian life which is supplied by the thought of a glorified Head and King living in closest connexion with her through each successive age, and able to meet each age's peculiar needs. Therein lies her power to convince the world that she is Divine. We talk of evidences of Christianity, and they have their value. They may satisfy historical inquirers, and they may meet intellectual difficulties. They will never make men Christians.[1] Nothing will do that except the recognition by those without that there is in those within the Church a brighter light, a higher life, than they have yet attained to; but which they feel, by the light and life within them, to be better, nobler, more worthy of pursuit, and more capable of producing happiness, than what they possess. If the poor, the suffering, the degraded, and the criminal do not behold in the Church as she exists before their eyes that which, by its nature, proclaims its Divine origin, we may spare ourselves the trouble of speaking to them of the Divine at all.

Nor will the Church attain her end by moderating her demands or toning down her life to something more on a level with the prejudices of the world. If by doing so she seems to be more successful than she would otherwise be, her success will only be superficial, shallow, and temporary, the prelude to a permanent and shameful defeat. The time is not long gone by when it was a common thing to encourage men to enter the mission-field by the promise of worldly comfort and short and easy service. An entirely different method is now adopted, and an attempt is made to win them by the thought of hard and, in this world, unrequited service. It is needless to say which of the two methods is the more Christian. We have reason to thank God

---

[1] "An age of apologetics has seldom been an age of spiritual power."—Young's *Fernley Lecture*, p. 10.

that the second has been the more successful.   As in the
mission-field abroad, so also with that at home.   The
Church's life, not her money, is there again her power.
"Thy money perish with thee" are words that she
ought rather to ring into the ears of not a few rich con-
tributors to her "Schemes."   We could dispense with
a few schemes; we want more inner life.   A tear, a
smile, a hand grasped in love, is often of more avail
than money.   Upon this point a complete revolution of
thought is needed ; and nothing will bring it about
except a profound conviction on the Church's part that
she has to represent her Lord among men, and that,
like Him, she is to do this by offering a Divine-human-
self-sacrificing life to the Father, for His glory and the
world's good.

LECTURE VI

THE glorified Lord in heaven is to be represented by His Church on earth ; and we have seen how this is to be effected by His people's life. We turn now to the second point proposed for consideration.

II. The glorified Lord is to be made manifest in His people's Work. At the right hand of the Father the Redeemer works; and, as His people are to represent Him in the world, they must represent Him not in life only, but in work. Their work also must be moulded upon His work, and more particularly upon that "Intercession" of His with the Father which consists, as we have seen, not in prayer alone, but in such a continuous and varied application of the blessings of redemption as may establish His Divine-human kingdom upon earth in all its completeness, strength, and beauty. One thing, however, the Church has to do which is not needed of her Lord. He is "perfected"; she is not. She has still to press on to the goal that has been already reached by Him ; and her work thus naturally divides itself into two great branches — first, for herself; and secondly, for the world.

1. The Church's work for herself. For it is a mistake to imagine that the activities of the Church are to bear only or even chiefly upon those who are beyond her pale; or that she has discharged her duty to her Lord when, by means of ministers, missionaries, and workers of many different kinds, she has become a centre of Christian action among men. She has another and still more imperative duty to perform — that of so building up, purifying, and adorning her own inner life that, in herself and by what she is, she may worthily represent that Redeemer who, in the combined perfection of His Divine and human natures, is ever before God, with His people in Him. But enough has been already said upon this point. What we have to think of now is the relation of the Church's Life and Work to one another.

Here it is of importance to remember that of the power by which the best work is done, character is always the highest and the noblest element. In that Sermon on the Mount in which our Lord unfolded the greatest mysteries of His kingdom, every one of the Beatitudes with which He begins has reference to character. For the activities of the Church there is no Beatitude. Our Lord would unquestionably have blessed these also in their proper place. Yet something more deserving of cultivation was to be first attended to; and not until the Beatitudes are ended do we read, "Neither do men light a lamp, and put it

under the bushel, but on the stand; and it shineth to
all that are in the house. Even so let your light (the
light of those in whom the Beatitudes are realised)
shine before men, that they may see your good works,
and glorify your Father which is in heaven." [1] Character
precedes power. The general teaching of the New
Testament is in conformity with this principle.

It was so in the case of our Lord Himself. When the
fourth Evangelist describes the deepest and most characteristic feature of His Person, it is in the words, " In
Him was life; and the life was the light of men " [2]—an
order of things which the Church of the present day
would be under a strong temptation to reverse. And
throughout the Gospel in which these words occur our
Lord Himself, in carrying on His work, continually
refers " the Jews" not so much to what He said as to
what they beheld in Him, for the manifestation of His
Father's glory and the revelation of His Father's will.

As with Him, so also with His disciples. The scene
of the Foot-washing, spoken of in the previous Lecture
for another purpose, is in this respect peculiarly instructive. Immediately connected with those parting
discourses by which the disciples were prepared for the
work before them, it comes first, not second, in the
transactions of the touching and memorable night when
it occurred. The disciples were to cleanse one another
before they proceeded to execute their task. It is
hardly necessary, however, to refer to particular passages. In the structure, strain, and spirit of every one

[1] Matt. v. 15, 16.   [2] John i. 4.

of its various parts the whole New Testament guides us to the same conclusion. Important as the sacred writers knew their message to the world to be, they never fail to exhibit the conviction that it was even more important to the churches; that, while they had no doubt to convert unbelievers, it was still more imperatively required that they should edify believers and carry them on unto perfection; and that the different members of the Body needed to be compacted into one, each working well in its own place, and all working smoothly together, before the Church could successfully accomplish her mission. Hence the exhortations to growth in every Christian grace with which the New Testament Epistles abound; hence the joy and thankfulness with which every manifestation of that growth was hailed by the Apostles and apostolic men who wrote them; hence the prominence continually assigned to that order of things which, embodying the precept of our Lord, first makes the tree good that its fruit may be good also; and hence, to take only one noteworthy example from the writings of St. Paul, when that Apostle tells us of the object which the ascended Lord had in view by the gift of His various ministries, the conversion of the world is not mentioned. Everything has relation to the Church. Apostles, Prophets, Evangelists, Pastors, and Teachers are given " for the perfecting of the saints, unto the work of ministering, unto the building up of the body of Christ: till we all attain unto the unity of the faith, and of the knowledge of the Son of God, unto a full-grown man, unto the

measure of the stature of the fulness of Christ . . .
from whom all the body fitly framed and knit together
. . . maketh the increase of the body unto the building
up of itself in love." [1]

The lesson taught by passages such as these had been
also taught by type and figure under the Old Testament
dispensation. The Golden Candlestick of the Tabernacle was, as we learn from the Apostle John, an em-
blem of the Church as well as of the Church's Head; [2]
and it was not the least interesting arrangement
connected with it that not only would its lamps appear
to have burned by night when no work needed to be done
within the sanctuary, but that the wicks of the lamps
were so trimmed towards the stem of the candlestick as
to throw their light upon it rather than into the surrounding space. Each lamp, to whichever side of the
candlestick it was attached, had the same commission as
its fellow-lamps, and all were to mingle their rays around
that elaborately wrought stem, the gold and knops and
flowers of which were seldom under any other eye than
that of God! What a lesson for the Church! Why shall
she concern herself so exclusively as she does about shining for the world's good? Why not shine for the sake of
shining, and without thinking of the world? Why not
send up songs in the night although there be no ear of man
to hear? Why not clothe herself in her bridal garments
although there be no eye of man to see? The Lord
Jesus Christ is the Bridegroom of the Church. Can
the Church be wrong in often thinking exclusively of

[1] Eph. iv. 11-16.   [2] Rev. i. 20.

Him, of the duty that she owes Him, and of the manner in which she can increase His happiness? Can there be either error or sin should lamp often shine on lamp, church on church, congregation on congregation, Christian on Christian, as if there were no one in the world but themselves? as if they had simply to rejoice in each other's beams, to heighten each other's brilliancy, and to create a larger, purer, sweeter body of light than there would otherwise be for God alone?

Thus it was in the bright dawn of the Church's history, when all that believed continued steadfastly with one accord in the temple, and, breaking bread at home, did take their food with gladness and singleness of heart, praising God and having favour with all the people. The infant community was not thinking then —it had, indeed, had no time to think—of anything beyond itself; but the Lord added to it day by day those that were being saved.[1] We need a revival of this spirit in our day. If, on the one side, the activities of the Church seem to increase her strength; on the other side, these very activities, by engrossing almost all her thoughts, are wearing her down to the level of the world, and thinning the heavenly life-blood by which alone she can be sustained. We have too little of the spirit of devotion, of meditation, and of prayer. Multitudes are ready to speak for Christ, or to sacrifice themselves in labouring for His cause. But the utterances are too few that come from sitting at His feet or leaning on His breast. Both the Church and the

[1] Acts ii. 46, 47.

world are the poorer for this. The home is not all that it should be when our attention is fixed mainly on the busy Martha. More even than of her ought we to think of Mary, who has chosen "the good part that shall not be taken away from her."[1]

Would that the different branches of the Christian Church could see this more clearly than they do! The late Dr. Arnold of Rugby said, "If half the energy and resources which have been turned to Bible Societies and Missions had steadily been applied to the reform of our own institutions, and the enforcing the principles of the Gospel among ourselves, I cannot but think that we should have been fulfilling a higher duty, and with the blessing of God might have produced a more satisfactory fruit."[2] Dr. Arnold did not, in thus speaking, undervalue either Bible Societies or Missionary exertions. But he felt that these, however earnest, depended for their strength upon a prior element—the vigour and purity and depth of the Divine life out of which they spring. What was true then is not less true now, when outward agencies have been indefinitely multiplied, and thousands are unceasingly endeavouring to discover what new agencies they can bring into the field. Let them do so, and may God prosper every genuine and wise effort of the kind. But, beyond and above them all, it is the primary duty of the Church to ask herself whether she *is* what she ought to be. Is she sufficiently "one, holy, Catholic, and apostolic"? Is she manifesting to men, as the chief features of her

[1] Luke x. 42.   [2] Letter to Rev. J. Tucker in 1826.

condition, to strike and win them, those beauties of holiness which sparkle like the dewdrops of the morning? To these things, more than to all Bible Societies and Missions to the heathen, the Church needs in the first instance to direct her thoughts. We may plant new churches both at home and abroad; we may gather increasing funds; we may employ fresh agencies till each sex and age and profession and condition of life has its special religious provision made for it; and we may be encouraged by the hopes and prayers of thousands of humble followers of Christ, who, amidst all discouragement, console themselves with the reflection that such efforts cannot be in vain. It is very touching and very beautiful; and doubtless the efforts are not in vain. But the result is trifling in comparison; and it will and must remain so until the Church sees more distinctly than she does that she herself, and not her work, is the great Mission to the world, and until she spares neither labour nor sacrifice to exhibit a more perfect representation of that Divine life and love without which all she either does or suffers, or tells of her doing and suffering, is no more than "sounding brass or a clanging cymbal." To her the conversion of the world has certainly been committed, but only to her while she reveals herself to it as the Bride of Christ. "Put on thy beautiful garments, O Jerusalem, the holy city." [1]

2. The Church's work for the world. The true rule, as we have seen, is, First be, then do. But the Church is not to delay doing. Her doing will even react upon

---

[1] Isa. lii. 1.

her being. So essentially is action involved in the
nature of her calling that, just as the discharge of every
separate function of the natural body tends to the
strengthening of the whole body, so Christian action in
any department strengthens life, even while it cannot
be efficient unless it springs from life.   St. Paul proceeded upon this principle when he commended the
Corinthian Christians, because they "first gave their
own selves to the Lord," and then "to him by the will
of God";[1] and when again, in exhorting the Philippians
to the cultivation of whatsoever things are true, or
honourable, or just, or pure, or lovely, or of good report,
he enjoined them first to "think" of these things, and
then to "do" them.[2]   After the "thinking" the "doing,"
and that both as to its matter and its manner.

For (1) as to its matter, the Church has to represent
her glorified Lord by carrying out, as His representative, the work of which He laid the foundation when He
was on earth.   It is true that He is now in heaven, and
that she represents Him glorified as well as Incarnate.
But that does not alter the character of her work ; it
simply increases her power in prosecuting it.   It gives
her a more elevated spirit, and more confident assurance
of success.   Whatever belongs, therefore, to the idea of
priestly work, belongs to her commission ; and a fundamental conception of that work is service of man—the
service of humility, gentleness, meekness, love, and
self-sacrifice.   Men tell us that it has not always been
so when the priestly idea has been rampant.   They bid

[1] 2 Cor. viii. 5.   [2] Phil. iv. 8, 9.

us look back upon the past that we may see there what
a Church calling herself a priestly Church became—
proud instead of humble, cruel instead of tender, selfish
instead of loving.   The charge cannot be denied ; and
from some sides of the picture the mind shrinks with
dismay and horror.   But there are other sides of the
picture to be kept in view when we endeavour to form
a general and impartial judgment.   Protestants have no
interest in denying the good that was done even by a
corrupt and worldly Church during the centuries of her
undisputed sway.   They can have no pleasure in believing that darkness then covered the earth, or that
selfishness ruled instead of love.   And, after all, the
picture when really studied is far from being one only
of gloom.   There was light in the midst of darkness,
and love in the midst of selfishness.   The secular world
then consisted for the most part of tyrants on their
thrones, and of fierce, reckless, lawless barons in their
castles.   The poor were ground to the dust by brutal
authority against which they had no protection from
the State.   They found protection in the Church.   In
her, notwithstanding all abuses, there was law, order,
mercy, charity ; and when men and women, weary of
the corruptions and abominations around them, sought
rest, they found it in her bosom.   There was help in her
for woes for which there was otherwise no helper ; and
when monks and nuns gave bread to the hungry, water
to the thirsty, and clothing to the naked ; when they
visited the sick man upon his bed of languishing, and
the prisoner in his loathsome dungeon, and told of **One**

who had loved His people even unto death, and of a
Church which was still His messenger upon earth for
works such as He had done, the hungry and the thirsty,
and the naked and the sick, and the prisoner, touched
by the living hand, moved by the living voice, looked
up and said, " We believe in the love of Him whose
love is taught us by your love, whose pity by your pity."
The representative of the dying, living Lord was fulfilling her commission, and the fruits appeared.

This was priestliness, that priestliness about which
so much is spoken without thought as to the real
meaning of the word.   Whatever may advance the
welfare of our fellow-creatures falls within its sphere of
operation, subject only to the condition that it exhibit
the spirit of a Master, not merely as He was on earth,
but as He is in heaven, spiritual and glorified.   When
the Church keeps this in view there is no human want
or weakness strange to her.   It is her part to heal every
wound and to wipe away every tear.

Of the amount of harm done by forgetfulness of this
truth it would be difficult to speak aright.   Both at
home and abroad ministers and missionaries are not
unfrequently driven by force of circumstances to make
the material welfare of those among whom they labour
one of the first objects of their regard.   On the mission-
field they have to teach men to plough, to sow, to reap,
to build, to clothe themselves, to read and write and
cipher.   At home they have to arouse a feeling on
behalf of elementary education, and light, and air, and
cleanliness, and efficient drainage.   They are apt to

enter upon all this work, questioning whether they are justified in doing it; while, on the other hand, multitudes around them cry, "Now, we understand and value you; this is practically to promote human welfare, and is far better adapted to human needs than what is called Preaching the Gospel." The workers may dismiss their hesitation. The patronisers of their work may withhold their compliments. When work of this kind is done from the Christian motive, and is animated by the Christian spirit, it is a preaching of the Gospel. Our High-priest in heaven—"the same yesterday, to-day, and for ever"—healed the sick and fed the hungry multitudes. He would do the same thing now through His people, as they carry on His priestly work. In His name they are still to help, strengthen, and comfort all. They are to find their joy in taking upon them the sorrows of others; in dying for others they are to live. A heavy responsibility has been incurred by those who have presented to men a different idea of priestliness. A no less heavy responsibility is incurred by those who disown the term because they say it has a different meaning.

The remarks now made apply with peculiar emphasis to the mission-field. To no part of their work are the thoughts of Christian men more earnestly turned at this moment than to that which bids them "go and make disciples of all the nations."[1] It cannot surprise us that it should be so, for the world is waiting to be christianised. The cry for help is heard from the darkest continents and the remotest islands of the sea;

[1] Matt. xxviii. 19.

U

while the taunts of the scoffer have been almost silenced
by the self-sacrificing lives and martyr deaths of many
devoted missionaries. The question is rising from innumerable lips, How shall we best advance the cause of
Missions? The true answer is by the Church's more
fully realising her relation to all human wants; in other
words, more fully realising her call to be the priesthood
of humanity. No lower thought, no thought of the
conversion of individual souls in one place or another,
will maintain the missionary spirit at its proper height,
or will clothe it with its appropriate power. The
Church must be animated by the belief that she is elect
not for her own sake, but for the world's; and that her
life is to be a priestly life, in the name of the Heavenly
Father, for the spreading of that "kingdom" which,
bringing men to God, brings them also to one another,
and lifts them into that ideal sphere of the holy, the
beautiful, and the loving which is as yet consummated
only in the Great High-priest in heaven. To the
missionary spirit "duty and reason and warm human
sympathies yield each their contributory native energy;
but more constraining than these, because more deeply
seated, is the sense of a personal identification with that
which impels towards a transcendent ideal, a vast
Unknown of God's embracing love as the historical
destiny of men.

> " For we spin the lives of men,
> And not of gods, and know not why we spin.
> There is a fate beyond us." [1]

---

[1] From a thoughtful paper on "The Missionary Appeal" in the

This "historical destiny" of the human race is but another expression for the Biblical idea, "The Tabernacle of God is with men";[1] and in that Tabernacle, wide as the world, and with its veil rent from top to bottom, the whole Church, when alive to her vocation, is to stand a ministering priesthood; until, in the most extended sense of the term, "all Israel shall be saved."

(2.) In connexion with the point before us the manner as well as the matter of the Church's work demands a moment's notice, for in the glorified Lord we see what the one no less than the other ought to be. Even upon earth our Lord paid supreme regard in what He did to the means as well as the end; and His Temptation in the wilderness, in the different parts of which were summed up all the trials of His approaching work, is in this respect peculiarly instructive. The third temptation in particular, in which Satan showed Him all the kingdoms of the world, and promised that they should be His if He would only fall down and worship him, was essentially a temptation to despise the means if He might secure the end. It was the greatest temptation of the three, and one which, yielded to by the Church in after times, has done more harm to the cause of Christ than all the efforts of her adversaries. Yet our Lord repelled it with indignant scorn, "Get thee behind Me, Satan: for it is written, Thou shalt worship the Lord thy God, and Him only shalt thou serve."[2]

Church Quarterly Review for July 1890. Comp. also *The Priesthood of the Laity*, by Bishop Webb, a small book full of valuable instruction.   [1] Rev. xxi. 3.   [2] Matt. iv. 10.

Were the means impure, the kingdom established through them would be impure also; were they of the earth, the kingdom could not be heavenly.   The lesson is needed now; for there are methods, too often resorted to by persons both clerical and lay, who from their position cannot fail to represent the Church, which have little correspondence with either the Person or the Work of the Church's glorified Head in heaven.   The sensational advertisement; the vulgar coarseness of not a little pulpit language; the appeals to sinful vanity or pride, for the purpose of forcing money out of the pockets of the miserly; the dexterous management by which godless patrons are obtained to countenance religious meetings —these and many devices of a similar kind are not the way to make a Christian impression on the world. They rather render any true conception of Christianity impossible.   They poison Christian growth at its very root.   They make truth a lie.   The Church of Christ will never accomplish her object by such means.

Apart, however, from all thought of methods of this kind, which would be unworthy of notice were they not so common, the point before us throws light upon the only means by which the Church can make a deep impression on the poor and outcast.   She is to represent the personal Redeemer.   How can she do it except through the persons and the personal exertions of her members?   We talk of salvation through a preached Gospel, but we have no right to expect the result of preaching from the outward word alone, apart from the living personality of those who utter it.   It is the living word, the Gospel as it comes in love from the loving heart, that speaks with power. We need not under-value great schemes of Christian benevolence. Love may proclaim itself from the platform, and vast assem-blies may be moved to tears and liberality. But the true work of love is personal. " Love suffereth long, and is kind ; love envieth not ; love vaunteth not itself, is not puffed up, doth not behave itself unseemly, seeketh not its own, is not easily provoked, taketh not account of evil ; rejoiceth not in unrighteousness, but rejoiceth with the truth ; beareth all things, believeth all things, hopeth all things, endureth all things." [1] Such love must be the soul of any work that is to leave a deep impression behind it, or in the spirit of our Lord to secure His end. Tears stirred in any other way will soon be dried, and a tide of liberality flowing from any other influence will soon ebb.

From the thought of the work of the glorified Lord, therefore, it would seem that many branches at least of the Church of Christ have a lesson to learn in our day which, when learned, may be the means of introduc-ing a new era in their history. Let us be thankful that they are learning it. Their brotherhoods, their sisterhoods, their " settlements," the dwelling of their ministers amongst the poor, the daily personal contact with hearts often more sad than wicked, or often sad-dest in their wickedness, the labours unseen by human eye, the sacrifices uncomplained of by those who make them—these and other efforts devised by the spirit of

[1] 1 Cor. xiii. 4-7.

faith and love are producing, and will produce, an effect, the extent of which we cannot as yet measure. While we guard against their abuse, let them grow. They have the thought of the personal Redeemer and the experience of many Christian centuries to commend them to our regard. They are an approach to the idea of the priesthood of the Church.

III. The glorified Lord is to be manifested in the Worship of His people. We can no more conceive of the Church without worship than without life or work. In nothing do Christian men find more necessary or suitable expression for their feelings. By nothing do they exercise a more powerful influence on the world. Let any branch of the Christian Church make the subject one of careful inquiry, with a view to the improvement of her worship, should improvement be thought necessary, and in doing so she takes a step that will certainly be followed by the most momentous consequences.[1] When, accordingly, we ask how the Ascended Saviour is to manifest His glory in His people, and by means of them to carry on His work on earth, the thought of the Worship of the Church immediately forces itself upon us. What are the principles upon which it rests? and What is the spirit which ought to mark it? The answer to the second question depends upon the answer to the first. In making this inquiry, too, it would be foolish to forget the lessons of Christian history, or to aim at the construction of theories

[1] This step was taken by the General Assembly of the Church of Scotland in 1889. The inquiry continues.

founded upon our own conceptions of man's religious need, and of the manner in which Christianity may be best applied to it. The Christian Church has worshipped, and has maintained her life by worship, for nearly nineteen centuries. During that long period we may rest assured that, under the influence of the Spirit, she has come to clearer conceptions of what her worship means, has eliminated mistakes, supplied deficiencies, and done much to shape her offices of devotion into a harmonious and consistent whole. When, therefore, we endeavour to ascertain the principles by which she has been guided in the construction and arrangement of her worship, our appeal must be less to abstract theory than to theory illustrated and enforced by historical fact. In making such an appeal several important considerations meet us; and all of them will be found to lead up to the exalted and glorified Lord.

1. The worship of the Church has always been and must be a common worship. There is no doubt a worship of the closet which is the Christian's "vital breath" and "native air," and without which the spiritual life cannot be maintained in health and vigour. There is also a worship of the family, arising out of those sanctified family affections which cannot tolerate the thought that any member of the home-circle shall be missed from the family in heaven.[1] Both these forms of worship the Church of Christ approves of and inculcates as most necessary and binding duties upon

---

[1] Comp. Lightfoot's remarks on the hallowing of Family life by the Gospel, *Comm. on Philippians*, Introd. p. 56.

every Christian man and Christian family. But neither the one nor the other, nor both together, are enough. Christians need a common worship. They are the Body of Christ; and only in that capacity can they either perform the functions of the Body, or enjoy the privileges which flow through the Body as a whole to its separate parts. They are not merely individual personalities, each having its own distinct line of connexion with the Head. They are sharers of a common life, and are united to one another by a bond similar to that which unites them to their Lord, and in their Lord to the Father of all. One of the truths most strenuously insisted on throughout the whole of the first Epistle of St. John is this, that only in the fellowship of Christian men with one another is their Christian standing realised and perfected : " That which we have seen and heard declare we unto you, that ye also may have fellowship with us "; " He that loveth his brother abideth in the light, and there is none occasion of stumbling in him " ; "Beloved, let us love one another : for love is of God ; and every one that loveth is begotten of God, and knoweth God." [1] From the beginning to the end of the Epistle the same strain of thought prevails. It is not in the fellowship of Christ alone that we fully occupy our Christian position. There must be added to this the fellowship of the saints. The latter as well as the former is necessary to the unfolding and perfecting of the Divine life within us.

If so, that common worship, which is as much the

[1] John i. 3, ii. 10, iv. 7 ; comp. also i. 7, iv. 11, 12, 21.

expression of common life as individual worship is of
individual life, is binding upon every Christian. It
depends in the first and highest instance upon no
thought of benefit received or to be received, but upon
the fact that, as Head of the Body, the Redeemer does
not stand alone. He has taken up all His people into
Himself, and His glory cannot be thought of without
them. Through them and in them He fills all things.[1]
Apart from them He has not that fulness, that fulfilling,
of all which was from eternity the predestined consummation of His Mediatorial Being.

The social element is thus as deeply involved in any
correct conception of Christ Himself the glorified Lord
as the individual element. We do not make it: it is
made for us. We cannot dissolve it without, in separating ourselves from the Body, also separating ourselves
from the Head, which acts through the Body. Just as
without the individual element there is no individual
life, so without the social element life, cut off from the
channel through which the grace of the Head penetrates
to every member, languishes and dies.

Nor is this to maintain in any objectionable sense
the proposition so frequently branded as narrow and
offensive, *Extra ecclesiam nulla salus.* It is only to
maintain that beyond the Church there can be no *salus,*
no salvation, worthy of the name. If that word means
simply escape from condemnation, it is impossible to say
by how many forms of a stunted or eccentric Christianity
salvation may be reached. It is even impossible to

---

[1] Eph. i. 23.

say whether it may not be reached without a conscious Christianity at all. But, if we interpret the word in its true and proper sense, as conformity to the will of God, to the example of Christ, and to the inheritance of heaven ; if we understand by it the redeemed life ideally perfected in the soul, then it may be truly urged that to such salvation communion with the Church is absolutely required. Only in fellowship with men can the human character be developed into the strength and harmony which it may naturally attain ; and any sound principle of nature is not less sound in grace.

Were there time to discuss the question, it might be shown that the considerations now adduced afford the only sure ground upon which to vindicate at least the partial use of prescribed forms of prayer in the public services of the Church. No argument against extemporaneous prayer can be safely rested either on the confusion of thought or tastelessness of expression by which it is too often marked, or on the need which the officiating minister has of help in the performance of his duties. Where such defects exist they may be corrected by increased spirituality of heart or by the study of the best models of devotion ; while a minister must be ready to bear any burden belonging to his office. But extemporaneous prayer, however tasteful, and however it may proceed from the most fervent spirit of devotion, can never be the Church's voice. We can never hear in it those common utterances that, sanctified by centuries of Christian usage, proclaim the faith and hope and love of ten thousand times ten thousand souls, which, amidst all the varieties of their outward condition, have been really one.

2. The worship of the Church is designed in the first instance to promote the glory of God rather than to procure benefits for His worshippers. This is, indeed, the mission of universal nature, and nature fulfils her mission. "The heavens declare the glory of God, and the firmament showeth forth His handiwork."[1] The sun and moon and stars, the multitude of the heavenly bodies, the unnumbered creatures that people earth and sea and air, the mountains and the valleys, the rivers and fountains of waters, the trees of the forest, the flowers of the garden, and the grasses of the field, with one voice proclaim His praise.[2] Amidst this general song man cannot alone be silent; and least of all man redeemed, taught to know God as a Father, and to look forward to heaven as a home. He must take his part in the universal choir. Even when he would ask no favour, when he would utter no want, when he would tell no tale of sorrow into a sympathetic ear, he must praise. "Let them praise the name of the Lord; for His name alone is exalted : His glory is above the earth and heaven. He also exalteth the horn of His people, the praise of all His saints; even of the children of Israel, a people near unto Him. Praise ye the Lord."[3]

If this be the spirit of Old Testament worship, the same spirit, though in a still higher degree, ought to mark the worship of the New Testament. And it does so. Upon this point the Revelation of St. John affords

---

[1] Ps. xix. 1.   [2] Comp. Ps. cxlviii.   [3] Ps. cxlviii. 13, 14.

us peculiar guidance. The worship there set before us is penetrated throughout by the thought of magnifying the name of God and of the Lamb for what they themselves are in all the glory of their perfections and works. In that book the four living creatures, representing redeemed creation, are introduced to us as having no rest day or night, saying, " Holy, holy, holy, is the Lord,— God, the Almighty, which was and which is and which is to come " ; and they are immediately followed by the four and twenty elders, who fall down to worship Him that sitteth on the throne, casting their crowns before the throne, and saying, " Worthy art Thou, our Lord and our God, to receive the glory and the honour and the power; for Thou didst create all things ; and because of Thy will they were, and were created." [1]   Nor is this all ; for no sooner has the sealed book been opened by the Lamb than a new note is struck, the note of redemption, but still in praise ; until gradually the song extends from the four living creatures and the four and twenty elders to the ten thousand times ten thousand and thousands of thousands of angels round about the throne ; and from them to " every created thing which is in the heaven and on the earth, and under the earth, and on the sea, and all things that are in them,"—all of which, now brought into the liberty of the glory of the children of God, unite in saying, " Unto Him that sitteth upon the throne, and unto the Lamb, be the blessing, and the honour, and the glory, and the dominion, for ever and ever." [2]   In scenes like these, whatever may be the

[1] Rev. iv.   [2] Rev. v.

peace, the joy, and the triumph of those who thus
praise God, it is not so much of themselves that they
think as of Him from whom flow all their blessings.

This, accordingly, has been the spirit of the Church,
in so far as she has expressed it in her Service-books,
throughout all her history. "Lift up your hearts unto
the Lord"; "We have lifted them up unto the Lord."
The low dull tone so often marking our Public Worship
has never been the tone of any Christian liturgy. Nothing strikes one sooner in the old Service-books than
the absence of confessions except on special days or
seasons of repentance. The service of the Church was
almost exclusively joyous. Her worship consisted
nearly altogether of Psalms, the Lord's Prayer, the
Creed (itself a Psalm)—

> Creed of the saints and
> Anthem of the blest—

a few versicles, a few Collects, the lections from Scripture, and these interspersed with anthems, responsories,
and hymns. It was one chant, culminating in the
Eucharist, the peculiar sacrifice of thanksgiving. It
was one effort to set forth "God's most worthy praise,"
when the Church forgot for the moment her own
necessities in contemplating the love which passeth
knowledge.

Here again, accordingly, we are led to the thought
of the glorified Redeemer. His life on earth was praise;
and when, in the Epistle to the Hebrews, the sacred
writer brings Him before us "crowned with glory and

honour," surrounded by His people, it is in the words of the Psalmist, "In the midst of the congregation will I sing Thy praise."[1] Suffering from many weaknesses and trials, the Church on earth has much to ask for. Even in heaven she will have constant need of that prayer which is the longing of her heart after the fountain of all goodness and beauty. But the first thought which she associates with Him in whom she stands is praise; and the more fully the Spirit of her Lord becomes her Spirit, the more must she feel that the keynote of her worship is not prayer for blessings needed in the future, but adoration and thanksgiving for those that have been made hers already.

3. The worship of the Church is primarily, and it has been historically, intended for the edification of saints rather than the conversion of sinners. Not to convert the world did Christians of old gather together in private chambers, or catacombs, or dens of the earth, or basilicas, or cathedrals, or parish churches, but to strengthen their own faith, to deepen their own convictions, and to enjoy the consolations provided for them amidst their trials. In very ancient times the place of preaching to the unconverted was even *outside* the Church, in the *narthex* or *atrium;* and hence St. Ambrose shut the doors of his church against Theodosius.[2] The principle has been too frequently lost sight of; many think too little of it even now. Multitudes regard the Christian

[1] Heb. ii. 12; Ps. xxii. 23.

[2] See an excellent paper on "The Principles of Christian Worship in the *Transactions of the Aberdeen Ecclesiological Society* for 1887, by the Rev. James Cooper of that city,

sanctuary as a place in which, if they have not to be converted, they have at the best simply to receive instruction. It does not occur to them that there is something strange in receiving the same instruction for fifty years, or even for a lifetime, in " ever learning, yet never being able to come to the knowledge of the truth."[1]

No doubt there is a certain amount of truth in this view of Christian worship. In every Christian congregation some are to be found who, though baptized, have practically fallen away from Christ, and who may be led by the services in which they take part to repentance and faith, while even the true members of Christ have in many ways to be edified and comforted by the preacher's words. Yet surely the conversion of men is not the chief thing aimed at in Christian assemblies. In no proper sense does such an aim express the idea of the Church. It is the idea of a mission to the heathen. Were the members of any Church in a condition of heathenism ; were the ministers who guide their worship missionaries to the heathen, the conception would be right. Such, however, is not the case. By the very fact of their coming together as they do, and prior to their doing so, both ministers and people are supposed to be one in Christ ; and their common function is to help one another to a deeper understanding of their Lord, and to bestow upon one another some gift of mutual faith.[2] In this lies the fundamental idea of their meeting as they do, and it is of no moment to them whether any part of the world is present with

---

[1] 2 Tim. iii. 7.   [2] Comp. Rom. i. 12.

them or not. Better, perhaps, if the world is absent. They may then be more unrestrained, more at ease, less liable to the chill which threatens to paralyse the heart when its emotions are certain to be misunderstood by those who witness them.[1]

Our Lord Himself appears to have felt thus at the institution of the Supper; for, as the Evangelist reports the scene, "When *therefore* Judas was gone out, Jesus saith, Now is the Son of man glorified";[2] after which He proceeded to pour forth upon His disciples, in a way previously unexampled, the fulness of His love. The conclusion is irresistible. The worship of the Church is the expression of Christian feeling for the edification of Christian men.

4. The Worship of the Church must express itself, as it has always expressed itself, in form. We are to serve God as men, with our whole nature, and not merely with a part of it. To say, therefore, that we will serve Him in spirit, though not in outward acts embodying that spirit, is to refuse to Him one great

---

[1] It is well known that the feeling of the Ancient Church did not allow her to go on to the celebration of the Eucharist till the heathen, and even the cate-chumens, had been sent out. The principle is to be found in our Lord's words in Matt. vii. 6. His example has been spoken of in the text.

Where the ancient Liturgies are used, the deacon still bids the catechumens depart, and it is generally allowed that the Mass has its name from a proclamation of the kind — in the Latin rite *ite, missa est.* The Mass followed that dismissal. Our children in Scotland remain in church dur-ing the celebration of the Supper, because they are not strangers. Those also are not strangers who, though they may not communi-cate on the special occasion, do communicate on other occasions or at other hours.

[2] John xiii.

part of the being which He has given us, and all of which He claims. Nature herself thus becomes our teacher as to the necessity, and even in some respects as to the regulation, of religious forms. And St. Paul recognised this when, referring to a disputed ceremonial at Corinth, he said, "Doth not even nature itself teach you"?[1] In Christian Worship, accordingly, as in all other worship, there has always been more or less form, ceremonial, ritual ; and it could not possibly have been otherwise. The instinct of the human heart was sufficient to be, so far at least, the Church's guide.

But the main principle, at once justifying and demanding form in the worship of the Christian Church, is the fact upon which her very existence rests—that of the Incarnation. Whether we think of our Lord's existence upon earth or of His glorified condition in heaven, the Incarnation involves as a fundamental verity that the outward, the formal, and the visible are the complements, not the opposites, of the inward, the spiritual, and the invisible. So far are the latter from losing their essential character when they pass into the former, that then only do they reach a stage in complete correspondence with our human condition. We may make them opposites. In the weakness of the flesh we may substitute the one for the other ; and the experience of many Christian centuries has warned us of this danger ; but the danger does not lie wholly in that one direction. It has also shown itself in an exclusive devotion to the spiritual in its narrower sense ; and, if

[1] 1 Cor. xi. 14.

X

consequences as fatal to the Church's life have not followed, it is probably because the last-mentioned tendency has been that of the few and, as such, checked by that of the vast majority of Christians.[1] In themselves the logical consequences of either error are equally dangerous and equally near. The duty of Christian men, therefore, is to guard against both errors, and only by recognising the claims of the outward as well as the inward can they be preserved from both. The *body* as well as the spirit of man has been for ever consecrated by Him who took to Himself a "true body" as well as a "reasonable soul," and who still retains the one not less than the other, even in that estate of glory in which man's nature has been for ever perfected. Outward worship is thus not something either devised by man or bestowed by God, in order that spiritual religion may be helped onward to perfection. It is an essential part of spiritual religion in its highest sense.

The appeal made to us by every flower of the field may thus with equal propriety be made by every well-considered arrangement of the sanctuary. In admiring the colours of the lily we may forget Him who has arrayed it with a greater glory than the robes of Solomon. Would we have remembered Him more if the glory had been less? The whole question as to the amount of form appropriate to the services of the Church is one to be determined by a Christian wisdom which remembers both that national temperaments

---

[1] Comp. Dorner, *System of Christian Doctrine*, iv. 153.

differ, and that what is suitable to men or congregations at one stage of progress is not always suitable to them at another. We may easily have too much ritual, but one thing we ought never to forget, that the spiritual is not secured by its absence, and that the carnal is not necessarily connected with its presence. As man the Lord Jesus Christ has consecrated ritual. As man exalted and glorified He has not less consecrated such elements of dignity, beauty, and glory as, appearing in it, may fittingly express these characteristics of His own exalted state.

We have seen that the worship of the Christian Church must be common worship; that its leading idea is the glory of God; that it is designed for the edification of believers rather than the conversion of unbelievers; and that it must find utterance in appropriate forms. But these general considerations, however important in themselves, only prepare the way for a true conception of what may be regarded as the central idea of Christian worship. In perfect harmony with what has been said of the Church's Life and Work, her Worship is a repetition by the Church on earth of all that is involved in our Lord's presentation of Himself in heaven to His Father. In His glorified condition our Lord is the first-born among many brethren. In His combined Divine and human natures He offers Himself as a continual oblation to the Father.[1] But His people are in Him, and He is in them. In Him they have access to the Father. In Him they

---

[1] 1 Cor. xv. 28.

have the support and nourishment of their spiritual life. And it is by now partaking, in ever-increasing measure, of His Spirit that they receive the spiritual education by which they approach continually nearer to the standard of the perfect man in Him. All education, however, proceeds upon the principle that the point to be ultimately reached must regulate the earlier steps by which we gradually reach it. From the fact that the public school is an image of the world in which the boy is afterwards to play his part, it derives its chief value as an institution for the discipline of the young. The more perfectly it reflects the future, the less it forgets that the boy is "the father of the man," the more successfully will it accomplish the end in view. The same rule holds in regard to the kingdom of God. That kingdom, as manifested in the future, will only be the development and completion of its manifestation now. We are as yet in the infancy of our being; our manhood is to come; but our infancy and manhood are bound together by the closest ties. The knowledge that we are to possess, the feelings that we are to cultivate, the hopes that we are to entertain in heaven are the knowledge, the feelings, and the hopes by which we are to be marked on earth. It follows that the scenes of our spiritual manhood must supply the rules for the training of our spiritual youth. As Christian worship here is a preparation for the worship of the Church of the first-born hereafter, the one must be a reflection or reproduction of the other in which we are to engage in the heavenly sabbatism. So far as the imperfections

of earth permit, the Church of Christ is already come to
the Mount Zion, and the heavenly Jerusalem, and the
innumerable company of angels; and, to be a meet inhabitant of such a dwelling and companion for such an
assembly, she must even now catch their spirit and sing
their song.

The worship of the Christian Church is thus again
no mere independent arrangement, provided by the
goodness of God to guide us to communion with Him.
It is no mere token of His love which might have been
replaced by another equally precious and effective.   It
flows from communion with the Father through the
Son as an already existing reality, and it is because it
flows from that communion that it leads us to it.
Hence it is that from the very beginning of her history
the Church has instinctively regarded the Sacrament
of Holy Communion as the central act of her worship.
The statements of the New Testament, with regard to
the religious exercises of Christians when they met
together for worship,[1] followed as they are by the
earliest accounts of these assemblies preserved for us
in Christian history, leave no possibility of disputing
the fact.   The question is, How are we to explain it?
And the only answer that can be given is, that in the
Sacrament of the Supper the Church realised to a
greater extent than in any other of her ordinances both
her own deepest, that is, her sacrificial life in her
glorified Lord, and His peculiar presence with her as
her nourishment and strength and joy.   She lived in

---

[1] Acts ii. 46, xx. 7 ; 1 Cor. xi. 20.

Him as glorified; and in a far higher than ordinary degree Holy Communion, by His own institution, gathered up into itself and applied to her the chief ideas and blessings of His glorified life. In heaven He was surrendering Himself, with all His people in Him, to the Father. Through the spirit of His own Divine-human being, He communicated from thence those Divine-human influences by which His people were enabled to make His surrender of them a free and cheerful surrender of their own. That sacred rite, therefore, in which all this was most clearly represented and most powerfully applied necessarily came to occupy its central position in the Church's eyes, and to be regarded by her as her " great, distinctive, and supreme act of service." [1] Not simply because it commemorated the most momentous event in the life of Jesus upon earth, and certainly not with the faintest idea that she was receiving benefits in a merely mechanical and outward way (*ex opere operato* [2]), was the Church led to her view of the Eucharist, but because the Communion Table was, more than any other spot, the meeting-place of heaven and earth, where the King met His guests in closer than common fellowship and with richer than common blessing. What was thus the case in early Christian times has continued to be the idea of the Church throughout her history. It was not on superstitious grounds, but as the most perfect expression by

[1] Freeman, *Principles of Divine Service*, i. p. 165.

[2] It is the thought of the dead Christ that connects itself with the thought of the *opus operatum*. The thought of the living Lord directly contradicts and negatives such an idea.

the members of the Body upon earth of the attitude in
heaven of Him in whom they lived, that the Eucharist
became the keynote of Christian Worship.

Not only, however, does the central position occupied
by the Holy Communion in the Church's services show
us, in the most striking manner, the light in which she
looked at her worship as a whole, the same thing is
hardly less strikingly illustrated by the tone and spirit
of her Common Prayer. Her ordinary offices for this
purpose would seem, in general character, often in the
very words, to be really an echo and reminder of her
sacramental office, to which they thus in turn became
tributary streams. And her acts of Public Worship
are felt, when the connexion thus pointed out is seen,
to be but a cementing of the eucharistically applied
union between the glorified Lord and the members of
His Body.[1]

From what has been said we learn the Church's own
testimony to her belief (whether reasoned out or largely
instinctive it is unnecessary to ask), that in its primary
conception her worship on earth is moulded upon the
worship of heaven,[2] and that its great aim is so to
manifest the glorified Lord that He Himself may be
more deeply rooted in that life of hers which is to be
the counterpart of His own.

One other remark upon this subject may be made.
It shows us not only what the substance of our worship,

---

[1] See this point treated with
great fulness and learning by
Canon Freeman in the work
above mentioned, vol. i.

[2] Comp. Medd, *The One Mediator*, p. 369 ; Wilberforce, *On the
Incarnation*, p. 209.

but also what the nature of its accessories ought to be—
of the buildings used for it, of the colours and orna-
ments employed in them, of the very tones of the
teacher's voice, and the style of the congregation's
music.   These ought all to be brought as near as possible to the harmony and beauty, to the liveliness and
joy, which we associate with the heavenly kingdom.
There are few things in the history of religion more
melancholy than to see multitudes led by the shoutings
of an ignorant fanaticism to resist the changes in this
direction which are urged wholly for their sakes, and
from which, if introduced without extravagance, they
would be the first to profit.   Let us not, however, be
afraid.   Let us only be more careful to test the purity
of our own motives.   Let us be tolerant to a spirit for
the nursing of which we are ourselves in no small
degree responsible.   Above all, let us build, in every improvement introduced into the Worship of the Church,
not upon the shifting sands of a superficial and, it may
be, temporary æstheticism, but upon principles lying at
the very root of the Christian faith, and flowing out of
our holiest and most reverential thoughts of Him who,
Himself the Rock of Ages, gives a rock-like stability
to every just expression of His Spirit.   Of that Spirit
Worship is an expression.   It may be the poetry rather
than the prose of the Christian life.[1]   But it is all the
more precious and powerful if it be :—

> We find within these souls of ours
> Some wild germs of a higher birth,

---

[1] Palmer, in Herzog's *Encycl. Gottesdienst.*

Which in the poet's tropic heart bear flowers
  Whose fragrance fills the earth.

God wills, man hopes ; in common souls
  Hope is but vague and undefined,
Till from the poet's tongue the message rolls
  A blessing to his kind.

IV. The glorified Lord is to be made manifest in the Confession of His Church.

Our Lord came into the world to confess His Father before men, to be a Witness to His being and character and aims. When defending Himself against the opposition of the Jews, He said : "I can of Myself do nothing : as I hear I judge : and My judgment is righteous ; because I seek not Mine own will, but the will of Him that sent Me."[1] When Philip in a moment of despondency exclaimed, "Lord, shew us the Father, and it sufficeth us," He replied, "Have I been so long time with you, and yet hast thou not known Me, Philip ? He that hath seen Me hath seen the Father."[2] And when Pilate asked Him, "Art thou a King then ?" He answered, "Thou sayest that I am a King. To this end have I been born, and to this end am I come into the world, that I should bear witness unto the truth."[3] St. Paul speaks of our Lord as having "before Pontius Pilate witnessed the good confession";[4] while St. John, in his Gospel, describes Him as One who has "declared the God whom no man hath seen at any time,"[5] and, in his Apocalypse, as "The faithful Witness," as "The

---

[1] John v. 30.   [2] John xiv. 8, 9.   [3] John xviii. 37.
[4] 1 Tim. vi. 13.   [5] John i. 18.

Amen, the faithful and true Witness."[1]   There is, indeed, no more characteristic aspect in which our Lord is set before us in the New Testament than that of witnessing.

A similar confession then, a similar witnessing, is demanded of the Church when she manifests her Redeemer's glory and carries on His work.   It is true that the Church of Christ bears this witness in everything that she is and does,—in her life, her work, and her worship.   But that she is to bear it also in word is clearly indicated by such passages of the sacred writings as speak not only of confession by the individual believer,[2] but of the open acknowledgment of a common faith.   Thus we read that Christians are to be baptized "in the Name of the Father and of the Son and of the Holy Spirit";[3] that to salvation a public profession of faith is necessary;[4] that we are exhorted to "hold fast our confession" and the "confession of our hope";[5] and that St. Paul even seems to present us with an early confession of faith in a rhythmical arrangement of parts, when the "great mystery of godliness" is described as "He who was manifested in flesh, justified in spirit, seen of angels, preached among the Gentiles, believed on in the world, received up in glory."[6]

Passages such as these point to an open proclamation of her faith on the Church's part, whatever be the particular purpose to which her Confession may be applied.

---

[1] Rev. i. 5 ; iii. 14.   [4] Rom. x. 10 ; comp. 1 Cor. xii. 3.
[2] Phil. ii. 9-11.   [5] Heb. iv. 14 ; x. 23.
[3] Matt. xxviii. 19.   [6] 1 Tim. iii. 16.

It could not be otherwise. All strong emotions of our nature find utterance in words as well as deeds. When we believe we speak.[1] Blot out to-day every Confession that the Church has framed in the past, she would be compelled to begin framing a new one to-morrow; and she would do this, in the first instance at least, with no thought of discipline, but simply to glorify God, to satisfy her own feelings, and to make her position known. Such is the general principle lying at the root of all Confessions of Faith. But the whole question is at this moment stirring so deeply the heart of the Scottish churches that it may be well to ask whether any light is thrown upon it by that work of the glorified Lord on earth which we are here considering. One or two preliminary observations must be made.

1. A Confession, properly so called, of the Church's faith is the Confession of the whole Church. To imagine that it may be the Confession of the office-bearers, though not at the same time of the members of the Church, is to limit it to a body which does not constitute the Church; is to draw a distinction between office-bearers and members in a way unknown to the New Testament; and is to say that that embodiment of Divine truth proclaimed to men in order to win them to Christ may cease to interest them as soon as they have been won to Him. To maintain, too, that a Confession is only for the few is to destroy its vitality, and to doom it to gradual extinction. The few will soon cease to care for what they are taught to regard as

---

[1] 2 Cor. iv. 13.

316 THE HEAVENLY PRIESTHOOD LECT.

316 THE HEAVENLY PRIESTHOOD LECT.

intended for them alone. The Church of the Lord
Jesus Christ does not live for the few. She lives for
all, and she proclaims One who is a Saviour for all.
She knows that, wherever there is a human soul, that
soul possesses faculties, affections, and feelings which
may be trained to the highest possible religious development, and she cannot for a moment acquiesce in the
idea that it is not entitled to the fullest light. From
the belief that her message is universal, she draws at
once her enthusiasm and her hope. Whatever cannot
tell on all must soon lose its value in her eyes ; and to
think that any part of her Confession is for her office-
bearers, but not her members, is to hasten the arrival
of an hour when that part shall be no longer regarded
as living and present truth.

2. A Confession thus intended for the Church as a
whole must spring from the Church as a whole. It
cannot be framed on the supposition that different
sections of believers, attaching different degrees of
importance to different parts of revelation, may each
contribute their share to that common stock of theological statement which is to be afterwards accepted
as the Confession of the Church's faith. So framed it
would fail in unity, and no attempt to arrange its parts
upon a definite system could be successful. Some parts
would almost necessarily be inconsistent with other
parts, and the document could not possess that logical
coherence which is essential to power over the minds
of men. It would also be no Confession of the Church,
and we could only learn from it that one section was

with equal right adopted by one party and another by another in the common Body.

3. For the same reason the relation of men towards a Confession, which is looked on as a test of membership, but parts of which perplex them, cannot be lightened by encouraging them to think that they are not bound to receive it all; and that they need only fix their attention upon those parts which, for one reason or another, have for them peculiar attraction. It might then easily happen that, while no single part failed to secure defenders, the sum of the parts had no defender. To avoid this danger it is difficult to lay down any other principle than that all the parts of a Confession which is regarded as a test must be equally authoritative. Even the attempt to distinguish between fundamental and non-fundamental articles will be useless, unless the Church in her collective capacity draws and expresses the distinction. The distinction is a sound one. It may be considered as an axiom of Protestant Theology, and its truth is not now denied. But it cannot be left to each individual to draw the line of distinction for himself, or we shall be in the same hopeless confusion as before.

4. The attempt often made at the present day to draw a broad line of demarcation between theology and religion is entirely irrelevant to this discussion. Who denies that theology is not religion, or that religion is not theology? Since the days when our Lord denounced the wise and prudent, and commended babes, the distinction has been illustrated and acknowledged by every

age; and to place it in the forefront of an argument
upon the question with which we are dealing is to resort
to what, in that connexion, is either a truism or a
delusion. It is a truism if it simply mean that religion
is an internal and spiritual, not a merely outward and
formal force. It is a delusion if it mean that we may
dispense with positive statements of religious truth, and
may be satisfied with cherishing pious feelings. Distinct
as theology and religion are, they are indispensable to
each other. To a greater or less extent they must co-
exist if the end of either is to be attained. Without a theology religion becomes a human speculation.
Without religion the most comprehensive system of
theology becomes a lifeless husk. The language often
heard, even from orthodox theologians, that all the
benefit to be derived from any doctrine of the Church
may be obtained by simply resting upon the fact contained in it, and without inquiry into the bond between
the fact and its result, is little better than the language
of indolence or despair. We must form an intelligent
conception of the manner in which a fact operates
before we can fully experience its effect. The doctrine of the forgiveness of sin is contained in every
theory of the Atonement, but to urge that we may
be content with this assurance, without asking how
the forgiveness is brought about by the means proposed, is to deny thought its rights, and can lead
only to a vague mysticism, or to the impression that
the whole matter is unreal. However true, therefore, in itself, the distinction between theology and

religion may be, it is of no value in the present argument.

5. It may be thought by many that more aid in the solution of the question before us is to be found from drawing a distinction between the words of our Lord Himself and the later and more elaborate statements of theology. Upon this point an eminent theologian of the Church of England has recently expressed the hope that "as the centuries pass Christian thought will . . . come nearer in love and insight to the simple teaching of our Divine Master." [1] Perhaps it will ; we may even share the hope that to some extent at least it may. But no equalising of the differences of different Confessions will be thereby effected. For, in the first place it is impossible to admit the desirableness of laying aside, as if it were without bearing on our present position, of the whole history of theological development between the time of our Lord and the present hour. And, in the second place, even were we to attempt to do so, we should not be successful. The words of the Divine Master cannot be understood by us in the more vague or general sense in which they were at first apprehended by His hearers. Words have no fixed meaning of their own ; and they can only be understood in the light of that condition of mind to which we have been brought by the course of past and present history. Unless, therefore, we use the words of Christ in an avowedly ambiguous sense they must be interpreted ; and, so interpreted, they will necessarily take the hue

[1] Bishop Moorhouse, *The Teaching of Christ*, p. 148.

of the theological propositions which, differing in different minds, have become a part of ourselves. We may have recourse to the simpler expressions desired, but we shall be compelled to interpret them, each for himself, by the lessons of his Christian experience. Why not do openly what we must do secretly?

Instead, then, of engaging in speculations like these, it may be suggested that an entirely different question ought to occupy the Church's mind. All past attempts to meet our difficulties in connexion with this subject have failed. May there not be a better way? Proceeding upon the views of our Lord and of His work taken in these lectures, we venture to ask,—not, How shall we distinguish between an elaborate and simple theology? but, How shall we distinguish between the conclusions of theology as a science, and the extent to which these conclusions ought to be embodied in a Creed or Test? Upon this important aspect of the question the following observations may be made—

1. The Church must have a Creed. It would seem to be impossible for her to do without one. In the first place, she has to proclaim her faith to the honour of Him from whom it comes ; in the second place, she has to make clear to herself what she believes; and, in the third place, she has to be a witness to the world that she knows her faith, and is not ashamed of it. To each of these ends a Creed is necessary.

2. Numerous doctrinal statements enter into the ordinary idea of a Creed upon which not only are Christian men not agreed, but upon which no agreement

can be looked for.   If these statements are to fulfil their
purpose they must come from the deepest convictions
of the Church, and must be clear to those who utter
them. They must also be adapted to the habits and modes
of thought by which those are marked who, whether
within or without the Church, are expected to acknowledge their power.   Ambiguity can never satisfy an
earnest mind, and to take refuge in it is simply a form
of dishonesty.   Both for her own and the world's sake
the Church is under the highest obligation to speak as
plainly and as incisively as she can think.   Her language,
too, must be cast in a mould corresponding to the general
mould of thought in her day, or she will make no impression.   The seed may be ripe and sound, but the soil
may not be adapted to its growth ; and, instead of ger-
minating when sown, it will in that case wither and
die.   The moment these principles are admitted, and it
is difficult to see how they can be denied, it will be seen
that men of different countries and of centuries far
distant from one another can never hold in a living way
a variety of minute doctrinal statements, the product it
may be of a peculiar country and a peculiar age.   Let us
take the case of the East and West, and let us suppose
that Christianity, in the early years of its history, had
penetrated the Eastern instead of the Western half of
the globe; that the Eastern instead of the Western
mind had formulated and arranged its truths into orderly
propositions ; and that, after centuries had passed, the
East had resolved to Christianise the West.   Can any
one believe that, in such circumstances, the Confession

brought by Eastern missionaries to the West would have resembled the Confessions of the Reformed or Lutheran Church ? Would it have been adapted to our minds, or to our way of looking at God, man, and the universe ? Would it even have been understood by us ? It would rather have been a strange tongue. The illustration may appear extreme, but it is undeniable that differences, if not quite so radical, yet hardly less important for the present question, meet us within the churches of the West.

They are not diversities of gifts with the same spirit, but fundamental antagonisms of thought. . . . What they really denote is divers modes of Christian thinking, divers tendencies of the Christian intellect, which repeat themselves by a law of nature. It is no more possible to make men think alike in theology than in anything else where the facts are complicated and the conclusions necessarily fallible. The history of theology is a history of " variations " ; not, indeed, as some have main- tained, without an inner principle of advance, but with a constant repetition of oppositions underlying its necessary development. . . . Men may meet in common worship and in common work, and find themselves at one. The same faith may breathe in their prayers, and the same love fire their hearts. But men who think can never be at one on the great subjects of the Christian revelation. . . . Of all the false dreams that have ever haunted humanity, none is more false than the dream of catholic unity in this sense. It vanishes in the very effort to grasp it, and the old fissures appear within the most carefully compacted structures of dogma.[1]

Nor are we entitled to say that the persons by whom these differences are exhibited have no right to a place

---

[1] Tulloch, *Some Facts of Religion and Life,* pp. 21-23.

in our Communion should they desire to join it. They embrace multitudes whose "work of faith and labour of love and patience of hope in our Lord Jesus Christ before God and our Father" call for the profoundest thanksgiving, and impose upon us the most solemn obligations both to be like them, and to hold Christian fellowship with them. Every Christian Church, however different from others, has produced men of the most exalted piety and self-devotion. We cannot even forget that differences quite as important as those spoken of existed among the Apostles of our Lord. Only a superficial examination of the facts would lead any one to maintain that the moulds of thought and types of teaching exhibited by St. James, St. Peter, St. Paul, or St. John are the same. They are not only distinct, but so distinct that it may be doubted whether either an earlier Apostle could have adopted the language of a later, or a later that of an earlier, as a satisfactory exposition of his own Christian views. The earlier might, indeed, have been educated to the platform of the later without abandoning one Christian conviction. The later might have recognised the truth of the earlier as a preparatory stage for his own higher development; but neither could have said to the other, Your Confession of faith, if extended into lengthened propositions, will be the same as mine. If then the mechanical mode of looking at the Bible, which has marked all branches of the Protestant Church to the present hour, has not only injured the Bible, but has seriously hindered the growth of the Church, the same remark may be made

as to the Church's creed. Scripture, Christian experience, and human nature teach us that to look for agreement in all the doctrinal statements of the Creeds of
our modern branches of the Church is to look for an
impossibility.

3. To what has been said it may be replied that
different churches, like different voluntary societies, in
order to fulfil the end of their existence, must express
their peculiar doctrines in a manner appropriate to
themselves. One great truth, or one particular aspect
of truth, has taken so powerful a hold of them that they
cannot be silent regarding it. For it their members
have toiled and suffered and died. It has been graven
with a pen of steel upon their memories. It has been
written on their records with the blood of martyrs.
Let them remember it; and let the remembrance stir
them up to walk worthily of their fathers. But a distinct
denial must be given to the statement that the Church
is a voluntary society, and that her members are bound
to submit to whatever conditions the society may
impose, or leave it. The Church is not formed by
believers who associate themselves together and lay
down rules for the guidance of their mutual fellowship.
The Church is founded and regulated by Christ, and no
privilege of her members may be taken away by man.
Each portion of the Church can only be what it claims
to be in so far as it is a portion of the universal Church.
Its members are baptized, not into the community to
which they may specially belong but into Christ and,
in Him, into the Church at large. When they sit down

at the Communion Table their communion is not only with the Head, but with all the members of the Body. Ministers are ordained to the ministry of Christ, and not merely to that of the Denomination in which they are to labour.   The reasoning now contended against proceeds upon the false supposition that the individual precedes the Church, whereas the Church precedes the individual.   When our Lord was in the world His whole Church was gathered up in Him, and His Apostles, in being united to him, were united to the Church in Him.   The same remark applies to all successive generations of disciples.   They do not create the Church.   They enter into the Church which has been waiting to receive them, and the privileges which they enjoy in her flow to them through her from her Head. The Church, therefore, is not entitled to lay down conditions which would exclude from her communion any of whom she has not reason to believe that Christ excludes them from communion with Him.   She acts only in her Redeemer's name, and in the exercise of an authority which He bestows.   For any particular Denomination to force out members on grounds on which it is not believed that Christ would Himself exclude them is to make light of those whom it may itself confess to be His little ones.   It is no answer to this to say that they may go elsewhere.   More cruel words could not be spoken by any theologian of that iron age of Creeds which we have not yet passed through.   Such persons may not wish to go elsewhere.   They may not have it in their power to go elsewhere.   They have no right, except under compulsion, to go elsewhere. Their dismissal may be equivalent to depriving them of the privileges of the Christian Church altogether.

4. These considerations point to the necessity of assigning a different place to those parts of the Church's Creed which are essential and those which are not essential to the unity of the Head and members. Not, indeed, in the sense of drawing that distinction between fundamental and non-fundamental articles of faith in the same Creed which, however true, we have already seen to be no practical solution of the difficulty. The non-fundamental articles ought to have no place in the Creed. They are not needed either for the fellowship of believers or for the manifestation of that personal Lord and Saviour on whom the Church calls the world to believe. The Church has other ways of bearing a testimony to them, and she does not depreciate them by declining to make them terms of communion. In the early Church the questions as to eating meats offered to idols, and the observance of the Sabbath, penetrated as deeply into the Church's life as most of those questions by which she has been rent asunder in later times. St. Paul recognised their importance, and maintained his own position in regard to them with a clear conscience and great firmness. But he did not allow them to break the Church's unity. "Let not him that eateth," he said, "set at nought him that eateth not; and let not him that eateth not judge him that eateth: for God hath received him. Who art thou that judgest the servant of another? to his own lord he standeth or

falleth.   Yea, he shall be made to stand; for the Lord
hath power to make him stand. . . . Let each man be
fully persuaded in his own mind." [1]

Nor is there any ground to fear that in such a case
those who attach importance to statements not made a
test of membership will lose interest in them.   There
is rather reason to fear such a result when they are
introduced into a Creed, but at the same time declared
to be non-essentials.   When they are grouped together
in another way and set forth for another purpose they
will retain their value.   In point of fact experience
teaches that refusal to admit the distinction now contended for has proved injurious to doctrinal theology,
and that every approach made to it has been favourable
to the study of doctrine.   Nowhere so much as in
Germany has theology in its wider sense been for long
so completely separated from the idea of testing by it
the right to either office or membership in the Church,
and nowhere has it been more honoured and studied.
We may disapprove of many of the conclusions that
have been arrived at, but it cannot be denied that in
that country the field of doctrine has been one of noble
effort and achievement.   Nowhere has theology, in a
wide extent of its conclusions, been made more a bond
of church communion than in Scotland, and nowhere
in later years has it been less studied in a worthy
manner.[2]   It became a dead letter, a formal lifeless

[1] Rom. xiv. 3-5.

[2] The one school of native
Theology which we had in Scotland (that of Aberdeen in the
time of Charles I.) was destroyed
by the enforcing of the National
Covenant.

system. Genuine delight in it, zeal in pursuing it, almost
vanished from the land ; and only now, when the bonds
of confessional stringency are at least practically relaxed,
are there on every side symptoms that theology may
revive, and once more become the subject of interest
and debate.   This result might have been expected.
Men cannot inquire with the necessary freedom when
every point of inquiry has been already settled for them
and publicly accepted by them.   They may be willing
to meet any loss of worldly goods, but they shrink from
the doubts and suspicions they may awaken.   They
have no wish to be branded with the odious term
Heretic.   Whereas, on the other hand, were the field
clear, and did they feel that they might be welcomed
as honest students in it, they could throw themselves
with all their hearts into those theological struggles
which have attracted so many of the best spirits
of the past, and the cause of truth would eventually
gain.

It is no sufficient answer to this to say, that " men
are intended to deal with temptations, to feel the force
of them, and to overcome them." [1]   There is a balance
to that truth in the words of the same writer, " Sources
of temptation wantonly or needlessly created, are
always to be condemned." [2]   The question indeed turns
upon the point, whether the temptation occasioned by
putting into the Church's Creed what ought rather to
find its place elsewhere is or is not a " wanton and
needless temptation."   Experience shows that it is, and

[1] Rainy, *The Development of Christian Doctrine*, p. 265.   [2] u.s.

that the Church ought to remove it. Nothing but un-
certainty and confusion can arise from the statement
that "in the confessions of the Churches there are two
elements or two strata of confessional matter." [1] The
remedy is to see that there shall be only one stratum, is to
put into the Creed nothing but what is essential to the
existence of the Church in the unity of her Head and
members. Let speculation be free upon all other points.

The conclusion to which we are thus led seems to be,
that a distinction ought to be drawn between Creed, as
a test of office-bearing or membership, and those larger,
wider, and more elaborate theological statements which
the Church may yet by a majority, and therefore speaking as a whole, put forth as the expression of her faith
on particulars not needed for Christian unity. Let her
utter her testimony upon these points with all plainness
and force ; let her proclaim her sense of their importance ; let her defend them in the face of opponents, and
let her spare no effort to make opponents friends ; but
let her not say, as say she must when she makes them
a Test, No one who does not receive them can be a
member either with office or without office in our
company.

To attempt here to draw the line between what is to
belong to the Creed or Test and what to the Confession
would simply be an act of inexcusable presumption.
No individual may dare to do it. All that can be done
is to indicate that there appears to be a principle involved in separating the two things from one another.

[1] u.s. p. 263.

When this is admitted the subject of these lectures—
the Ascended and glorified Lord—may come in to help
us.   In Him—risen, ascended, glorified, Son of man as
well as Son of God, the revelation, the manifestation, of
the Father—believers live.   They live not in Him only
as He was on earth but as He is in the heavenly
and invisible world, as He is in a new super-earthly
existence, and as, in that existence, He is now by His
Spirit present in His Church, as fully, distinctly, and
powerfully, nay, more fully, distinctly, and powerfully
present than when He tabernacled upon earth.   It
follows that this nature of the Lord's Being, in which
is expressed not merely what He was but what He is,
and out of which flows the existence, the nature, and
purpose of the Church, ought to be the essential constituent of her Creed.   Whatever else is there ought to
range itself around a truth which is not only the first
but the last, not only the beginning but the end, of the
Church's faith.   It was so once.   The three ancient
Creeds are full of the Person of Christ.   Both in these
and in the other parts of their contents they deal also
more with facts than with speculations upon facts.   Let
speculation " grow from more to more," but let it belong
as much as possible to the region of theology, as little
as possible to that of Creed.

With what has been said the language of Scripture
strikingly agrees.   When St. Paul speaks of the confession which is " made unto salvation," he fixes at once
on the thought of the risen or glorified Lord as its substance, " If thou shalt confess with thy mouth Jesus as

Lord," [1] where the whole context shows that the word
" Lord " expresses Jesus as one whom " God raised from
the dead." [2]   To the same effect the same Apostle, in
another Epistle, describes his preaching, " We preach
not ourselves but Christ Jesus as Lord "; [3] declares in a
third that " no man can say that Jesus is Lord, but in
Holy Spirit "; [4] and, when referring in a fourth to the
glorious issue of Christ's work, sums it up in the words
" that every tongue should confess that Jesus Christ is
Lord, to the glory of God the Father." [5]   In all these
passages, dealing expressly with the public profession
of the Christian faith, that faith is set before us as an
acknowledgment that the Church believes and lives in
an exalted and glorified Lord in heaven.

Along with this, indeed, it lies in the nature of the
case that the Church ought to confess the practical
purpose of her calling, in order that she may deepen her
own sense of it, and let men see more clearly at what
she aims.

How much more is to be taken into her Creed or
Test the Church must herself determine.   It will probably be found that much of what now claims entrance
there belongs to the province of Testimony, of Confession in the larger sense, and that it may be safely left
in the hands of theologians for further examination and
definition.   Thus we shall gain the two points mainly
necessary to the soundness and progress of the Church's
thought—fixity with regard to the great facts of Revela-

---

[1] Rom. x. 9.   [2] Comp. Godet *in loc.*   [3] 2 Cor. iv. 5.
            [4] 1 Cor. xii. 3.   [5] Phil. ii. 11.

tion, and freedom within her borders to discuss all else. Without the former there can be no such thing as a Church. With the latter, discussion and debate within the Church will be full of promise. When different disputants have accepted the Church's main propositions as a Creed; when they are animated by the spirit of the Christian home which the Church opens to her children; when they have learned to sympathise with her perplexities, and to trust to the illuminating power of the Spirit promised to guide her into all the truth, then let them work out the problems which Christianity suggests. They will do so with profit to all, with harm to none. Remaining in connexion with the Church, and, through her, with her living and glorified Head in heaven, they will rest in peace until difficulties needing to be resolved and questions demanding an answer meet them. Then, in the bond of the Church's unity, let them struggle with these, and face every problem of the Christian faith. The scene of controversy may prove stirring; but, unity being still unbroken, the combatants will find that, so far from destroying one another, they will each rather sharpen, as iron sharpeneth iron, the countenance of his friend.

These lectures must close. They have been occupied with one of the greatest subjects to which we can direct our thoughts,—the Ascension, the Glorification, and the Heavenly Life of One of whom both Scripture and experience testify, that to Him the hopes of Humanity point, and that in Him alone its glorious destiny can be fulfilled. To this very greatness of the subject much of the imperfection of the lectures may be traced. True theological definition, the true unfolding in ever larger measure of the height and depth and length and breadth of the Divine counsels for the race, must always be preceded by a wide religious movement of the mind. All that any single person can hope to do is, amidst innumerable shortcomings and imperfections, to direct men's thoughts to topics worthy of their regard, although they may be at the time neglected. If he can succeed in this he may prepare the way for that larger leavening of the Christian society out of which aspects of the truth may spring adapted to his particular generation or demanded by its peculiar problems. For every hint, therefore, helping us to a fuller conception and appreciation of God's plan for that education and perfecting of humanity at which its deepest instincts compel it to aim, it is our duty to watch and wait, " as they that wait for the morning." Of the ancient prophets, as they looked forward to the age which they had not yet seen, it is said in one of the most touching descriptions of the Bible : " Concerning which salvation the prophets sought and searched diligently, searching what time or what manner of time the Spirit of Christ which was in them did point unto, when it testified beforehand the sufferings of Christ, and the glories that should follow them. To whom it was revealed that not unto themselves, but unto us, did they minister these things."[1] In a lofty discontent of soul with what was immediately around them they eagerly anticipated a better and a

---

[1] 1 Pet. i. 11, 12.

brighter future. That future, indeed, may now be said to have come, because Christ has come. Yet our Lord said even to His own disciples, " Can the sons of the bride-chamber mourn, as long as the bridegroom is with them? But the days will come when the bridegroom shall be taken away from them, and then will they fast." [1] Under the Christian as well as under the Jewish dispensation there were to be dissatisfaction and discontent with the actual state of things, as well as longing for a more perfect manifestation of the Divine power and goodness than had yet been seen. Not that a more perfect revelation of the Divine Kingdom was to be expected than had been given in Him who was "Son of God and King of Israel" (that was impossible), but that the revelation in Christ Jesus was to penetrate the world until by means of it humanity reached its full-orbed life, its weaknesses overcome, its hopes fulfilled, and its longings satisfied.

Is there no cause now why the children of the bride-chamber should still fast and mourn? Can we say that we are at this moment satisfied with the state of Christendom, contented with our Christian privileges, desiring only to be quiet till the end comes with noise-less step, and we may close our eyes in peace, to open them in a still happier home? It cannot be. The world is around us in its misery. The ear is pained, the heart is sick, with its tales of wrong and infamy, with its dark places the habitations of horrid cruelty, with its oppressions that make wise men mad, with its

[1] Matt. ix. 15.

myriads of innocent children trained up in every form of vice and steeped in wretchedness. Worse than this, the very Church of Christ to which we would naturally turn for help seems powerless; the light of men, but her light dimmed; the salt of the earth, but the salt with its savour lost; hardly to be distinguished from a world that cares for little else than the newest luxury or folly; often ignoring if not denying the most characteristic doctrines of her faith, and eager to make that best of both worlds which seldom has any other meaning than making the best of this world, and letting the next world take its chance, while at the same time her different sections are busier contending with one another than with the common foe, without mutual forbearance, or sympathy, or helpfulness, or love.

Can we see all this without feeling that in the condition of things around us there is something wrong, that we need more than the repetition of the story in the midst of repeating which this state of things has come about, that fresh aspects of the truth are demanded upon which a fresh life may rest, and that we are all interested in discovering whether we have given His real place in what we are and do to Him in whom are hid all the treasures of wisdom and knowledge ?

Among these aspects of truth, too much neglected, but full of power, the Ascension and Heavenly Priesthood of our Lord may certainly be included. The Ascension of the Great Head of the Church, in His human as well as His Divine nature, to the right hand of God, opens up to us a boundless prospect of what our humanity shall yet be in Him, and conveys to us the assurance that whatever He desires He is able to effect, while there is nothing more imperatively demanded of the Church of the present day than the revival of that idea of her priestliness which flows directly from the fact that she lives in him who is our High-priest in heaven.   This idea has been left too long associated with periods of unscriptural domination on the part of the Clergy, and of ignorance and superstition on the part of the Laity.   In spite of this it is alike true and fundamental.   A clear perception and a bold enunciation of it lies at the very root of all that is most real, most forcible, and most valuable in the Church's work. Her duty is not to abandon a position to which she has been divinely called, because it has been abused, and may be abused again.   It is rather so to occupy it that the fears of timorous friends may be dispelled, and the reproaches of opponents silenced.   The aim of true priesthood is not money or station or power ; it is love, work, self-sacrifice.   The Anointing in Bethany was accepted by the Redeemer as His consecration, not to worldly honours, but to His " burying " ; and to such a burying, not to ease and the high places of the earth, is the Church in her turn consecrated.   She has not gained much by casting the thought of her priestliness aside Let her return to the proclamation of it both in word and deed ; and it may be that, when she again anoints her Lord, men will be more ready to listen to her message, till the world is filled with the odour of the ointment.

NOTES

NOTES

NOTE A, p. 6.

IT has not been thought necessary to allude in the text to the old objection, that the two narratives of the Ascension in the Gospel and in the Acts of St. Luke are inconsistent with each other, inasmuch as the one is alleged to place the event on the very day of the Resurrection, the other forty days thereafter. But, as this objection has been recently revived by Pfleiderer in his *Ur-Christenthum* (p. 548), it may be proper to say a few words regarding it. Pfleiderer, indeed, does not directly urge that the two accounts are contradictory. His inference rather is, that a comparison of the two shows how lightly St. Luke regarded such contradictions in narratives of the same event ("wie leicht es Lukas mit solchen Widersprüchen bei der Wiederholung einer und derselben Erzählung nahm"); and in proof of this he refers to chaps. ix., xxii., xxvi. of Acts, meaning, without doubt, the three narratives of the conversion of St. Paul contained in these chapters. As to this last point, he has not adverted to the fact that only one of these is from St. Luke's own pen, the other two being given as St. Paul's statements before different audiences, and bearing precisely such slight marks of divergence as might be expected, and as strengthen rather than weaken our confidence in the main accuracy of a narrator. He has also paid too little heed either to St. Luke's preface to his Gospel or to the general style of both his books, which demonstrate that whatever complaints may be made of their author, indifference to historical details is the last charge that ought to be brought against him. In the present instance also we may well ask why Pfleiderer should not allow what he had allowed in an earlier part of his work

(p. 478), when speaking of the same fact, that St. Luke's brevity in his Gospel, if certain words are not genuine, arose from this and this alone ("wohl nur darum"), that he already intended to give a fuller statement in his second book.   Here, at any rate, the explanation of the apparent divergence is to be found, and this all the more if the words of Luke xxiv. 51, καὶ ἀνεφέρετο εἰς τὸν οὐρανόν, are to be treated as a gloss.   With much more propriety might it be pleaded that the Gospel places a *first* Ascension on the Resurrection day, and that that placed in Acts, forty days afterwards, is the *final* and formal departure. In any case there is no contradiction between the two accounts.

NOTE B, p. 149.

The view taken in the text as to the Offering of our Lord has so important a bearing upon the great doctrine of the Atonement that it seems desirable to enter somewhat more fully into it in a note.   Not that the substance of that doctrine, as generally held by the different branches of the Church of Christ, and stated in their symbolical books, is affected by what has been said.   Let us apply the Saviour's test, "By their fruits ye shall know them" (Matt. vii. 16); let us reason as does St. Paul when he appeals to the practical experience of the Galatian or the Corinthian Christians (Gal. iii. 1-5 ; 1 Cor. i. 4-8, xii. 1-3); let us believe that the promise of our Lord to His disciples has not been an illusion, "Howbeit, when He, the Spirit, is come, He shall guide you into all the truth" (John xvi. 13), and we shall be constrained to admit that the doctrine of Christ's sacrifice of Himself for the sins of men, acknowledged and taught by His Church, cannot have been false.   As "the power of God" it must also have been "the wisdom of God."   It does not, however, follow from this that the doctrine may not be looked at from different points of view, or even that the form in which it is expressed may not be to some extent changed.   It has been so in the past, and may be so in the future.   A distinction may be drawn between the substance of any condensed statement of Scripture teaching and the mode in which the substance of that teaching is set forth.

Proceeding upon this principle, the aim of the following remarks is to endeavour to place the view presented in this volume of the Offering of our Lord in its right relation to one or two leading ideas deeply embedded in the experience of Christian men; to the demands of the heart seeking after salvation; to the teaching of Scripture; and to the religious life and theology of the Reformed Church. The aim is so wide that what is to be said on these points must be stated briefly.

I. Any just conception of the Offering of our Lord ought to recognise and take up one or two leading ideas embedded in the experience of the Church. The ideas here particularly alluded to are those of the *Substitution* of our Lord as a victim for us, and the *Imputation* of His righteousness to us.

(1.) Substitution. It is hardly necessary to say that the thought of Christ as a Substitute for His people, as One who in their stead endured the penalty of the Divine law which they had violated, and at the same time rendered to it that perfect obedience of which they were through sin incapable, has always been largely entertained in the Christian Church. Dr. Buchanan speaks of it as one of the "fundamental principles which cannot be discarded without undermining the ground on which the Scriptural doctrine of pardon and acceptance with God must rest" (*The Doctrine of Justification*, p. 190), and by the popular mind it is generally supposed to contain the very essence of the Gospel. To what extent is it allowed by the view taken in the Lectures? The term "Substitute," it may first be observed, is ambiguous. In its strict sense it means one who does something for us that we cannot do for ourselves, and who, by doing it, makes it unnecessary for us to repeat the act. No one contends that this full meaning of the word is applicable to the case before us. On the contrary, all admit that the highest end of the work of Christ is to make us like Him, in the virtues not less than the privileges of the Divine life. By what our Lord does for us we are not relieved from doing: we are the more bound to do. A similar remark applies to suffering. We are not released from suffering because Christ has suffered. On the contrary, all allow that, while the Christian has to meet the ordinary sufferings of this life, he has over and above them to bear a cross, and to make a sacrifice of himself for his own and his brother's good, the value, and even the necessity, of which he learns from Christian faith alone. To the true disciple of Christ suffering may have changed its character; or rather, it should perhaps be said, there are consolations and hopes afforded under it which enable him even while he sorrows to rejoice. But suffering continues. Nor only so. Suffering can never be separated from the thought of the wrath of God against sin, or from the thought of penalty. The solidarity of the race, the intimateness of the bond uniting each man to all his brethren, alike in their sins and in the consequences of their sins, is enough to render the thought of this connexion necessary. Our suffering for sin is not removed because Christ suffered for us. As with suffering, so with death. The two accompany each other. Had there been no death, there would have been no suffering. But death reigns though Jesus died. Its character, like that of suffering, may have been changed to the believer; or rather, it should perhaps be said, the believer gains such a victory over it as enables him to cry, "O death, where is thy victory?" Death, however, not only still asserts its power; it must always be associated with the thought of what it is in itself, "the wages of sin." Dying as a consequence of sin is not removed because Christ died.

The term "our substitute" cannot, therefore, be applied to our Lord in its strictest and most proper sense, and theologians seem to have felt this. Nothing is more common than to find them combining the word Representative with the word Substitute. They speak of our Lord as our "Representative and Substitute" (Buchanan, u.s. p. 330), and they leave the impression upon the reader that the two words are regarded by them as synonymous. The theology of Scotland, too, does not use the word in any of its more formal documents. We meet it neither in the Westminster Confession of Faith nor in the Larger or Shorter Catechism of the Scottish Church.

Here, then, the view taken in these Lectures of the work of Christ on our behalf appears to lend us aid. It enables us to present to ourselves that work in a manner by which we escape the difficulties of a merely popular theology, while at the same time we retain the truth of which that theology is an imperfect and onesided expression. It would certainly avoid the word "Substitute," because that word is ambiguous and misleading. But it is *grounded* on the idea that Christ is the Representative of sinners. It acknowledges that there is no part of His work in which Christ stands alone, and that He enters upon and executes that work not for Himself but *for us*. It allows that He does for us what we cannot do for ourselves, and that His relation to His people is altogether different from that of a mere Friend or Benefactor or Example. He represents them; yet by a representation which is more than one of outward appointment, which rests upon an internal reality, and an internal correspondence with the essential elements of their state. He becomes what they are, that they in Him may become what He is. Through faith in the Personal Redeemer, brought before them in the message of the Gospel, they are made members of His Body, and one with Him the Head. They accept Him as their Representative. They go to the Father not in their own name but in His.

All this, it may perhaps be said, applies to the life of Christ; but where, upon the supposition now made, is that death which is the wages of sin? The answer is not difficult. Christ does die. It is true that physical death does not constitute the essence of His atoning work. That essence lies in the surrender of His will to the will of God, in the love which led Him to the Cross in order to execute, at the cost of life itself, the counsels of the Father's love. But still He does die. He passes through death in order to satisfy the great law of righteousness. He bears the punishment, the " curse " of a broken law, and what He offers is the life bearing that penalty, and reaching, while it bears it, its most glorious perfection. With Him and in Him His people also die. While by a living act they appropriate Him they both live and die. Their life is a life which passes through death. There is death for them as well as life.[1]

(2.) Imputation. Here again it is of importance to distinguish between the popular conception and the scientific statement of the truth. According to the former it is generally supposed that the righteousness of Christ, both active and passive, having been wrought out in our room and stead, is imputed or reckoned to us in our natural state of sinfulness on the sole condition that we accept it ; and that the Judge of all

---

[1] On the question of substitution the writer would refer his readers to an elaborate and able work by the Rev. G. Jamieson, D.D., first minister of Old Machar, Aberdeen, entitled, *Discussions on the Atonement.* The writer may not have brought out the different senses in which the word " substitution " is to be understood, and he may have devoted himself at unnecessary length to an argument against it when only taken in its narrower sense. With some positions too laid down by him in the course of his argument it may be impossible to sympathise ; but the work is full of valuable thought, and deserves the careful attention of the theological student.

the earth, then beholding us clothed in it as in a spotless robe,
is well pleased with us for His righteousness' sake. The figure
of a robe indeed is that most frequently employed to give expression to the idea. Naturally we are naked, but we put on
Christ's righteousness as a garment, and we are saved. From
this conception the scientific statement of the truth wholly
differs. "The Reformers," says Principal Cunningham, and
his words may be quoted as authoritative, "taught that, when
God pardoned and accepted any sinner, the ground or basis
of the Divine act—*that* to which God had directly and immediately a respect or regard in performing it, or in passing a
virtual sentence cancelling that man's sins, and admitting him
into the enjoyment of His favour—was this, that the righteousness of Christ was his, *through his union to Christ;* that
being his in this way it was *in consequence* imputed to him,
or put down to his account, just as if it were truly and properly his own; and that this righteousness, being in itself fully
satisfactory and meritorious, formed an adequate ground on
which his sins might be forgiven and his person accepted"
(*Historical Theology*, ii. 46). The words of this extract,
"through his union to Christ," which are italicised by Dr.
Cunningham himself, imply much more than a mere outward
relationship between Christ and the believer at the moment
when Christ's righteousness is imputed. Union, by its very
nature, supposes in the case of living persons an internal movement, a movement of the heart of man towards Christ, and a
communication to some extent at least of the affections of
Christ to man. Imputation of Christ's righteousness thus
follows and does not *precede* our union to Christ; and it
becomes an expression, not for that by which we are saved
(for we are saved by union to Christ), but for that by which an
absolutely holy and righteous God is enabled to deal with us
as though we had, what we have not, the perfect righteousness
which the law requires. When the word "imputation" is
understood in this sense not only is there no ground of objection to it, it must be accepted even in those lower theories of
justification on which we have no space to enter. (Comp.
Buchanan on Justification, Part I. Lect. vi.) It even offers a
point of connexion between Roman and Protestant theology.
The Roman Church maintains that "the meritorious cause of
justification is our Lord Jesus Christ who, by His own most
sacred passion on the Cross, merited justification for us, and

satisfied the Father in our room ";[1] and, however unhappily it introduced confusion into the subject by its definition of "the formal cause" of the same great act of God, confusion is not contradiction. It may be removed by a proper definition of terms, and a fuller consideration of what those employing them intended them to convey.

The idea of "imputation" then, as above explained, belongs essentially to the view of Christ's Offering taken in the Lectures. When the sinner believes in Christ he is united to Him; but not outwardly only. He lays hold of Christ as a living Redeemer who passes through a penal death for his sake. He is with Him in that death. In other words, He lays hold of the life of Christ in its aspect as an offering to God. His life has moved to Christ's life, and Christ has identified Himself with him. But he is not perfect. How is he then accepted? The Father beholds him in His "beloved." So beholding him, He beholds him truly united to the Son of His love; in that union He beholds also the germ out of which the life of a complete sanctification will spring; and He turns away from the sins and weaknesses which still cleave to him. In other words, He imputes Christ's righteousness to the believer for that particular purpose, and to that particular extent.

It is no doubt true that, while thus retained in their theological and scientific import, the popular misconceptions as to Substitution and Imputation perish. But can any one regret that they should do so? Do they not go far to account for those hypocrisies and vices by which even Office-bearers in the Church have too often done dishonour to the Christian faith, and for that separation between Christianity and the daily life which marks too many professing followers of Christ in Scotland at this hour?[2]

II. The view now taken of the Offering of our Lord gives

---

[1] The following are the words of the Council of Trent: "Meritoria (causa) autem, dilectissimus unigenitus suus, dominus noster Jesus Christus, qui cum essemus inimici, propter nimiam caritatem, quâ dilexit nos sua, sanctissima passione in ligno crucis nobis justificationem meruit, et pro nobis Deo Patri satisfecit" (Sessio Sexta—See *Chemnitii Examen*, p. 127).

[2] The wide prevalence of this conception, and the mischief done by it are strikingly illustrated by what the writer has been told, upon apparently the best authority, was everywhere said in Glasgow after the failure of the City of Glasgow Bank with all its disastrous consequences. See "*the fruits of Imputed Righteousness*."

prominence to that moral or religious element in the plan of our salvation which is not less needed than the legal element to satisfy the conscience and the heart of man. Of its retention of the legal element little further need be said. It recognises the claims of the Divine law, and the satisfaction rendered to them by Him who gave Himself for us, the Just for the unjust, that He might bring us unto God. Upon the Cross the Redeemer dies no merely martyr's death; nor does He die only that He may seal His testimony with His blood, or that He may open for us the gate of heaven. There is a penal element in His death. Bearing their sins in His own body on the tree, He takes up into Himself, and, with their full and free acceptance of His work, represents before the throne of God those who have the sentence of death in themselves, and who cannot be delivered from their bondage unless they see that the claims of law are satisfied, and that that eternal righteousness which fills them as much with admiration as with alarm is vindicated. Thus the legal element finds its place.

It is of more consequence to turn to the fact that, when our Lord's Offering is regarded not as an Offering of death but of life in and through death, it includes in it as an *integral part* of the gift bestowed, a moral or religious element, not less necessary to appease the awakened conscience than is the assurance that punishment has been endured for sin. A sense of guilt, or of liability to just punishment because of the violation of the Divine law, is not the only thing in our natural condition for which a message of good news is wanted. In innumerable instances such a sense is far less oppressive than the consciousness of sinful tendency, and for this no merely external atonement will suffice.[1] No change in our legal relation to the Almighty can meet that want. Awakened to see what sin is, we long even less for pardon than for reconciliation to God, and, reunion to Him in a willing and welcomed sonship. It would be unjust to the Prodigal Son in the Parable to imagine that, when he resolved to return to his father, he thought only of his own bodily wants, and nothing of that fulness of his father's love which, caring for the humblest domestics of his family, had so richly encompassed his children. And when the Publicans and Sinners "were drawing near unto our Lord for to hear Him" (Luke xv. 1), they were attracted to Him, not

---

[1] "The mind shrinks from a purely external atonement."—Lyttelton, *Lux Mundi*, p. 296.

so much by the hope of pardon, as by a dim perception that in One so holy yet so loving they might find a guide to that better life for which they longed. And so always.[1] We need to be saved out of our sins themselves, before we can be at peace. This, however, cannot be effected by a mere change in our legal relation towards God. Nor is it enough to say that, the legal relation being changed, the practical obedience which flows from gratitude must follow. What the sinner feels most powerfully that he requires to receive is life, spiritual life, and with that life strength to lead it (Rom. v. 6, viii. 3) ; and to this primary want the message of salvation must be able to address itself. The thought of such life and strength must lie *in the very conception* of that redemption which is made his in Christ. It is not enough to grope after them, to reason to them, or to hope that our feelings will soon be so quickened as to justify a persuasion that we have them. They must be then and there bestowed upon us as a part of the Divine gift, if we are to be at peace. So important does this point seem that one or two other considerations may be briefly adduced in its elucidation and defence.

(1.) Thus alone is justice done to the Person of the Saviour. So long as we occupy ourselves solely or even mainly with legal relations, the Redeemer who reconstitutes these is not embraced by us in that light in which He appears in the New Testament. He is there a spiritual Person who unites His people to Himself by such a real transmission of His Spirit to them that they may be identified with Him, and He with them. But this transmission cannot be made ours without a spiritual activity of the soul which we do not naturally possess, and which must be freely bestowed upon us as a gift. In other words, Christ cannot be to us the Redeemer that He is unless He be as much our religious Representative as our legal Substitute. Then only do we receive Him in the completeness of His character and work when we behold in Him One whose representation of us is made real by His impartation to us of His Spirit in the very act of our receiving Him.

(2.) Thus alone is justice done to the great principle of faith.

---

[1] "Propitiation is not enough by itself, though propitiation is the necessary first step in the process of reconciliation."—Lyttelton, *Lux Mundi*, p. 284. "The Gospel of happiness and misery is not true to the heart of man."—Hinton, *Man and his Dwelling Place*, p. 119 ; comp. also Jukes, *Law of the Offerings*, p. 201.

For the faith in the Person and Work of Christ, which we are called to exercise, is a faith which possesses in it a moral or religious element ; and such faith can only have scope when it is directed not simply to a legal transaction by which we are to profit, but to a living personality which meets and, in meeting, nourishes it into a continually increasing power within us. To think of faith as a mere hand, it might even be an artificial hand, stretched out to appropriate salvation is to mistake its nature. Faith implies trust in the object of faith, and must correspond to that object. In its proper meaning it supposes interchange of sympathy between the person in whom we believe and ourselves ; and it is thus more than a principle apprehending a change of legal relation to God, from which the fruits of righteousness ought to grow.

(3.) Thus only is justice done to the true nature of that ground of confidence towards God which the revelation given us in Christ is intended to supply. For this ground of confidence is not any process of reasoning upon our part, or any exercise of feeling by which we respond to the great acts of God's mercy towards us. It is these acts of mercy themselves. This truth is especially apparent in the Sacraments. In them, according to the teaching of the New Testament and of the Standards of the Scottish Church, Christ comes to us as much as we to Him. In them He is by His own appointment "represented, sealed, and applied to believers." They are channels of His grace, so that, when we seek for assurance of salvation, we are to find it in what He does for us, and not in any inward persuasion of our own that we have accepted Him. Such a persuasion enthusiastic or presumptuous persons easily find, and are too frequently puffed up ; the modest miss, and are too frequently thrown into agony or despair. Christ Himself is with and in His Sacraments, to make them not only a sign, but a seal to us of "engrafting into Christ, of remission of sins by His blood, and regeneration by His Spirit, of adoption and resurrection unto eternal life" (*Larger Catechism, Question* 165).

So also in the case before us. If Christ is to be our life (and surely that is the light in which He appears chiefly in the New Testament), He must be presented to us and appropriated by us in that character. Our life cannot consist in feelings, emotions, and purposes awakened in us as logical inferences from a work which He has executed in our room and stead. It must be part of the life summed up in Him and in Him made ours ; and this implies the existence of a moral and religious, as well as of a legal element, in that action of the Redeemer by which, through union with Him, we obtain salvation.

The analogy of human affairs appears to sustain this contention. A prisoner at the bar of an earthly judge may hear a sentence of acquittal pronounced over him, while his heart remains unchanged. The sinner is such a prisoner. He has been brought trembling into the midst of a great assize. An awful Judge is upon the bench, and thousands of spectators are around him to justify his doom. He is suddenly and unexpectedly acquitted. He hails his deliverance with joy, and he resolves never to forget the Judge who in his clemency forgave when he might justly have condemned him. Good so far ; but the sinner's acquittal brings him into no heart-relation to his Judge. Is the man changed? He may be, or he may not. If he is, there have been deeper thoughts at work within him than he was aware of. What relieves his fears and breaks his bondage is not simply the thought that his relation to the sentence of the law is different from what it was, but that in closest connexion with his pardon full effect is given to his union with One who yielded perfect obedience to God, and in whom he now receives strength to obey.

From all this it follows that the spiritual wants of the sinner, seeking after salvation, are provided for not by the death of Christ alone, but also by the life of Christ as it passes through that death. It has been truly said that "the crucifix with the dead Christ obscures our faith. Our thoughts rest not upon a dead, but upon a living Christ." [1] No doubt the crucifix is to thousands upon thousands a spiritual help, and the figure of our Lord upon the cross preaches to them of the love of God with a power which the words of men can rarely if ever equal. Yet the empty cross is to be preferred, "as being a symbol, not a representation ; as symbolising, moreover, the resurrection as well as the death of the Redeemer. He has borne the cross, and passed from it for ever " (Rev. Jas. Cooper, in *Transactions of the Aberdeen Ecclesiological Society*, Part I. p. 13). Few things, indeed, are more striking than the manner in which the sacred writers lead us to the living Christ, and not merely to His death. Even when they speak of Him as the propitiation

---

[1] Westcott, *The Victory of the Cross*, p. 96.

for our sins, they think of Him as alive. Let one passage from St. John suffice : "And He Himself" (not merely "and He") "is the propitiation for our sins ; and not for ours only, but also for the whole world" (1 John ii. 2). "He Himself"! Yet not only as a living Lord since His Ascension into heaven, but at the first moment when He was such an offering. Even upon the cross what He offered was "Himself," His life on our behalf ; and, if we are His, we are in the life then offered as well as in the death then died.

Perhaps it may be well, before passing on, to say in a single word that, notwithstanding the importance here attached to the moral element in the offering of Christ, the light in which that element has been regarded is not merely different from, but entirely at variance with, the theory known as the Moral Theory of the Atonement. More, however, need not be said. This is not the place to discuss that theory ; and the reader may be referred to Dr. Crawford's volume on *The Atonement*, and to Dr. Dale's Preface to the seventh edition of his work on the same subject.

III. The view now taken of the offering of our Lord not only combines the legal and the moral elements necessary to make that offering satisfactory to the conscience : it does justice to an aspect of apostolic teaching too frequently forgotten, and harmonises not a little in the sacred writers that is apt to appear discordant. If there are in the New Testament, upon the one hand, many texts which seem to connect the offering of our Lord more peculiarly with the pardon of sin, or with the removal of our sense of liability to punishment, there are also, on the other hand, texts not less numerous, which describe the chief purpose of that offering as the restoration of man's moral nature, his deliverance from the power of sin, and the implantation of a new Divine life within him. The question to be answered is, Whether, by dwelling too exclusively upon our Lord's death as a penalty for sin, and by failing to associate it at the same time with His offering of life, we do not draw this distinction far more sharply than Scripture does ; or whether in Scripture the two elements are not fused more completely into one ? Some facts bearing upon the point may be first adverted to.

(1.) The light in which sin is regarded by the sacred writers. It is not merely an act ; it is a power within the soul. That ἁμαρτία may be used to express an act of sin is indeed true, although it is characteristic of St. Paul's tendency to penetrate beyond the outward manifestation to the inward principle out

of which it springs, that the word appears to be employed by
him in this sense only once, in 2 Cor. xi. 7 (Rom. iv. 8 is a
quotation from the Old Testament). It is thus used, however,
in Matt. xii. 31 (generally in the Synoptists in the plural),
Acts vii. 60, 1 John v. 16, as also in the phrase ποιεῖν τὴν
ἁμαρτίαν, John viii. 34, though in the last case the article may
lead us to think of the sinful spirit which makes itself manifest
in the evil acts of men rather than of these acts considered separately. But, however this may be, there can be no doubt that
the word is most commonly employed to denote not sinful acts
whether single or continuous, but a force, a power, in the heart
by which they are produced. Thus it is equivalent to ἀνομία
(1 John iii. 4), which never means mere living without law or
an act of disobedience to law, but a condition or spirit of direct
opposition to it. Thus also its influence is illustrated by many
different figures in the writings of St. Paul. It is something
that dwells in us (Rom. vii. 17, 20); it uses the body as its
instrument (Rom. vi. 6); it possesses a craftiness by means of
which it is accustomed to deceive (Heb. iii. 13); it holds man
down (Rom. iii. 9); reigns over him (Rom. vi. 12); exercises
a lordship over him (Rom. vi. 14); makes him its slave, one
sold to it (Rom. vi. 6, John viii. 34, Rom. vii. 14); it is
further the direct opposite of righteousness (1 John iii. 7); and
it has a law contrary to the law of the spirit of life (Rom. viii. 2).

These passages are sufficient to show the light in which sin
is regarded in the New Testament. It is not a mere trans-
gression, and, as such, deserving of punishment. It is something which no remission of punishment can cure. It is an
active principle of evil, of selfishness and rebellion against God
in the moral nature, something, therefore, which needs to be
destroyed or rendered helpless in itself. There is, in short, a
compound conception in the Scriptural thought of sin ; and, if
it is to be overcome by a message of Divine mercy and an
exercise of Divine power, these must meet directly and imme-
ately each of the two factors that make it up.

(2.) The light in which the sacred writers regard the putting
away of sin, or in other words the sense in which they understand the ἄφεσις ἁμαρτιῶν or τῶν ἁ., or ἄφεσις παραπτωμάτων.
These important expressions, of which the first occurs frequently
in the New Testament, the last only once, while in Heb. x. 22
ἄφεσις stands alone, are generally understood to mean " forgiveness of sins " in the sense of removal of guilt, without

thought of the removal or putting away of the sins themselves.
It may be doubted if this interpretation is correct.   Trench,
indeed, in his *Synonyms* (First series, p. 131), defends it : " He
then, that is partaker of the ἄφεσις, has his sins forgiven, so
that . . . they shall not be imputed to him, or mentioned
against him, any more."   But it is to be observed that in the
section referred to Trench is almost wholly occupied with the
distinction between ἄφεσις and πάρεσις, and that he does not
even allude to the question whether or not there lies in the first
of these words the idea of removing sins themselves, as well as
the idea of forgiving them.   The meaning of the verb is properly
" to send away," and in this sense it is frequently employed
(Matt. xiii. 36, 1 Cor. vii. 11, 12, 13), the sense of " leaving "
being only secondary.   But to send away sins is to do more than
to leave or not impute them.   It is to cancel sins, so that they
shall no longer exist, just as one cancels a debt (Matt. xvii. 27, 32),
i.e. so that the debt is completely blotted out.   When thus sent
away sins are extinguished, are wholly removed from the sight of
God so that they cannot be punished.   There is thus a clear
distinction between ἄφεσις and πάρεσις (Rom. iii. 25), the sins
in the latter case, though the guilt of them was not imputed,
remaining to rise up, it may be, against the sinner at a future time.
In ἄφεσις ἁμαρτιῶν sins are regarded in a deeper light than as
only bringing condemnation, the thought of their extinction as
offensive in the sight of God and hurtful to the sinner being
included.   The old sins are completely put away, and the sinner
is placed in a position from which he can start upon a new life,
free not only from punishment but from the " bondage " which
sin as a power had brought with it.
       This view of the effect of ἄφεσις is confirmed by the lan-
guage of St. John in his first Epistle, " If we confess our sins,
He is faithful and righteous to forgive us (ἵνα ἀφῇ) our sins,
and to cleanse us from all unrighteousness " (1 John i. 9).   The
cleansing (καθαρίζειν) here spoken of is undoubtedly a moral
cleansing, and that not in the mere sense of leaving us in a
negative condition, but in the condition of persons who have
had a positive communication made to them of Divine light and
life (1 John i. 7, Acts xv. 9, Titus ii. 14, Heb. ix. 14, Eph. v.
26, 27).   The " cleansing " referred to is not, however, to be
so separated from the previous clause as to constitute a distinct
act performed at a moment subsequent to the first.   The usage
of καί in the writings of the Apostle (comp. John xiv. 1, xv.

26, 27) forbids this. The two things, though they may be distinguished in thought, go together. Both are the one acting to the sons of light of Him who is light. The moral element in the second thus belongs also to the first. In forgiving sin God's sentence is not only judicial but moral : in imparting life it is not only moral but judicial. The sinner who confesses his sins has, through the blood of Christ, separated himself from them, and the Righteous God pronounces His judicial sentence accordingly, bestowing upon him at the same time, through the blood of Christ, His own perfectly holy and, because perfectly holy, therefore also judiciously righteous, life (comp. Haupt, *Der Erste Brief des Johannes, in loc.*)

(3.) The light in which "salvation" is presented to us in the New Testament. As a remedy it corresponds to the disease. Two individual texts may first be noticed. (*a*) "Thou shalt call His name Jesus, for it is He that shall save His people from their sins" (Matt. i. 21). It will hardly be contended that in these words of the angel to Joseph we are to understand by the word "save" either deliverance from the punishment of sin alone, or moral renewal alone. Both are obviously included. The Captain of our salvation, the Joshua, the Jesus of the New Testament, leads His people out of bondage not only as pardoned but as redeemed to their new and higher life. They are delivered from sin itself as well as from its guilt. (*b*) "Behold the Lamb of God, which taketh away the sin of the world!" (John i. 29). The word αἴρων here is not (with Luthardt) to be understood as applicable to the removal of guilt alone. The use of the verb in 1 John iii. 5 (comp. the context there) is decisive upon the point. It signifies the removal of sin itself as well as of its punishment. Christ "came to remove all sin even as He was Himself sinless" (Westcott on 1 John iii. 5 : comp. Godet on John i. 29). If the comment by Milligan and Moulton on the distinction between the language of ver. 29 and ver. 36 be allowed to have validity this interpretation is confirmed. In ver. 29 the Christian is supposed to be placed in his *full* Christian position ; in ver. 36 he is nourished and maintained in it. The "taking away" of sin spoken of by the Baptist is a compound thought ; and, if we analyse it, it includes the removal of sin itself as well as its pardon by means of the expiatory sacrifice of the Lamb of God.

It is not possible to dwell further upon individual texts, but

2 A

it may be well to quote a few in which clear expression is given to the *immediateness* with which the introduction of men to a new life is bound up with Christ's work on our behalf, in which that work is represented as directly affecting the removal of sin as well as its pardon. Thus St. Paul, instructing Titus as to the things which he was to "speak with all authority," gives prominence to the truth that "our Saviour Jesus Christ gave Himself for us that He might redeem us from all iniquity, and purify unto Himself a people for His own possession, zealous of good works" (Titus ii. 14, 15). Thus the same Apostle, writing to the Galatians, speaks of "our Lord Jesus Christ who gave Himself for our sins, that He might deliver us out of this present evil world" (Gal. i. 4). Again, he declares to the Ephesians that "Christ loved the Church and gave Himself up for it, that He might sanctify it, having cleansed it by the washing of water with the Word, that He might present the Church to Himself a glorious Church, not having spot or wrinkle or any such thing; but that it should be holy and without blemish" (Ephes. v. 25-27); and, once more, writing to the Romans, he says, "For what the law could not do in that it was weak through the flesh, God, sending His own Son in the likeness of sinful flesh, and as an offering for sin, condemned sin in the flesh; that the ordinance of the law might be fulfilled in us, who walk not after the flesh but after the Spirit" (Rom. viii. 3, 4). To the same effect St. John, referring to the removal rather than the pardon of sin, or at least implying in his words the first not less than the second, says in his first Epistle, "If we walk in the light as He is in the light, we have fellowship one with another, and the blood of Jesus His Son cleanseth us from all sin" (1 John i. 7). St. Peter follows in the same line of thought, "knowing that ye were redeemed . . . from your vain manner of life handed down from your fathers" (1 Pet. i. 18). The writer of the Epistle to the Hebrews also shows what he means by the words "take away sins," when he confirms his statement as to the offering of Christ by a passage from the Old Testament in which the moral element predominates, introducing it by the word "wherefore" (Heb. x. 5-7); and when, contrasting that offering with the offering of bulls and goats, he again exclaims, "How much more shall the blood of Christ, who through Eternal Spirit offered Himself without blemish unto God, cleanse your conscience from dead works to serve the living God?" (Heb. ix. 14): while in the Apocalypse the song of praise to the glorified Redeemer with which the book begins is, "To Him that loved us, and loosed" (not "washed") "us from our sins in His blood" (Rev. i. 5). Add to these the whole train of apostolic thought with regard to that ordinance of Baptism by which we are engrafted into Christ, so that we begin to receive the full communications of His grace ; and the language of the sixth chapter of the Epistle to the Romans will show us that the very purpose of that Sacrament is not only to signify and seal our pardon but our being buried with Christ through Baptism unto death, that we may walk in newness of life, that the body of sin might be done away, that so we should no longer be in bondage to sin.

When we look at these passages, and there are many more to the same effect, we are at once struck with the moral and religious aspect in which the atoning work of our Lord is set before us. There is no mention of any change produced on our legal relation towards God. We know, indeed, from other passages that there is such a change at the time when the new life is given. But in the texts now quoted it is not spoken of, and the fact that it is not is a strong warrant for saying that the writers of these texts did not regard the religious life as a *consequence* of our being saved. That life was a part of the salvation. Salvation is again before us as a compound thought.

It is not only, however, to individual texts that reference may be made. The point now under consideration may be illustrated by the tone and spirit of Epistles as a whole. Let us take the Epistle to the Galatians. Does the Apostle deal in this Epistle only with legal relations, with justification considered simply as a forensic act ? or does he deal also with the moral and spiritual life of those to whom he addresses words which are "living creatures, with hands and feet" ? The use made by Luther of the Galatian Epistle is well known ; and the question is not whether the Reformer was right so far as he went, but whether he unfolded the whole meaning of the book on which he was commenting. So far he was right. He found in the Epistle what is really there. But by treating one side of the truth as if it were the whole truth he has in no small degree contributed to diminish the force of an appeal worthy of all the enthusiasm which it stirred within his own breast. For it is a narrow view of this Epistle which leads us to imagine that the law is spoken of in it merely in its relation to the sinner's justification, and not also as it affects the state in which man is to live before God,—whether in obedience to outward and constraining statutes, or in the free unfolding of a spiritual life from within, when the Spirit of the Lord dwells in the heart, and inspires and regulates the life of faith. The latter of these thoughts penetrates the Epistle as deeply as the former. There was a dispensation of the law; What is its true place in history? It was to be our tutor to lead us to Christ, yet not only that we might be justified by Him alone, but that He, living in us, might unfold and perfect in us that manhood of the Christian life which can be reached in no other way. Now that He has come, and that we are united to Him in faith, we are no longer under the tutor. We are sons who have attained to the privileges of sonship; the Spirit of God is in our hearts; and the fruit of the Spirit is manifest to the spiritually enlightened mind. This is not Antinomianism. Is there no reality, no truth, in the Spirit? Is there no clear decided answer to be obtained from the Spirit—the Spirit, let us remember, who is the Spirit of Christ—when we ask what, as the sons of God who cry, Abba, Father, we are to do? The Apostle says, "Walk in the Spirit, and ye shall not fulfil the lusts of the flesh"; and again, "If we live in the Spirit, let us also walk in the Spirit." Was he wrong in thinking that to walk in the Spirit was as definite and intelligible as to walk according to the law? Men do not believe in the reality of the Spirit's influence. They say, We must have the law to tell us what we ought to do; to speak of the Spirit is vague; every man will have a spirit of his own. But if we "love our neighbour as ourselves," surely that is not vague, loose, indefinite. St. Paul tells us that "the whole law is fulfilled in that one word" (Gal. v. 14). He evidently connected with the Spirit something quite as distinct and definite as the law. Through all this argument, which it is impossible to follow out in detail, careful consideration will show that St. Paul is not dealing with justification alone, but also with the life of the justified man. This, indeed, may be said to be the keynote of the Epistle, in so far as it is grounded upon the Apostle's personal experience, "Far be it from me to glory, save in the cross of our Lord Jesus Christ, through which the world hath been crucified unto me, and I unto the world" (Gal. vi. 14). Two sides of truth are again united in one.

(4.) A similar combination of particulars, often separated, is to be seen also in the account given us in Scripture of the

manner in which salvation is applied. The words of St. Paul
upon this point in Rom. i. 17 are so important that it will be
unnecessary to refer to others, "For therein is revealed a
righteousness of God by " (or out of) "faith unto faith ; as it is
written, But the righteous shall live by" (or out of) "faith." No
one denies that these words constitute the theme and kernel of
the Epistle in which they occur ; or that, by the manner in
which we understand them, we must understand the reasonings
of the Epistle as a whole. What, then, does the "righteousness of God" mean? It is unnecessary to linger on the fact
that Protestant Commentators almost invariably maintain
that, as used here, it expresses not a Divine attribute but a
condition of man. To use the words of Godet (*in loc.*), it is
"The relation to God in which a man would naturally be
placed by his righteousness, if he were righteous, and which
God bestows on him of grace on account of his faith." There
are various grounds on which it seems impossible to accept
this rendering.

(*a*) The correct translation of the words demands the indefinite not the definite article before "righteousness." The
Apostle speaks of "a righteousness," not of "the righteousness," of God. In other words, he speaks of a righteousness
which God might have manifested in some other way. He
might, for example, have done it by a revelation of His wrath
against sin (comp. ver. 18), but then it would have been something in Himself, not in man. That the way spoken of is one
of different ways which God might have adopted "to declare
His righteousness" shows that the Apostle could not have
been thinking simply of a saving relation of man to God.
There is only one way of salvation.

(*b*) This meaning is inconsistent with the verb "revealed"
(ἀποκαλύπτεται), which never signifies to bring into existence
an entirely new state of things, but only to uncover, to bring
into light, what was previously hidden.

(*c*) The expression used by the Apostle has an abstract
form. Let us ask him to make it concrete, and we learn from
chap. iii. 25, 26, where, after a digression, the argument has
been resumed, that he would at once have answered "Christ,"
—"For therein is revealed Christ." He could not have so
spoken had he not been thinking of something in God rather
than in the relation of man to God ; and, accordingly, though
nothing can be clearer than that the "His righteousness" of

chap. iii. 25 is precisely the same as the "righteousness of God" in chap. i. 17, Godet is compelled to make them differ, —in chap. iii. 25 "An attribute of God," in chap. i. 17 a relation of man.

(d) The thought of the "power" of the Gospel is what is most present to the Apostle's mind. But the word "power" is more properly applied to that in God by which He makes man righteous than to that by which He declares him righteous.

(e) Throughout the whole passage St. Paul deals not simply with the guilt of man, but with his condition as a creature who, whether Jew or Gentile, leads naturally a sinful life. For this disease the remedy is especially provided; and, although the application is not yet made by the Apostle, the thought of the new and higher life in contrast with the old and lower life, is from the first in his mind, and cannot be separated from the statement of those contents of the Gospel by which it is brought about.[1]

The words "a righteousness of God" must therefore be understood in their natural and simple sense. As employed by St. Paul, and before we begin to analyse them, or to mark by theological terms the separate parts of the analysis, they mean God's own righteousness, which is offered to us in the Gospel, and is made over to us on the only condition on which such a gift can be received—faith. We can neither separate the "righteousness of God" from God's personal righteousness, nor can we regard man as possessing no personal righteousness when the righteousness of God is made his.

Take one to whom the "righteousness of God" spoken of in Rom. i. 17 has been communicated, and consider what we see. A complex state is presented to us. As one who had sinned, violating the holy law of God and unable to make any atonement for sin, he is yet a child of God in Christ Jesus, and to this aspect of his state the term *justification* is applied. Into it there enters no thought of imparted righteousness. But that is only one aspect of his state. He cannot be in a condition of acceptance with God without having been so united to Christ as to be beheld in Christ, and he cannot be so united to Christ without having been inwardly changed from what he was, and to that aspect of his state the term *sanctification*, at least in

---

[1] On the whole of this point comp. the admirable discussion by Professor John Forbes in his *Commentary on the Romans*, p. 102, etc.

germ, is applied. But neither the one term nor the other is the same as the term *salvation*. Both must be combined if the whole condition of the person referred to is to be described. Unless this be done our description is imperfect, although each part of it is true so far as it goes. Nor are we entitled to say that the second part followed the first, for at the same moment that the sinner was—by that union with Christ, without which he can receive no spiritual gift—brought into a state of acceptance, he, by the same union, had the beginning of spiritual life infused into him. We are only entitled to separate in thought the one part from the other, because doing so helps to make our conception of the whole process clearer, and because we agreed at the beginning to apply a single term to each single part. But we have carefully to distinguish between salvation on the one hand, and justification and sanctification on the other. Salvation includes both these last.[1]

[1] The question may be asked, Whether, if it be so, the preacher of the Gospel is under any circumstances entitled to preach justification by faith alone? The question can only be answered in the affirmative; but why? Not because such a lesson is a complete expression of the truth, but because it may be that aspect of the truth which is peculiarly needed by those whom the preacher is addressing at the time. The preaching of Wesley, Whitefield, the brothers Rowland and Richard Hill and many others bears striking testimony to this. Men are not always alive to their disease, any more than they are always alive to the nature of the remedy, as a whole. There are many whose consciences are shaken and whose hearts are torn by dread of the punishment their sins deserve at the hands of God. To urge upon them the thought of that inward righteousness which they require would only increase their terror and drive them farther from all hope of peace. They are dwelling too exclusively upon one aspect of their disease and, to meet that, they must have enforced upon them, with more than ordinary earnestness, one aspect of the remedy. Again, there are many not so much overwhelmed by dread of punishment as bowed down under the thought of their own unfitness for anything that is good; and what they require is the assurance that in Christ Jesus there is a Divine strength provided for them by which they may overcome the World.

Both these are special cases. The general duty of the preacher is to bring together into one what the theology of the schools has separated. He is, in short, as a rule to preach Christ, leaving it to his hearers to make the application to themselves of the side of the complex truth which their condition peculiarly needs. *After* men have been brought into the Church's fold, and when it is desirable to lead them on to a more intelligent perception of the grace in which they stand, they may be taught what justification and sanctification mean, and what is the relation between them. There is but small risk then that they will become either antinomian or self-righteous.

In confirmation of what has been said as to the importance of looking at salvation in the synthesis of its parts, it may be worth while to observe that to such an extent is this the habit of the sacred writers that, when they do allude to the parts, they sometimes place them in an order different from that of logical thought. Thus, for example, St. Paul writes to the Corinthians, "But ye were washed, but ye were sanctified, but ye were justified in the name of the Lord Jesus Christ and ir the spirit of our God" (1 Cor. vi. 11), while St. Peter addresses his readers as "Elect . . . in sanctification of the Spirit unto obedience and sprinkling of the blood of Jesus Christ" (1 Pet. i. 2). No one worthy of being listened to will say that either Apostle was illogical, the truth being that they viewed salvation as a whole, and that even after they had separated it into parts they did not think it necessary to ask, in re-combining them, whether they were doing this in a manner perfectly logical, or not.

Failure to observe the distinction for which we have contended, a distinction deeply embedded in Protestant theology, vitiates Newman's otherwise able volume on Justification. When he starts with the idea that that word expresses our whole relation to Christ, he has of course no difficulty in proving that righteousness imparted as well as imputed is necessary to our being justified.

From all that has been said it will be seen that the Apostles proceed upon a double view of the necessities of man. On the one hand, man has sinned : he has rebelled against his righteous King and Governor : and he feels this. "When the commandment comes sin revives" (Rom. vii. 9). A guilty conscience makes him afraid, and he has neither confidence nor hope in the thought of the presence of God, until he sees that there is a way by which he may draw near to Him in *that very character which had impressed itself upon his conscience and awakened his fears.* He cannot rest on any assurance of mere change in God. The voice within had testified that his former conception of God was right. It testifies still to the same truth. He cannot hold at one and the same instant two views of God which are inconsistent with each other, and he must choose between them. But if he chooses that which puts the justice of God into the background, he must, in doing so, acknowledge that his former fears were groundless, and that the religious experience which made him cry after reconciliation to a holy and just God was false. On the other hand, man has not merely sinned. He goes on sinning; and again he feels it. He knows that within him there is an evil heart which is the root of his most poignant sorrow. Pardon of past offences will not cure that. A spiritual change in himself is requisite. He must have a new life given him in which he will hate the evil that he formerly loved, and love the holiness that he formerly shunned. These two states of man's spiritual consciousness, it is further to be observed, go together. They are simultaneous rather than successive. Neither of them is simply a deduction from the existence of the other. Each rests upon an immediate experience of its own, and both experiences must be satisfied, each in its own way, before the sinner can be at peace.

To these two states of human experience, practically combined in one, though they may be separately viewed, the sacred writers apply the two divisions of the work of Christ, to which reference has been made; and what is demanded of the theologian who would arrange and systematise the revelation of the New Testament upon this point is, that he shall find some conception of the work of Christ on our behalf which shall include what is necessary for both. He was not wrong in dividing. It is the very business of theology to divide that she may command, to separate a complex truth into its parts that she may determine with greater clearness and accuracy the force of each, together with the nature of the tie by which the parts are bound into a whole. Her mistake is apt to lie in carrying back to a Scripture statement, containing the whole truth, only the single side of the truth into which she has been inquiring, and thus narrowing the meaning of the original revelation in a way not contemplated by its Author. Her danger is less that of reading into the New Testament what is not there, than in not reading out of it all that is there. In earnest times, and it is only in such times that theology comes into existence, theology is necessarily one-sided. The mass of men cannot occupy themselves with more than one aspect of the truth at the same instant. They labour at, they determine, they fix that, intending it to apply to the special error against which they contend, and they conquer in the struggle. Another generation takes up the fruits, and is content with them, as if victory had been won over the whole field. The balance of the different parts of the truth is immediately disturbed, and truth suffers from the want of a comprehensive and uniting grasp of its various portions. In such circumstances the duty of the theologian is to go back to the fountainhead, before the waters parted, one stream in one direction, and another in another; and there to estimate the nature and capabilities of the waters as they issue from their perennial spring. He has not to discover what certain words of Scripture *may* mean in certain circumstances, or what special applications may be made of them. He has to discover the full meaning of the words, or all that was in the mind of their writer at the moment when he employed them.

We are thus brought back to the question, Is there any conception of our Lord's work on our behalf which fulfils this end, which may enable us to feel that, in appropriating that work, we appropriate it as one? It would seem as if such a conception were to be found in the view that our Lord's offering of Himself to the Father is not that of death alone, but of life passing through death. In that thought we have at the same instant both life and death. After the manner of Scripture we combine what the Church has divided.

IV. The view now taken of the offering of Christ is supported by the theology and religious life of the Reformation. These two things ought not to be separated from each other, when we would determine what the religious ideas of the Reformers were. There is even a probability that in a time of excited controversy men will express only half their mind. A great error is before their eyes, and so intent are they on its defeat that they can think of nothing else. They do not know all that is working silently in their own minds, and contributing to make them what they are. But what is thus unappreciated may not be the less real, and those who would afterwards judge them rightly must take it into account.[1]

Looked at in this light, it may perhaps be said that there were two theologies of the Reformation. There was the theology of the controversy with Rome, of polemical tracts, of books, of creeds, of intellectual statements. But there was also the theology of the hearts of those by whom that controversy was carried on, as the fire of Divine life burned within them in zeal for God's glory and the good of man. But the heroes of

[1] "Our futile and mistaken understanding of truth does not hinder our being indirectly and unconsciously benefited by it." *The Gospel of Divine Humanity*, 2nd edition, p. 160.

the Reformation did not think of the latter. It was too real, too true, too much the very condition of their life and action to be thought of. It was *themselves ;* and the existence of themselves had to be taken for granted in what they did. They thought therefore mainly, perhaps only, of the former ; and the theology which they handed down to subsequent generations, highly valuable as it was *in its own place and for its own work*, became narrow and one-sided when those who followed them took it for the whole. A true Systematic Theology must always be the living expression of the age in which it appears. The Reformers wrote only half of what they were ; they lived the other half without knowing and reading, and consequently without writing it. The effect appears to have been that the Church of later times, in devotion to what the Reformers taught, has not sufficiently considered what they would have taught had they foreseen that their teaching was to be the norm for times less earnest and for hearts less glowing than their own. She has too often dealt with Christianity as if its essence were a thing of legal forms, and as if its demands were a deduction from certain legal observances. In this respect she seems to need reviving ; and one of the first great truths to produce such a revival may be said to be, that the Offering to God on the part of the Lord who is the Head of the Body was not completed on the cross, but was, after the cross, and is, even now, made by Him who is our Living High-priest in heaven.

We cannot, however, hold this without at the same time holding that the essence of our Lord's offering consists in the fact that it was an offering of life, and, because life, therefore in its own nature perpetual. Regard it as an act in which life is only given up in death, and it is difficult to see how the perpetuity of the offering can be distinguished from that repetition of which Scripture condemns. Thus an able writer, justly defending the idea of perpetuity, has lately said that the argument of the Epistle to the Hebrews "yields this result : Christ the High Priest with the blood of His sacrifice is entered into the Holy of Holies, *i.e.* heaven itself. He is there at this moment making atonement, and we, His Congregation, are waiting without. We are waiting till He comes forth, which will be at the Second Advent. Till that time the atonement goes on " (*Church Quarterly Review*, April 1891, p. 18). But that is not the teaching of the Epistle ; for no lesson is more distinctly impressed upon it than that the whole Congregation have even now "boldness to enter into the holy place" (*i.e.* the Holy of Holies) "in the blood of Jesus" (Heb. x. 19); that they are even now come unto "Mount Zion, and unto the city of the living God, the heavenly Jerusalem, . . . and to Jesus the Mediator of a new covenant, and to the blood of sprinkling that speaketh better than Abel" (Heb. xii. 22-24). They are not "without." That was the case with the Israelitish (Luke i. 10), it is not the case with the Christian Church. Yet if, in thinking of the Offering of our Lord, we view it simply as an act, an act of death, it is not easy to escape one of two conclusions— either, that as an offering it is still incomplete, or that it is, as yet at least, constantly repeated in heaven, and that it ought therefore to be constantly repeated on earth in the service of the Mass. On the other hand, let us look upon our Lord's offering as an offering of His life, and the difficulty disappears. In the very nature of the case it is then complete, but it goes continually forward. In it also we are "complete," [1] and by it we approach with boldness to the throne of God as a throne of grace, "that we may receive mercy, and may find grace to help us in time of need." [2] Nay, not only so. We may then adopt the ancient idea that the words "for ever" stretch even beyond the Second Advent; and we may believe that in Christ's offering for ever His people for ever stand.[3]

[1] Col. ii. 10.

[2] Heb. iv. 16.

[3] The difficulties besetting any one who, upon the ordinary view that the death of Christ is merely a satisfaction to Divine justice, would attempt to explain how that bodily death upon the cross becomes, in St. Paul's reasoning upon the subject, identical with the dying of the "old man" in Christians, are well illustrated by Pfleiderer's effort to trace the genesis of Pauline thought upon the subject. His explanation, as given in his *Paulinism* (vol. i. chap. 2, translation by Peters), depends mainly on the assertion that, between the writing of 2 Cor. and Romans, there was on the Apostle's part an "advance" in "the formalisation, and at the same time the externalisation, of a fact of religious experience which is in itself purely inward and of psychological origin" (p. 112). In so speaking, Pfleiderer refers to the grateful devotion awakened in the believer by the thought of Christ's dying for him, and he supposes that the believer is led by this into the further thought of a mystical union with Christ, in which the death of Christ, already accomplished in him as a spiritual fact, "comes to be represented as a fact accomplished externally and to the senses in that very death of Christ." The explanation thus given can hardly be called simple or clear, but, apart from that, it is inconsistent with St. Paul's teaching as to the *unio mystica*. According to the Apostle this union with Christ is rather the offspring of a faith in, and a love to Him in, His Divine-human personality. It rather pre-

The conclusion to which we are led by a consideration of the whole matter is that the older theology, which deals with the ideas of sacrifice, of vicarious suffering, and of penal consequences to our Lord, is substantially true. It needs only that the element of life shall be allowed its proper place in the conception of sacrifice, and shall be made an integral part of the Atonement made on our behalf, and not a merely logical consequence deduced from it. The effort to introduce this thought probably lies at the bottom of those theories of the Atonement, differing from that generally held in the Church, which exercise more or less influence in our day. With the spirit leading to such efforts it is impossible not to sympathise. The Church has had bitter enough experience of the evil effects of that system of legal theology which has so long held possession of the field. She has seen a wide gulf opened between a supposed salvation in Christ and life in Him. She has seen a so-called orthodoxy, cold and hard, reigning in her pulpits and her pews, until at last many of the occupants of both, unable to endure their dissatisfaction longer, and having no better substitute, have been constrained to abandon theology, if not also Christianity, altogether. She has seen words expressive of the most solemn realities of the eternal world played with as if they were a set of counters without meaning. She has seen a preaching, boasting itself to be that of the only gospel, so separated from

cedes than follows the thought of Christ's giving Himself for us, and only at a later stage is it connected with a process of analysing what is meant either by Christ's dying for us or our dying with Him.

In his most recent work (*Ur-Christenthum*, p. 211, etc.) Pfleiderer returns to the subject ; and, forced to attempt an explanation of the fact that St. Paul should have thought of God as one to whom the bloody sacrifice of Christ was necessary before He could save men, while He was yet at the same time a God of love, he declares the contrariety (Gegensatz) to be logically insoluble, and only psychologically soluble when we remember that two souls dwelt in the Apostle. One of these, springing out of his Judaism and Pharisaism, led him to think of God as a God of avenging justice. The other, springing out of his Christian consciousness, led him to see in God a God of compassion and love. It must be obvious that this is no solution of the difficulty. It simply removes the difficulty a step farther back. But, not to dwell upon this, it is rather to be observed that all these laborious speculations are unnecessary, if we realise the fact that it is not the extinction of Christ's physical life that is our atonement, but rather His life thus surrendered in death, so that in the act of becoming partakers of his death for us we become also partakers of His life in us. The two contrarieties cease thus to be contrarieties, and coalesce in one truth with a double bearing upon men.

sweetness of moral tone and beauty of moral conduct that the faith of weak Christians has trembled in the balance, while a merely outward formalism has passed gaily through the Church and the world, smiling at its own accomplishments. All this the Church has seen, until it may be doubted whether her life, looked at on a large scale, has not become an obstacle to the progress of Christianity, instead of being, as it ought to be, the most powerful argument in its favour. No wonder that so many of her best children have sighed and cried for life, and that in the effort to reach it they have often been led to give utterance to views supported by neither Scripture nor experience.

We need, therefore, at this moment a restatement of the great doctrine of the Offering of our Lord for sinners ; and, although that proposed in these pages may be rejected as untenable, any one that shall be more fortunate in obtaining the acceptance of the Church will probably find it necessary to have regard to its leading principle. In one way or another life will have to be included in the essence of the sacrifice made on our behalf. The conscience will never be satisfied while life is viewed simply as a consequence deduced from a change in our legal relation towards God.[1]

[1] That the Church is feeling her way towards some such view of the doctrine of the Atonement as would follow from the principles here laid down seems to find an illustration in words that may be quoted from a sermon recently preached in Aberdeen by the Rev. Robert A. Mitchell, one of the ministers of the Free Church of Scotland there. The sermon was preached before the Free Church Synod, and was published at *the Synod's request*. The text was Rom. viii. 3, 4. The whole sermon is interesting and able, and one or two sentences may be quoted. "Why not read the passage before us, then, in the light of that previous passage (Rom. vi. 2), and regard it as meaning this, that the condemnation which rested upon us on account of our sin, by bringing about the death of the Son of God made for our sakes in the likeness of sinful flesh, has inflicted a death-blow upon the sin rooted in our flesh, and so has secured our deliverance from the ruling power of sin ?" (p. 13). Again, referring to Rom. vi. 10, the writer explains our dying unto sin, as "a sharing with Christ in his dying, by being conformed to the likeness of His death, by entering, so to speak, into the *spirit* of His death. And His death is *nothing* to us, and can avail us nothing, unless we do so. . . . In the view of Paul it is one of the Christian's greatest privileges that he is *dead with Christ* (not merely legally but morally); he has died to sin by taking on the likeness of His death, by entering into the fellowship of that *death to sin* which the incarnate Son of God, the second Adam, the true Son of Man, consummated once for all in the agony of the cross" (pp. 19, 20. The italics are the author's.) The difference from the common way of

Note C, p. 203.

A striking illustration of what is said in the text is afforded by words of Laurence Oliphant, quoted by Mrs. Oliphant in her beautiful biography of that noble and pure soul. In a letter, explanatory of his faith, to her who was to be his future biographer, Oliphant says : " The breath of Christ descending into the organisms of men to meet the invading force from below, makes known its presence also by *physical* sensations of a blessed and life-giving character, conveying with irresistible force the consciousness that Christ is actually descending with power and great glory a second time to dwell with us." Again, in a letter to another friend, he speaks of himself and those who agree with him as enjoying " evidences both of an *external* and internal character, which the world would call supernatural, encouraging us when we are obeying His will," etc. And, once more, he thus describes our Lord : " He is the connecting link between us and the great Unknowable, and for this cause He came into the world, that he might unite us *sensationally* to His father and our Father " (vol. ii. pp. 18, 34, 335. The italics are not in the original). To the many supposed experiences of this kind in the so-called Revival Movements of the day it is not necessary to refer.

stating the truths involved in this momentous subject which appears in these extracts can hardly fail to be recognised. Dr. Macleod Campbell's work on the Atonement, even when the theory contained in it is not adopted, has exercised a powerful influence over modern thought.

INDEX I

TEXTS MORE OR LESS DISCUSSED IN THE LECTURES AND NOTES

INDEX II

of the gift, 172 ; dwelt in fulness in our Lord, 173; but did not take the place of His Divinity, 176 ; His human nature still pervaded by the Spirit, 178 ; nature of the indwelling, 179 ; the gift of the Spirit is the gift of Christ's own Spirit, 179 ; this Spirit also the gift of God, 181 ; doctrine of the procession of, 182 ; must be made ours inwardly, 183 ; Spirit of Christ and spirit of man, interpenetration of, 184 ; yet the spirit not incarnated, 189 ; function of the Spirit to reveal Christ Himself within us, 194 ; not an independent authority, 200 ; cannot be substituted for Christ, 201 ; when bestowed, 204 ; the Holy Spirit before the Christian dispensation, 206 ; during our Lord's earthly ministry, 207 ; after the Incarnation, 209 ; influence of our Lord, after His Ascension, in relation to the Spirit, 211 ; on whom is the gift of the Holy Spirit bestowed, 216 ; His actual work, 217 ; belongs in fulness only to Body of Christ, 221

Stanley, *Lectures on the Eastern Church*, 192

Sternness, value of, in Christian truth, 54

Substitution, idea of, discussed, 341

Suffering, Christian, for others, 267; a necessary part of salvation, 268 ; necessary to power over others, 270 ; a conveyance of Christ's life to others, 274

THEOLOGY, relation to religion, 317 ; not to be forsaken because elaborate, 319 ; how much necessary for a test, 320 ; of Germany, 327 ; of Scotland, 328, 329 ; different aspects of any truth of, to be combined, 359, 361 ;

the older substantially true, 365

Thomas Aquinas, 110

Trent, Council of, on Justification, 344

Truth in Christ never a mere dogma, 51

Tulloch, Principal, *Facts of Religion*, 322

UNION of believers with their Lord, 196 ; place of, 344

WARDLAW, *Syst. Theol.*, 196

Webb, Bishop, 117,191,260,263,291

Weiss on the Ascension, 14

Westcott, 68, 73, 77, 92, 116, 117, 120, 121, 123, 132, 134, 138, 144, 150, 218, 273, 349

Wilberforce, *On Incarnation*, 100, 202, 311

Will, human, force of, in Gospel of St. John, 186

Work, Christ at His Ascension enters on, 57

Work of the Heavenly High-priest, 113 *et seq.*

Work, Church representing her Lord in, 278 ; her work for herself, 279 ; for the world, 285

World cannot receive Holy Spirit, 218

Worship, Church representing her Lord in, 294 ; must be common, 295 ; without it life languishes, 297 ; end to promote God's glory, 299 ; importance of praise in, 301 ; for the edification of saints, 302 ; expressed in form, 304 ; Incarnation demands form, 305 ; outward, essential, 306 ; a repetition of the Lord's presentation of Himself in heaven, 307 ; accessories of, 312

YOUNG, *Fernley Lecture*, 276

"Yourselves," force of, in fourth Gospel, 187

Printed by R. & R. CLARK, LIMITED, *Edinburgh*.

OTHER FINE VOLUMES AVAILABLE

1980-81

TITLES CURRENTLY AVAILABLE

0101	Delitzsch, Franz	A New Commentary on Genesis (2 vol.)	27.75
0201	Murphy, James G.	Commentary on the Book of Exodus	12.75
0301	Kellogg, Samuel H.	The Book of Leviticus	19.00
0601	Blaikie, William G.	The Book of Joshua	14.00
0901	Blaikie, William G.	The First Book of Samuel	13.50
1001	Blaikie, William G.	The Second Book of Samuel	13.50
1801	Gibson, Edgar	The Book of Job	9.75
1802	Green, William H.	THe Argument of the Book of Job Unfolded	10.75
1901	Dickson, David	A Commentary on the Psalms (2 vol.)	29.25
2301	Kelly, William	An Exposition of the Book of Isaiah	13.25
2401	Orelli, Hans C. von	The Prophecies of Jeremiah	13.50
2601	Fairbairn, Patrick	An Exposition of Ezekiel	16.50
2701	Pusey, Edward B.	Daniel the Prophet	19.50
3801	Wright, Charles H.H.	Zechariah and His Prophecies	21.95
4101	Alexander, Joseph	Commentary on the Gospel of Mark	15.25
4301	Brown, John	The Intercessory Prayer of Our Lord Jesus Christ	10.50
4401	Alexander, Joseph	Commentary on Acts (2 vol. in one)	27.50
4402	Gloag, Paton J.	Commentary on Acts (2 vol.)	27.50
4501	Shedd, W. G. T.	Critical and Doctrinal Commentary on Romans	15.75
4601	Brown, John	The Resurrection of Life	13.25
4602	Edwards, Thomas C.	A Commentary on the First Epistle of Corinthians	16.25
4801	Ramsay, William	Historical Commentary on the Epistle of Galatians	15.75
4901	Westcott, Brooke F.	St. Paul's Epistle to the Ephesians	9.75
5001	Johnstone, Robert	Lectures on the Book of Philippians	16.50
5401	Liddon, H. P.	The First Epistle to Timothy	6.00
5601	Taylor, Thomas	An Exposition of Titus	17.50
5801	Delitzsch, Franz	Commentary on the Epistle to Hebrews (2 vol.)	29.95
5802	Bruce, A. B.	The Epistle to the Hebrews	15.00
5901	Johnstone, Robert	Lectures on the Epistle of James	14.00
5902	Mayor, Joseph B.	The Epistle of St. James	19.25
6501	Manton, Thomas	An Exposition of the Epistle of Jude	12.00
6601	Trench, Richard C.	Commentary on the Epistles to the Seven Churches	8.50
7001	Orelli, Hans C. von	The Twelve Minor Prophets	13.50
7002	Alford, Dean Henry	The Book of Genesis and Part of Exodus	11.50
7003	Marbury, Edward	Obadiah and Habakkuk	21.50
7101	Mayor, Joseph B.	The Epistles of St. Jude and Second Peter	15.25
7101	Mayor, Joseph B.	The Epistles of St. Jude and Second Peter	15.25
7102	Lillie, John	Lectures on First and Second Peter	18.25
7103	Hort, F.J.A. & A.F.	Expository and Exegetical Studies	29.50
7104	Milligan, George	St. Paul's Epistles to the Thessalonians	10.50
8001	Fairweather, William	Background of the Gospels	15.00
8002	Fairweather, William	Background of the Epistles	14.50
8003	Zahn, Theodor	Introduction to the New Testament (3 vol.)	48.00
8004	Bernard, Thomas	The Progress of Doctrine in the New Testament	9.00
8601	Shedd, W. G. T.	Dogmatic Theology (4 vol.)	49.50
8701	Shedd, W. G. T.	History of Christian Doctrine (2 vol.)	30.25
8702	Oehler, Gustav	Theology of the Old Testament	20.00
8703	Kurtz, John Henry	Sacrificial Worship of the Old Testament	15.00
8901	Fawcett, John	Christ Precious to those that Believe	9.25
9401	Neal, Daniel	History of the Puritans (3 vol.)	54.95
9501	Shilder, Klass	The Trilogy (3 vol.)	48.00
9801	Liddon, H. P.	The Divinity of our Lord	20.25
9802	Pink, Arthur W.	The Antichrist	10.50
9803	Shedd, W. G. T.	The Doctrine of Endless Punishment	8.25